THE
DAY THAT CHANGED MY LIFE

THE
DAY THAT CHANGED MY LIFE

INSPIRATIONAL STORIES FROM IRELAND'S WOMEN

CAITLIN McBRIDE

BLACK & WHITE PUBLISHING

First published 2019
by Black & White Publishing Ltd
Nautical House, 104 Commercial Street
Edinburgh, EH6 6NF

1 3 5 7 9 10 8 6 4 2   19 20 21 22

ISBN: 978 1 78530 265 7

This book is a work of non-fiction, based on interviews about the lives,
experiences and recollections of its contributors. In some cases names have been
changed solely to protect the privacy of others. The author has stated to the publishers
that the contents of this book are true to the best of her knowledge.

The publisher has made every reasonable effort to contact copyright holders
of images in this book. Any errors are inadvertent and anyone who for any reason
has not been contacted is invited to write to the publisher so that a full
acknowledgment can be made in subsequent editions of this work.

A CIP catalogue record for this book is available from the British Library.

Typeset by Iolaire, Newtonmore
Printed and bound by CPI Group (UK) Ltd, Croydon, CR0 4YY

To my sister Maura,
I could never have done this — or anything — without you.

Contents

LISTEN TO YOUR HEART

WOMEN AT WORK

SLIDING DOORS

~

Introduction

Hello and welcome to my book.

In my head, I have written that first sentence hundreds of different ways, but I've come to believe that life is much simpler than we give it credit for. It's simple in that most of us want love, security, health and happiness and that applies no matter your age, profession, socio-economic status, sexuality or any other box society tries to put you in.

The Day That Changed My Life started with a seed of an idea in 2017. I read an article in a magazine and someone used the phrase 'that day changed my life' when referring to a major life event of theirs. I can't remember the person or their story, but the concept stayed with me. I began to scratch my head to think of moments that changed my life: could I narrow it down to just one? Did I feel there was a defining time in my life that led me to the path I'm on now?

I became obsessed. I asked friends and family about their life-changing day; some I already knew would be too painful to relive, others I was desperate to know. Could there be one specific point in our life that changed everything, whether we realised it or not?

In my work as a journalist, I began asking interview subjects the question to see what answers would arise. The answers were – as expected – fascinating. I did short and longer features with this key question and unlocked not only some insightful responses from people, but the self-reflection I always wanted from my writing.

Over the next two years, I continued my day job — as executive style editor at Independent.ie — but I stored the idea for the right moment; unaware what exactly that moment might be. In 2018, I co-wrote a book with Conor and Hugh McAllister, two brothers from Co Meath, who co-own the Grafton Barber chain, with Black & White Publishing, an independent publishing house based in Edinburgh, Scotland. The Grafton Barber project went well and afterwards, my new publishers asked if I had any ideas for a book of my own. Suddenly, that seed of an idea had been watered.

I shared my fascination and my belief that the life-changing concept could make for a very strong book and, perhaps most pertinently, serve as a vehicle to tell women's stories. Thankfully, Black & White agreed and before I knew it, I was writing the early draft of what now appears on these pages.

I can't help but think it was serendipitous timing. The way in which society speaks about women has seen great positive change and our work is now being valued in new ways. I've always written for (and through) the female gaze, but my own writing shifted, and improved exponentially, once I began to focus on topics affecting women the world over. As it turns out, my calling is to tell women's stories, including my own.

Women's magazines now cover wide-ranging issues from abortion rights and sexual misconduct cases to beauty and fashion advice. The truer range of women's multi-faceted interests are being recognised in mainstream magazines, newspapers, websites and . . . this book.

The Day That Changed My Life is anchored in my belief that everyone has a story. In this book's early stages, I began compiling a list of women's names who I hoped would feature. My initial criteria were that they are (a) women who inspired me and (b) women of real significance. Whittling them down to thirty-one seemed an impossible task.

How was I going to pick just thirty-one women in a country filled with extraordinary talents? And how would I get interview time with some of the busiest and most impressive people I could think of? It seemed a gargantuan task, but I could feel in my bones that this was something worth doing – and doing well.

I found myself reaching for the sky and finding there was room for this book in the clouds: government ministers, Oscar nominees, world champions, Paralympian medallists, human rights campaigners and women from around the island of Ireland breaking barriers in their walk of life were all saying yes to me. Once the confirmations started pouring in, I wanted to push the deadline further and further. I wanted to do it bigger and better. I thought thirty-one was never going to be enough to shout these stories from the rooftops.

But it was a great place to start.

When it came to it, there was one thing of which I was certain: it *had* to be a compilation of stories of substance. In our world which encourages a mentality that those who shout the loudest are heard the most, I felt it was in a position – however small – to contribute towards change. I work as a journalist with a national newspaper and so, my voice, whether my Irish self-deprecation will allow me to say or not, is one of the loud ones; so why wasn't I doing some good with it?

Many of the women featured in *The Day That Changed My Life* also have voices that reach far and, together, we could celebrate and inspire women in Ireland and beyond. This made it an even more exciting experience for me as a writer and a reader. I could bring these stories in one place with a piece of their heart and soul in every word, on every page.

One book to rule them all!

What I never could have expected is the personal satisfaction I have found in writing this. I have been working as a full-time journalist for the past ten years and I have written about everything you can imagine: terrorist attacks, human interest, court cases, celebrities, red carpets, sport, fashion, cars. You name it, I've done it – and there's probably embarrassing photographic evidence to prove it.

This project was on another scale. Granted, it was a scale of my own making, but it was a responsibility that I felt and took very seriously.

I had a duty to honour these women who gave up their time and spoke with a candour I can only hope one day to possess, because they also believed in The Book. So, in 2018, I began researching, reading, writing (and researching some more) in order to determine a roll-call of women whom I admire and whom I feel are representative of modern Ireland.

I needed those who encapsulated the message I wanted to send: everyone has a story and now is the time to make theirs heard. Over the last decade of my career, I have spent countless hours listening to those stories – happy, sad, awe-inspiring and some to make you go home at night, kiss your loved ones and count your blessings. I'm proud to say this book has a lot of that.

I'd be lying if I said I didn't cry during the months of creating *The Day That Changed My Life*; not because of the hard work – although there was plenty of that – but because of the sheer joy and privilege of telling these stories. It has left me humbled and inspired.

Every woman met me with open arms; some of whom I knew and others who treated me like a friend having never met me before in their lives. Some of these women had never heard my name before and yet, they cried, laughed and reflected with me. I had the same conversation with everyone: it started with an email pitch, then a phone call and then a yes.

Women I'd never met welcomed me into their kitchens, their 'good' rooms and introduced me to their family and closest friends. We bonded as they shared some of the darkest moments of their lives, which now feature in these pages. There were endless cups of tea in hotels, cafés and restaurants around Ireland to hear about the highest of highs and lowest of lows.

And there were Skype interviews where we both held back tears (and some where holding back just wasn't realistic). These women gave up time out of already jam-packed schedules dictating national agendas, starring in TV shows and raising their families to speak with me. And their only payment was the desire to help and trust that there really is comfort in sharing.

Time became the most valuable currency in my life. My sister Maura, with a newborn daughter at home, spent countless hours counselling me over the phone and in person. She became a de-facto researcher, sending me stories of interesting women she came across and offering valuable advice in driving through writer's block or feelings of being overwhelmed. Two of the women she recommended feature here. In a way that only a sister can, she has taken as much joy from this as I have.

My fiancé Guy, a life-long good sport and my pillar of support, agreed to postpone our wedding planning to accommodate *The Day That Changed My Life*. For months, there wasn't one day he walked through our apartment door and I didn't wax lyrical about everything related to The Book. He listened to my accomplishments and setbacks, retaining enthusiasm for this — and me — in a truly beautiful way. I lost count of how often I'd call him after an interview, shedding a few tears (I'm a cryer), and telling him, 'I really think this can *be* something good.' A piece of my heart is on every page and writing this has been the greatest honour of my life.

In my pitches to agents, managers and the women themselves, I wrote that I wanted readers to 'feel they can take on the world after' and that goal has only become more ingrained at each stage of the process.

When I spoke to Georgie Crawford, a breast cancer survivor who was diagnosed just six months after giving birth to her first child at the age of 31, she said she had a new lease of life after successfully beating the disease. "Mondays don't seem so bad when you've survived cancer," she told me (over one of the aforementioned cups of tea on her lunch break in a small café in Stephen's Green shopping centre in Dublin).

And she's right. If there's one thing I've gained, it's a renewed outlook on my life. Some of these women have been to hell and back – they have survived abusive marriages, wrongful deaths of newborn babies and cancer diagnoses. They have also reached a glorious assortment of personal and professional accomplishments like realising they're gay, becoming a mother for the first time, victory in a world championship, winning a Paralympic medal and meeting the love of their life.

My own life experiences are mirrored in some of the stories they've shared and there have been more than a few nights where I've had a good cry reflecting on things I had long since buried; but I also gained a sense of healing that I could never have foreseen.

This book isn't about me, but I do bring my experiences as a writer, as a woman and a survivor into these pages and I'm thrilled we can begin this next chapter together. Now, join us with your drink of choice and, if you're a cryer too, know that you're in good company.

REWRITE THE RULES

~

**TRAILBLAZERS
CHANGE MAKERS
GROUNDBREAKERS**

She found her *ikigai*.

Sabina Brennan

Neuroscientist and psychologist

'The day I left acting and fell in love with academia.'

~

A famous actress turned world-renowned neuroscientist sounds like the stuff of a Hollywood producer's far-fetched imagination. But unlikely scenarios often make for the most gripping stories, as is the case with Sabina Brennan's career.

~

For a significant portion of her acting career, Sabina was best known for her portrayal of Tess Halpin on *Fair City*, a soap opera beamed into Irish homes three nights a week. It is still one of the highest rated shows on national broadcaster RTÉ and it has seen typically salacious storylines, like a woman's affair with a priest and a kidnapping, but it has also tackled these – and other – issues with taste and dignity.

Sabina's work falls into the latter category.

For nearly two years, Sabina played the part of a domestic abuse victim, whose on-air husband, Marty, eventually strangled her to death.

When she first joined the television show in 2001, she became an overnight star. In the early days of the internet and at a time when

RTÉ remained the biggest player in town, she was in the spotlight. She had landed what for many actors is the dream role – the chance to explore a character and to be a key role in a highly popular show that's broadcast frequently and regularly.

In the acting community, *Fair City* is seen as a solid gig – not only do you receive a coveted regular pay cheque, but you also become instantly recognisable and, if you're lucky, get a juicy storyline that shows off your acting chops.

The show's popularity turned out to be a blessing and a curse at first for Sabina, before later becoming simply a blessing. After working on the programme for nearly two years, her agent pointed out that most *Fair City* actors tend to be typecast in Ireland's already small acting pool and advised that it would be wise to diversify into something new until producers – and the public – had stopped associating her with that particular part.

'I knew I wasn't good at sitting around doing nothing and that tended to be the hardest part about acting for me,' Sabina says. 'It's hard to do nothing. So I rang Trinity [College Dublin] about a psychology course which looked interesting. They said that was the last day for applications for full-time mature students. I had about forty minutes to put together a personal statement, then take the entrance exams and wait to see if I'd be called for an interview. I'd never been to university before. I had done my Leaving Certificate at sixteen and went straight to work after that.'

Part of Sabina's motivation to pursue psychology was driven by her son, Darren, who has dyslexia and wasn't being given the appropriate resources in school to allow him to thrive in his education. Prior to that, she'd been exploring academic research in order to better understand her son's condition and ways to improve his learning experience.

'The school system was completely failing him. I couldn't stand by and watch it happen,' she says. 'When I was on *Fair City*, I started working with him on his reading and I found academic papers to try and make sense of it myself. He had a diagnosis under the dyslexia umbrella, but he had issues around sequencing and planning and organising. I was told that he should consider leaving school at the age of fourteen and learn a trade.'

But not only did her son thrive in secondary school, successfully completing his Leaving Certificate; he went on to study Biochemistry and Immunology at Trinity College Dublin (TCD) and from there, a degree in medicine.

So, one of the unexpected side effects from working so closely with her son in this was a newly discovered love of academia and, specifically, the study of the brain.

Having jumped through all the necessary hoops for entry to the course with flying colours, Sabina began the journey which would lead to the day that changed her life. She fell in love with psychology and academia and, as an added bonus, it just so happened that she was naturally gifted at analysing the human brain.

'I absolutely loved it,' she says. 'I turned into this complete and utter nerd and I would read everything I could get my hands on, oftentimes even before the lectures had covered the subject. For me, it wasn't a huge change from acting: I was an actor because I'm inter-ested in human behaviour. Theatre was never my thing, but I loved film and television because it was all about the discovery – figuring out what makes a person tick – and so the study of psychology became a dream.

'It opened up a whole new world for me. When you become an actor, you can become very blinkered in that it's always about chasing the next job and that can leave you feeling very unhealthy. You can't act until somebody gives you a part. If I'd been able to write, maybe I could have written something for myself, but I couldn't.

'That was a real change for me: to learn about stuff that I found exciting, and sitting exams, writing essays. I'd never done anything like that before. I loved it.'

~

Sabina and her son both wound up studying at TCD – where Sabina enjoyed an illustrious career after graduation and is now working as an adjunct assistant professor, on course to be a principal investigator and research assistant professor.

'He's really smart,' Sabina says of her son. 'I'd read about children who were failed by the system and how it can lead to mental health issues and I wasn't going to let that happen. So I worked with Darren in a way that was right for him. We worked on trying to understand his condition through studying academic papers and scientific research. Because I'd never gone to university, I didn't know how much I liked studying and the organising of it all until I was given the opportunity to try it.

'Now he's a doctor. Can you imagine? I always knew how smart he was and that he'd have to master his challenges and, to do that, he'd have to work extra hard. He did very well in the process.

'Darren's success is integral to my story. Helping him sparked my fascination in the human brain.'

~

As a mature student, Sabina had that much sought-after balance where she was exceptionally devoted to her subject matter, but also incorporated outside life into her studies. And, after finishing her psychology undergraduate degree, she was awarded a scholarship for a PhD in the area of cognitive ageing.

'I was hooked from the word go,' she says, 'when "I" started to look at brain function and how it changes with age. Then I got drawn into literature around risk for dementia: what exactly happens and how we assume the brain changes because we age but then looking underneath it, is it because we age or is it because of our behaviours?'

> I loved film and television because it was all about the discovery – figuring out what makes a person tick – and so the study of psychology became a dream.

Sabina's specialty is now dementia studies, an area she found herself 'drawn into' during the normal course of her psychology studies. She is actively involved with the Alzheimer Society of Ireland and is a global leader in the field of better brain health. Not to mention that, in 2018, she published her first book *100 Days To A Younger Brain*, which became a number one bestseller.

While she studied, Sabina worked at the Institute of Neuroscience and, after her PhD, she began working directly with the dementia research programme in Ireland. If further proof was needed that she had found her calling, she has successfully brought world-leading research to the fore and made the world of research far more transparent to the public.

'There was this amazing work being done, but scientists spent most of their time talking to one another at niche conferences or publishing their findings in academic journals that were usually inaccessible to the general public because they were behind paywalls. And even if they weren't behind paywalls, and you knew where to look – once you find them they're written in what can feel like an entirely different language that the ordinary reader can't understand.

'That's something that really bothered me and I felt almost a compulsion to improve this. I felt an ethical, moral responsibility; maybe because I had once been a member of the public – with no academic background or understanding of the scientific method to try and make sense of it – who was trying to search for that information so as to help my son.

'I felt that people deserve to know this information, about the relationships between lifestyle factors and risk factors and all the things you can do to just keep your brain healthy.

'It was about translating research into easy-to-understand information for the general public – that was the principle that I wanted every project to abide by.

'There is still a real stigma around dementia. Too much misinformation and misunderstanding. People often think the illness is a normal part of ageing or that it's genetic; they just put their head in the sand and don't want to know about it. That's an awful place to be as there really are preventative things that can be done.'

So began the next part of Sabina's efforts. First, she found a funding grant for a communications-style project from the European Commission and proposed they increase the social impact of their funding on health research and increase the visibility of their medical research through a brain health awareness programme, and then she was awarded the one million euro in funding. She was also a member of the applicant team that secured the biggest philanthropic grant in Irish history, totalling €138 million.

In looking back over Sabina's extraordinary career, it shouldn't come as a shock to learn that it's never been an accident, but rather a series of happy surprises.

In Ireland, to declare that you want to be an actor when you grow up certainly used to be akin to wanting to be a rock star or the president – there's no obvious career path one could pursue to achieve that goal. So, Sabina did the smart thing and followed in her father's footsteps and took a job working alongside him at the insurance and pensions company, Irish Life Assurance plc; a fine, pensionable job complete with perks. (Not to mention that she met her husband David there while playing for the Irish Life soccer team, another day that changed her life which we will get to in a moment.)

At the age twenty-seven, after getting married and having two sons, Sabina was offered a place at the renowned Gaiety School of Acting. One of the biggest regrets of her life is that she had to turn it down. At the time, she simply couldn't afford not to work (there was a mortgage to pay), though she is particularly proud of the fact that she would have been studying alongside Colin Farrell had she accepted.

Sabina then left Irish Life and trained as a speech and drama teacher at the Guildhall School of Music & Drama in London. At which point she realised, '*Oh, actually, ordinary people can be actors*. I just had no connection with that world.

'We had no internet so the obsession we have now with celebrities didn't exist on the same level. There just wasn't the access to information. If you want to find out something, you had to go to a library and if somebody hadn't written a book about somebody's life story as an actor, you couldn't find out anything about them. I didn't even know there were acting schools.'

But Sabina did know the importance of following one's heart, and she was determined to encourage her two sons to do that too.

'All I ever wanted to be was an actor,' she says, 'but it never entered my head that it was a possibility. It was a dream, but not an actionable one where I knew I could plan a certain way to achieve it. The decision to follow it later in life influenced how I parent my children. I told them to find something that they love and then find a way to get someone to pay them to do it. My other son is a musician, a classic saxophonist.'

Sabina credits her husband David, and her sons, Darren and Gavin, and his husband Jamie, as being crucial to her success. For example, they helped pick up the slack when she locked herself away writing for much of 2018.

This is a support network she wouldn't have had if she hadn't taken that initial 'safe' job at Irish Life, the one that provided a pension and made her a shoo-in for mortgage approval and, though it didn't have the pizzazz of being a TV star, it gave her the family she cherishes so much today.

'Anyone who is around my age will understand this – back then, your only real employment options were working for the civil service, as there were just an elite few who went to university and they were generally sons and daughters of professionals like lawyers and doctors.'

Sabina isn't the impulsive type, but she does know when to listen to her heart and when to her head. And when she met David, she followed her heart in what would become another life-changing day.

'After I met my husband, he asked me to marry him within six weeks; we got officially engaged a couple of months after that and then we got married the next year. Then I had my first baby and the year after, I had my next baby.

'There are ten months between my sons – that's a timeframe that really focuses you as a mother and as a person.'

Sabina says that through her work in brain health, she has found her 'ikigai', a Japanese word which is considered to be the source of value in one's life. It's the reason you get out of bed in the morning, your raison d'être. It's fitting that she has taken an interest in Japanese culture. The Japanese Okinawa islands have the largest population of centenarians in the world.

'Not only do they live long, but they live very well. There's a lot of information around their diets and different things they do, but their philosophy is that they have discovered a concept of something which there's no translation for... they don't retire, nor do they have a word for retirement.

'People have found their purpose and so they keep working right up until the end. They have found their "ikigai" and I feel I have found mine.'

She shattered the glass ceiling.

Judith Gillespie

Former Deputy Chief Constable
of the Police Service of Northern Ireland

'The day I was finally made a police officer.'

~

Judith Gillespie is the first of her kind.

She's a trailblazer and policy-maker who made history in 2009 when she was the first woman to be made Assistant Chief Constable and then later promoted to Deputy Chief Constable of the Police Service of Northern Ireland (PSNI), becoming the highest-ranking female police officer in the force.

~

Judith's impressive career began in 1982 when she was finally accepted into the Royal Ulster Constabulary (RUC) [which became the PSNI in 2001] after two previous attempts. For her, it was a dream come true, and she credits the day she was accepted as the day that changed her life.

Judith always knew she wanted to be a police officer, inspired by her father's measured approach to conflict working as a Presbyterian minister in Belfast during the Troubles.

'We lived right on a sectarian interface, so trouble was never too far from our door,' Judith recalls. 'I watched my dad get involved in some pretty tricky situations and always negotiate his way out through his very calm demeanour, being very courteous to people, listening to both sides and finding some way through that involved a level of a compromise.

'For example, he was about to conduct an evening service one Sunday evening and there was a lot of tension just outside the church and the start of a riot. My dad went out in his ministerial gowns and spoke to some of the guys on the street saying, "Folks, I'm trying to conduct a service of worship, is there any possibility of you showing some respect?"

> **I had a very strong sense that I was going to be a police officer, but of course those were very difficult times in Northern Ireland.**

'And I think my mother was sitting with her head in her hands. But they said "Okay", and the guys went off the streets. About an hour and a half later, they were back out, but he'd earned their respect for the way he approached them. He was able to conduct the church service and people got home safely after. I'm not saying it always worked that way, but on that occasion I witnessed how it could be a successful approach.'

Judith is similarly impassioned about the strength and the importance of community, a passion she built on throughout her work as a police officer – and particularly in those tricky situations and neighbourhoods.

'I learned a lot from my dad's real heart for community,' she says. 'He would have chased young fellas vandalising property or spraying graffiti on the walls – he would jump out of the car and run after them.

'He wasn't Superman – he was only about 5 foot 6 – but he had great spirit. And I learned from him that if you want to make your community a better place, you've got to get up off your backside and do something about it instead of sniping from the side-lines at the people who do.'

When she was eighteen, Judith was completing the A Level quali-fications required for secondary school students to enter third level education in the United Kingdom. But her heart wasn't really in it. So, while studying, she also applied to join the police force.

'My older sisters and brother had all gone to university and pursued academic careers,' she explains, 'but I knew that wasn't for me. I had a very strong sense that I was going to be a police officer, but of course those were very difficult times in Northern Ireland.'

It was the height of the Troubles, there were fourteen long years ahead until the ceasefire was signed, and the idea of Judith being a police officer – already a dangerous career no matter what part of the world you work in – in the midst of constant civil disruption was a cause of concern for her parents Dermot and Janet.

Both were supportive and appreciative of the police, but they wanted something more stable and safe for their daughter. So, it may have been fate at play that it was when her parents were away that she finally received her letter of acceptance.

'They were away on holiday – in Tenerife, I think – and I got this letter to say, "Dear Ms McMorran" – as I was back in those days – "We have a vacancy for you in the RUC and you start in the training centre in Enniskillen in January, 1982."

'My older sister, Heather, was still at home at the time and she just laughed when she heard the news. I only received six days' notice so

I'd gone to the training centre in Enniskillen by the time my parents were back from holiday. They came home and asked where I was.

And Heather said, "She's in Enniskillen."

"What's she doing in Enniskillen?"

"Oh, she's joined the police."

'I'd love to have been there!' Judith laughs. 'They forgave me some years later, and have got over it now.'

When Judith received her letter, she had just finished her first semester studying French and German at Queen's University Belfast. She upended her life to make her long-held dream come true.

'My parents were hoping and praying that this silly notion of joining the police would go out of my head so I hadn't told them that I'd applied for what was actually the third time.

'It didn't go down very well that I'd left Queen's to join the RUC – especially during such dangerous times,' she says. 'They were concerned about my safety; it wasn't that they thought policing wasn't an honourable profession or a good career. I think they might have preferred I became a French teacher, but the police was my chosen path.

'I did enjoy university to a certain point, but I knew it wasn't for me. I never really settled at Queen's and I was always looking forward to the day I would get that acceptance letter in my hand. I'm not really sure what I would have done if I'd been turned down a third time.'

At the time, her then-boyfriend (now her husband) had also applied to the force and was accepted – on his first attempt.

~

Even before she shattered the glass ceiling and became something of a feminist icon, Judith knew that her fight for equality was an uphill battle. At the time, only around 10% of uniformed officers were female, while it was more like 60% of police staff in specialist functions. So, once she'd risen through the ranks, Judith requested access to her personal file, dating back to the early 1980s. It confirmed her suspicions that the reason she was initially refused (twice) was because of her gender.

'I'd always suspected I was turned down because I was a woman, but it was only later in my career once I'd got to a certain level in the organisation that I could request my personal file,' she says. 'As I read through the file, I saw right at the very back of it was a comment from the recruiting sergeant to the recruiting superintendent. It said: "While this woman has all the characteristics that we expect in a competent police officer, due to the levelling of female recruitment, there isn't a vacancy for her." So, because I was a woman, there wasn't a vacancy for me.' And of course if Judith had been a man, it would have been a different story.

Judith audits the good, the bad and the ugly of her time in the force with a steely temperament that clearly shows why she was appointed deputy chief constable. After being accepted into the RUC in 1982, she knew she would have to work twice as hard for half the job. But, as Eleanor Roosevelt said, 'No one can make you feel inferior without your consent.' Inferior she was not and the fire in Judith's belly was stoked before she even began her first day on the job.

'I joined with real vision and with the purpose of proving them wrong for turning me down those first two times. Whatever I was asked to do, I was going to do it to the very best of my ability. I won the Battle of Honour for the best all-round recruit in my squad and training centre; there were ninety recruits made up of eighty-six men and four women.

'Sadly, the other three women in my group all left pretty early in their service because they married and had children and found balancing career and family in those days so challenging. I would say the organisation made it hard for women with children – and it wasn't a passive strategy; women were actively and consciously moved to challenging posts to make it more difficult for them to raise a family.'

On the flip side, Judith sought out those particularly challenging posts, seeing them as opportunities to bolster her experience and gain more qualifications; when she applied for leadership positions, she ensured she could never be accused of benefiting from gender balance ratios in her career advancement.

'I spent a lot of time working in Belfast, in Andersonstown for example, where it was pretty challenging policing terrain and a dangerous area. I patrolled accompanied by the army. A police patrol consisted of ten police officers – one female officer – and four soldiers. It always struck me what an intrusion of privacy it must have been, for the courageous people who, through their taxes, funded the police, to have such a huge patrol rock up to your door. Everyone would know who'd been visited by the police – people are always curious about what a police visit means, curious about other people's business – and I felt this especially in the case of domestic abuse or sexual offences.

'But, that level of patrol was all there for very good reason – it was a challenging and dangerous area to police.'

While Judith was assigned to Andersonstown, the station didn't employ a full-time cleaner because it was logistically impossible for someone to commute to the station or too difficult for them to live nearby. So, on days off, officers were given fatigues and called in to clean on designated shifts; a practice which educated Judith on the intricacies of running a successful station at all levels.

'When it was my turn to clean the station, I would do it to the best of my ability – as I had decided I would do no matter what. Nobody was going to complain about the station being grubby when I was on fatigues that day. It put me in very good stead to understand what it's like to work in a large bureaucracy as a cleaner because I've done it myself.'

Over time, Judith moved to the traffic unit, which exposed her to the media. As an inspector and young sergeant, she was put forward to speak about road safety awareness and make appeals to the public, which not only gave her a higher profile, but also allowed her to explore a new layer to her work. Her public profile was so well-received that she was asked to co-host *Crimecall*, a television show which re-enacts unsolved crimes and seeks public assistance in solving particularly difficult cases that are in need of eyewitness accounts and tip-offs. Judith is acutely aware of the dangerous position she was in as a public police figure, regularly appearing on television, before the ceasefires had taken place – always 'with an implicit threat going on in the background'.

'But, as I say, I always step up to challenges and try to see them as positive rather than as threats. Yes, of course, I was possibly exposing myself to risk with *Crimecall*, but what an opportunity I would have missed if I hadn't done it.'

Judith communicates via a language that most high achievers seem to be fluent in: interpreting everything as an opportunity and not dwelling too long on perceived obstacles. She even sees her first two rejections from the RUC as the gateway towards her eventual unprecedented success as a woman in the organisation. During her career, she was part of a team constructing a gender action plan, reflective of a modern PSNI:

'Being turned down and turning it into a positive drove me to do my best to make sure that experience of unfair rejection wasn't had by others. It was deliciously ironic to finally get to the stage of being assistant chief constable and be asked to lead on the organisation's gender action plan.

'Here I was, a woman who the organisation had turned down, not once but twice. I'd experienced all sorts of direct and indirect discrimination, and I was being asked to make a plan. I remember thinking back to my first sergeant's interview. I had reached this fabulous level in the organisation through, it has to be said, the encouragement and support of many men who could see potential in women, who could see potential in me. But I was still asked, "How's a wee girl like you going to control a section of men?"'

'So, I was in the right position to be in charge of the gender action plan looking at recruitment, retention, deployment – all elements of the force that I personally had experienced in a very negative way.'

While Judith's experiences were in keeping with those of a lot of women in male-dominated industries, she is quick not to denounce the organisation as a whole, which she clearly values and respects above all else. She is also thankful to the men who supported her along the way and to the other female officers who paved the way for her. 'Sometimes it was unconscious and sometimes it was definitely conscious,' she admits. For example, in the 1980s, female officers weren't armed and it's down to the bravery of Marguerite Johnston, who took a case against the RUC for this fact, which she won at the European Court, that this practice was changed. However, although the case was won in 1986, it wasn't until 1994 that women were finally armed.

Ending this inequality ended another hugely discriminatory aspect of the police force. In order to be eligible for promotion, officers had to take an exam, which was comprised of three papers on traffic, crime and general police procedure.

'The first question on the general police procedure paper was, "Describe the safety procedures for the Walther pistol,"' Judith explains. 'The Walther pistol was a general police personal protection weapon issued to the men. Women didn't get trained in it. So I couldn't answer the first question in the promotion paper. I hadn't been trained in the Walther pistol. It was discriminatory from the outset.'

After that, the fight for equality was full steam ahead to the point at which men in power understood the benefits of inclusivity. Now, test scores are not only fair from the get-go, but every effort is made to encourage women to not only join, but stay, with the PSNI.

'For me, changing the procedure around arming female police officers was the last barrier of inequality to be broken. Female officers in Northern Ireland today carry the same equipment as their male counterparts. They wear trousers (back in the day, when I was a young constable, women had to wear skirts) and they have their own uniforms that are actually designed for women and not "mini-men". We're not issued with what I call a "man blouse" anymore, they're proper, fitted short blouses that don't go down to your knee. There's now maternity leave, there's two-piece public order suits. It's much more women-friendly.'

Judith is both self-deprecating and self-aware enough not to take credit for any strides made during her tenure. She is the first to praise the force's growth, however. Particularly in Europe, the PSNI is regarded as one of the most effective and forward-thinking police services.

For more than thirty-two years, Judith's work included stints as head of the Drugs Unit and coordinator of the Child Abuse and

Rape Enquiry Units, but she served across a number of different roles 'where I worked with my many inspirational people, both as my leaders and as people I led'.

'I tried to be professional, positive, and prepared. I took the opportunities that came my way, and my advice to people starting out on their career would be to never get too comfortable, and to never let opportunities pass you by.'

Now retired, she is a member of the Policing Authority in the Republic of Ireland. She is also responsible for improved working conditions for women in the force, as well as ensuring effective methods are in place for dealing with sensitive cases like domestic and child abuse; none of which would be possible without Judith's dogged determination to follow a course she knew she was meant to.

'Would I always have kept going after the second rejection?' she wonders. 'Yes, I probably would have. But it's just as good I got that letter on the third application.'

The green jersey of Ireland.

Ciara Griffin

Irish women's rugby captain

'The day I made the Irish rugby squad.'

~

If good things come in threes, Ciara Griffin is in for quite the windfall. She is one of Ireland's most revered athletes. She has represented Ireland at the World Cup and during a Six Nations tournament. She is captain of the Irish women's rugby team – an incredible feat no matter your age – but it's made all the more impressive when you realise she was given that call at the tender age of twenty-four.

~

To say Ciara has earned this glory is an understatement. The blood, sweat and tears that went into making her such an incredible athlete represent a lifetime of effort.

'For me, there are three stages that led to this end goal,' Ciara explains. 'It took me three attempts to make the Irish training squad. I grew up in Kerry where there's a big football background, but I always loved rugby and it was always my dream to wear the red jersey of Munster and the green jersey of Ireland.

'From a very young age, that was what I wanted. The first two times I went for the Irish rugby trials, I didn't make it. As you can imagine, if that's your dream growing up, that was hard to take. The first time I put down to still being too young, but I saw the second time as my chance and I still didn't get it.'

Instead of wallowing, Ciara looked within herself for the mental and physical strength that would later prove so valuable when she went into action on the pitch. She simply wouldn't accept defeat or give up on her dream. Her only option was to simply work harder.

'What I took from my second rejection from the training squad was: I could sit on the couch and cry or I could ask them for feedback. I worked my arse off for two and a half years to be better and to work on my weaknesses.

'It made me tougher. Part of the joy of sport is knowing you can't control everything. Once I realised that, it was a turning point in my mindset. It's very easy to give up, but you should keep aiming towards your goals, no matter what they are.'

The emotional stamina it took to come back from a disappointment like that not once, but twice, is wholly reflective of who Ciara is.

Since she was seven years old, growing up in Castleisland, Co Kerry, playing rugby with her sister, Aoife, in her family's back garden, she had two professional goals: wear the red jersey for Munster and green for Ireland.

There was no plan B.

'After I didn't make it the first two times, it would have been easy for me to not push myself forward. I already had the red of Munster and I was thrilled with that, but I needed to constantly work towards a new goal.

'I could have stayed in the Munster bubble where everything was going well. I might have been good in my eyes, but at the national level it wasn't good enough. I was still quite green in rugby terms.

'It would have been easy for me, after the first two attempts at the squad, to say I tried and that was that. But I didn't. I just kept going. If you want something hard enough, you do everything within your power to achieve it.'

> Part of the joy of sport is knowing you can't control everything. Once I realised that, it was a turning point in my mindset.

So Ciara got to work.

Before her third trial for the national squad, she was studying for her Master's in Education at Mary Immaculate College in Limerick – where she had already completed a Bachelor in Education – and was balancing training with studying full-time.

She was already adhering to a strict, nutrition-rich diet with intensive training sessions, but needed to push herself harder than before to achieve her life goal. Ciara spent two and a half years either with her head buried in books or strategising her training regimen – researching new, innovative ways to increase her strength and speed. Good wasn't good enough. Now it was time to be her best.

To increase her speed while training, Ciara began wrapping a weightlifting belt around her waist, which was fitted to a chain attached to a tyre, and then she would sprint; this is a hardcore, old-school technique preferred by elite athletes and military divisions around the world. She began racing against her now-fiancé, Damien, and friends to get used to pushing herself in a competitive atmosphere when she was already operating at a loss, because of the weight and bulk of the tyre.

'Things like that paid off. I was trying to get better and stronger and get into that mental space where you keep going even when your legs and lungs are burning. Those techniques kept me going all that time.'

And they worked. The third time was the charm.

'I very clearly remember getting a phone call when they said they wanted to bring me onto the training squad and see what I could do. I'll never forget. I bawled my eyes out that day. All my hard work had paid off for that one phone call. I can't describe the joy I felt.'

Ciara showed up on her first day of training alongside veteran players and trailblazers like Fiona Coghlan, who had represented Ireland at three World Cups, and Lynne Cantwell, Ireland's most capped female player. They were in their natural habitat and Ciara was awestruck that she was now playing alongside her heroes.

It would have been a monumental life moment for anyone, but the glory was horribly short-lived as she wound up breaking her leg the first day of training.

'It was typical. I finally got my chance and that happened. It was during contact – something I do every day. I thought I could run on it and so I ran for a bit but my leg kept giving way and I knew something was wrong. It just broke. It was a freak accident that could have happened to anyone at any time.'

Niamh Briggs (who represented Ireland at two World Cups) made sure she was taken care of and showed her extraordinary care for which, Ciara says, 'I'll never be able to thank her enough.'

Ciara's leg was put in a cast on Sunday and on Monday she was back training with her local club, Munster, focusing exclusively on upper body strength.

'I could focus on lifting, handoffs, and get stronger in general. I saw that as an opportunity.'

The glass wasn't half full so much as it was pouring over with potential for Ciara. Every obstacle became an opportunity, every achievement a well-earned gift.

'You can look in the negative side and get bogged down or you can look at the positive and get the best out of it,' she says. 'It's only going to do you well. I focus on things I can accomplish and control.

'I got great at hopping on one leg. I'm a very independent person and I knew I had to keep going, put my head down and focus. Those were the best five weeks of training I had done in a long time because I was so focused on getting fitter and stronger. Even though I'd broken a leg, it wasn't an excuse to slow down.

'When I went on the rowing machine, I would put my broken leg on a skateboard and row away like that with my hands; I did the assault bike but you can do it with hands only; I set up circuits with boxing and ropes; the gym was so accommodating to me. The time flew because I was so focused on setting new goals for myself, like upping my reps and weights.

'My leg was sore, sure, but I knew I was going to do better after. I couldn't start from scratch again; I wanted to catch up with the girls who had been training all along for those five weeks.'

Ciara's dogged determination was formed at an early age, encouraged by her parents Kathleen and Denis, who drove her around the country to train and never let anything get in the way of following her dream.

'There was never anything I couldn't achieve because they supported me one hundred per cent. I played handball a lot as a child and teenager and they drove me all around Kerry to play football.'

Ciara was in her first year of college when she decided she wanted to try out for Munster's Under-18s rugby squad, but she didn't have a car and had no way of getting to the venue at Cork Institute of Technology from her college accommodation in Limerick, which was nearly two hours away. So, her dad drove the two hours from Kerry to Limerick, drove her to Cork, dropped her back to Limerick and then went back to Kerry again. 'Just so I could get a trial.'

On another occasion, she had returned home from college for Christmas and had to train in Fermoy, Co Cork (approximately 90 minutes from her home in Castleisland). Her mother simply volunteered to drive her to and from the training ground with 'no questions asked'.

Kathleen and Denis were well accustomed to their daughter's athletic ambitions, but when she began playing rugby competitively at the age of fourteen, they realised how deep her love ran for the game.

'It wasn't until I was fourteen that we got a rugby club set up in Castleisland. Being able to train every week, and the possibility of playing a match, was incredible. I used to play all the time at home with my sister, but it was a novelty to train, hitting the bag and running through the muck – it's muck so obviously it's not nice but because it's training, it's brilliant.

'It just clicked. I used to play football for a long time, and handball and soccer for many years. When you play a team sport, you get that camaraderie. You're killing each other one minute and having the craic the next.'

It's not just the activity, competition and teamwork Ciara loves, but the life experiences you gain as a result.

'I like rugby because of the discipline. It teaches you great life skills: you never talk back to anyone, or argue with the captain, you speak with respect to your teammates and coach and you don't give out to each other. You always have each other's backs.

'You're going hard tackling one another and then, afterwards, you shake hands with your opponent. When you come off that field, it's done. There's no animosity – only teamwork and respect for the game and the players.'

It's easy to feel Ciara's deep-rooted passion for rugby; a sport which is open to men and women but is still ridding itself of the shackles of gender bias from the past. In 2017, women's rugby competitions began airing on national broadcaster RTÉ after years of being exclusively streamed online.

The women's squad in particular have brought Ireland some of its most noteworthy sporting moments. In 2013, they received a Triple Crown and Grand Slam; they finished fourth in the World Cup in 2014 and won the 2013 and 2015 Six Nations Championships.

'Growing up,' Ciara says, 'I was always led to believe I could do, and achieve, what I wanted. I'm very lucky in that people around me know and understand the kind of person I am. Even my neighbours are used to seeing me running at all hours of the day and doing all sorts of training on the side of the road.'

Perhaps because of this, Ciara is quick to dismiss any of her experiences of sexism, saying the only struggle she experienced back at home was setting up a girls' rugby team, which, of course, she eventually did.

'Here I am living the dream playing rugby under the floodlights of Castleisland. I was very lucky growing up. I think it was the outlook at home was simply do what you want to do: I grew up helping my dad on the farm. Back then, a woman working in agriculture wasn't very common but, thankfully, it's becoming more common now.

'I was always supported and there was never the attitude of "boys can do this and girls can do that". I was never taught that and I've brought that into my life now, the fact that you can't be held back by your gender. It's up to you. If you want to do it, go out and do it.'

It's as if every day Ciara can't quite believe her luck that she is living her own dream. She most certainly never takes even a second for granted, knowing exactly what it took to get there.

'After I made it on the training squad and was working hard, I got my first cap in my first match in 2016 and I was delighted. A few games later I got my first start at Twickenham, which was a real "pinch me" moment – I couldn't believe it was happening. Things just started going up from there.

'It was always a dream of mine to play in a World Cup,' she says, 'and I got to play the World Cup match at home, which made it even sweeter. The result didn't go our way and we didn't play the way we wanted but still, the chance to say you played in a home World Cup wearing the green jersey while playing against such amazing athletes from other countries is something I'll always cherish.'

Getting the call to play for the Irish squad may have been the day that changed Ciara's life, but after that she never dreamed she would become captain. In 2018, she got the life-altering call which asked her to step up to the team's most senior leadership position. It was a move that 'blindsided' her.

'I was blown away. From a girl aged five or six playing rugby on the back lawn to wearing an Irish jersey – I never thought I'd get the opportunity to captain such incredible players.

'People get so scared of following and committing to their dreams, because they've worked so hard and there's a lot to lose – they want to continue on that path. Remember you're there for a reason and trust yourself. That applies to more than just sport; it applies to life in general.

'Just be you. There's only one of you.'

Ciara's emotional intelligence and mental strength are traits worth admiring, but ones that came as the result of just as much emotional hard work as that sprint-training with the weight of a tyre dragging behind her.

'It took a lot for me to feel like this. When I was younger, I was very hard on myself and I always saw the negative in things – sometimes I am still too hard on myself. It took a lot for me get to this point. I suffered a lot with confidence, but through sport and backing myself, I got there. I want all girls to feel the same and believe in themselves.

'I pinch myself every day that I'm here and I'll do everything I can to stay on this road.'

Passionate about chocolate.

Mary Ann O'Brien

Founder, Lily O'Brien's Chocolates and
the Jack & Jill Foundation

*'The day I learned about chocolate . . .
and the day my son Jack was born.'*

~

This entire book is grounded in the idea that each person knows a day, or moment, that they feel changed the course of their life. For Mary Ann O'Brien, one of Ireland's most successful businesswomen and generous philanthropists, there are two equally important days that sent her life in two new directions. The first being a chance encounter with a chocolatier in South Africa, a moment which would empower her to launch Lily O'Brien's Chocolate, and the second being when her son Jack was born in 1996.

~

To understand Mary Ann's life as a mother, one must first understand how her extraordinarily successful business came to be and how it affected her personal life. Parents the world over who are facing difficulties with their children understand the feeling of having to put on a brave face in the boardroom only to go back home and sob.

Mary Ann's story starts in 1992, when she and her husband, Jonathan Irwin, were on holiday in Cape Town, South Africa. She was recovering from a two-year bout of chronic fatigue, triggered by the Epstein Barr virus. It left her feeling constantly exhausted and so the idea of tagging along with Jonathan for some much-needed R&R on his work trip was too tempting to turn down.

'I didn't want to go initially because I was very worried and upset about the reality of apartheid, but Jonathan persuaded me to come along and little did I know it would change the course of my business life for ever.'

The couple arrived at a 'charming boutique hotel' in Hermanus, a seaside town in the Western Cape Province, intent on spending as much time relaxing as possible.

'It was a tiny hotel overlooking the cliffs and, the first day I arrived there, I was restless straight away,' Mary Ann recalls. 'I wanted to play chess and gamble with other guests and I came across the owner's daughter Mandy – who has remained a firm friend – and I asked her if I could borrow the chess set I saw in reception. She said, "You could but you'd melt it."

'It was the most beautiful chess set I'd ever seen and it was entirely made of chocolate; including the board and the pieces, which had been made using dark and white chocolate. I'd never seen anything like it. From that moment, I spent the rest of my holiday going from my bikini, straight into the kitchen to join Mandy.'

At the time, Mandy was making champagne truffles for BMW, one of the hotel's clients, and within a few minutes of seeing Mandy at work, Mary Ann was hooked.

'That day I learned how to make champagne truffles and I declared to God that I wanted to go home and start a chocolate business. It's 2019 now and I never dreamed on that day in January 1992 that we'd end up with Lily O'Brien's [so named after her oldest daughter], a business that turns over €30 million, which exports chocolate all over the world and has more than two hundred employees.

'If you'd told me how it would all turn out in 1992, I'd have said you were crazy. That day turned out to be the start of a journey. I wasn't Steve Jobs or anybody special in the world of business. Until then, I'd had no training and I didn't have a great business brain, but I was a lover of people and knew I had good emotional intelligence.'

At the time her chocolate passion was sparked, Mary Ann was working as the marketing manager for the Phoenix Park Racecourse, and horse racing was her main love. To say food and cooking were very low on her list of priorities would be polite.

'You wouldn't have come to my house expecting a beautiful meal,' she says. 'And if you were looking for the best mother at the school gates in the baking competition that really wouldn't have been me. I'd have been the mum at the back of the local bakery trying to re-ice the buns so it looked like I might have made them.

'But you can train any dog to do any tricks.'

And so Mary Ann was swept up by Mandy's work into a world of chocolate. Seeing the joy she could bring to someone's life with some baking, she decided she was going to spread that joy at home in Ireland. However, with her lack of experience, she needed to charm the chocolate masters around the world into training her and sharing their secrets to grow her burgeoning business.

'I saw what beautiful chocolates Mandy was creating and the pleasure she was giving to everybody and it seemed like such a fabulous idea. It's a very pleasurable business to be in.

'From that, I became a seeker of excellence in chocolate. I went to Belgium, Germany, France, San Francisco – anywhere I could find a chocolatier who I thought was working outside of the box. I camped outside their door, I brought them flowers, I brought John Donoghue books from Ireland . . . whatever I could think of just so I could learn.

'I totally immersed myself in the world of chocolate. I was overly enthusiastic and I had a huge amount of self-belief – I don't quite know where that came from.'

Within three years, Mary Ann was making such a name for herself in Ireland that Aer Lingus took notice at a time when airlines had money to burn. That first contract gave her the ambition to go even further.

'I got my first Aer Lingus contract in 1995, which was quite a surprise because I was still very small in business terms. In those days, the airlines were very wealthy. If you were flying to London, which is a 55-minute flight, you were given breakfast on the plane and if you were lucky enough to be up towards the front of the plane, there were flutes of champagne with it. They commissioned chocolates for every meal on every flight.

'An annual order from Aer Lingus at that stage was €2.2 million for two types of chocolates and €6 million for chocolates in the shape of a horse's head for those customers at the front of the plane. I thought, if I can get a contract with Aer Lingus, why wouldn't I get one with British Airways?'

After a convincing pitch, British Airways also commissioned her and the Lily O'Brien's business was booming; so much so that Mary Ann had to emergency-employ people from her village overnight because the BA order was so large.

A number of companies began seeing the brand on BA flights at Heathrow Airport and soon she was fulfilling orders from around the world with particular stakes in the United States and Canada.

'We still, to this day, travel to Paris, Vienna, New York, London, every November and December and immerse ourselves in those cities to see what's going on. What are the chefs up to? What are the cosmetic designers up to? What are the fashion people up to? What are the florists doing? And we try to weave that into the brand. Because you know, it is all about touchy feely.

'We're not the sort of high-end, most expensive chocolate on the market, but when I started people were beginning to aspire towards hand-crafted items and so my timing was very good. Always keeping the best ingredients in there is key and the rest is actually very easy.

'I think it's important to get the message across that it's about staying still sometimes when you're travelling or whether you're writing, or whatever it is you're doing, because you never know what's awaiting you. That day was a huge opportunity for me.

'I've made so many friends, including my employees, and we've had a great journey, but that's all because of that single day, so you never know. It could be this day or tomorrow that it will happen to you. Opportunity strikes when you least expect it and you don't even necessarily know it's an opportunity at first.

'I'd like to say it was a long, enjoyable journey but if I can do it, anybody can do it. The chances of me being in that hotel wanting to use that chess set; meeting Mandy who was incredibly generous sharing all her chocolate secrets with me was serendipitous.

'I got quite the education and I'm a very fortunate girl because I turned it into my career and it's been a great success for me and you can imagine all the people I've met along the way.'

~

That year in 1992, Mary Ann and Jonathan were parents to their then baby daughter Lily, their son Phonsie was born in 1994 and in 1996 she became pregnant again.

'To my joy, I got pregnant again, but this time, this was a life-changing day of a more personal nature – a game changer arrived in the shape of a beautiful twelve-pound baby called Jack, who appeared to be born perfect.

'The first evening, he suffered a near-miss cot death when he choked on his own mucus. The best way to describe his condition is like someone whose telephone wires have been completely jumbled, never be sorted out again. He was having multiple epileptic fits every few minutes. He couldn't swallow, and he couldn't see or hear. He was a very distressed little boy and went into intensive care for two months.'

It took up to twenty hours per day to feed him because he was having such frequent epileptic fits and they had to be so cautious about his feeding tube so as not to put it in his lungs.

'It wasn't a good situation. I obviously would give anything to have him here now and see him in college and running around having a great time. But he's not. Jack died when he was eighteen months old. But he did give us the idea to start the Jack and Jill Foundation.'

With all that was happening, Mary Ann and Jonathan were on the verge of divorce, they were barely sleeping and their two older children were struggling. 'They were only small but we were a disaster of a house,' Mary Ann remembers.

Their home was set up like a hospital, but in the 1990s there was no formal assistance for children with severe illnesses or disability. Until a friend, a former neonatal nurse, saw they were struggling and asked if she could help.

'For a mother it's like having a dagger stuck in your back that's twisted deeper every hour. Jack wasn't having a great time. But again, Lily O'Brien's kept giving me gifts because it introduced me to a woman who knew we were struggling to keep it together.

'She said, "Can I come out and see him? Up to two years ago, I was a neonatal nurse working in intensive care. I'd love to give you a few hours a few nights every week."

'I was so grateful that someone knew his needs. Straight away, she said the tube should be taken out of his nose, she recommended a little operation for him and then he could crawl and be put on his tummy.

'That stopped him having rashes. She recommended giving him a warm bath with lavender oil to get him out of a very bad epileptic fit and he loved the bath. We got to the stage where Jack had some decent quality of life. We got him giggling and we got him knowing us. We got him settled. And he lived the best life he could.'

She and a few others rallied together to improve little Jack's quality of life and help stitch their family back together, and then, in his passing, his memory for ever remains in the enormous work of the Jack & Jill Foundation.

The idea came about as a way of helping families in similar situations, who needed a solid support network of professionals, parents who had been through it themselves, or neighbours and friends who could assist. The public health nurses were well-intentioned and kind-hearted, but caring for a child with such severe needs required certain levels of expertise.

Mary Ann and Jonathan pleaded for assistance from the health service and, when they were repeatedly rebuffed, decided to start their own way of gaining and giving help.

'We would bump into people who had been through so much with their children, we came across some appalling stories. We also heard some good stories; we have kids who have survived when their prognoses didn't look good and we discovered with our little baby, of course, that they do much better at home than they do in hospital. And you as a parent will also do much better minding your child at home with support.'

Jonathan left his job to focus on the foundation full-time and Mary Ann returned to the helm of Lily O'Brien's, with the relief of knowing her baby son was comfortable.

Jack's quality of life improved and Lily and Phonsie's lives were also improving as they were able to pursue extracurricular activities and enjoy their own special family time. 'Because we were receiving help with Jack,' Mary Ann says, 'we were able to actually smile and speak and engage with our other children too.'

> In this world what we need is kindness and compassion and care. We need the time to allow ourselves to live and breathe.

Since 1997, over 2,400 families around Ireland have been helped by the Jack and Jill Foundation. And now, in 2019, thirteen nurses work full-time with the foundation, in addition to 600-plus community nurses, and there are local volunteers, too, who aren't specifically medically trained but can help in other ways.

'The Jack & Jill club perhaps isn't a very nice club to be in because it means you have a child who is suffering,' Mary Ann says. 'But it's great to have other members to turn to for support. It's a lovely community. It was just something that happened naturally and it was the right thing to do at the time.

'I'm probably the most grateful person you'll ever meet. I live in a beautiful place in Kilkenny, in the middle of nowhere. I grow all my own vegetables, I have six dogs, my children have grown up. I'm just so grateful and so lucky.

'A bit of compassion goes a long way. You know, a lot of people would say it's easier for me, but I don't believe success and money is what shapes people. In this world what we need kindness and compassion and care. We need the time to allow ourselves to live and breathe.'

An A-grade student
in the school of life.

Kirsten Mate Maher

Rose of Tralee 2018

'The day I decided not to go to college.'

~

Kirsten Mate Maher has a tendency to make history. Not only is she the first African-Irish woman to win the Rose of Tralee, but at twenty-one, she is also one of the youngest.

~

She possesses the type of quiet confidence you would expect from such an accomplished young woman, but without any arrogance. She speaks in soothing, soft tones and seems wise beyond her years, speaking in affirmations like: 'Even though I'm out of my comfort zone, I feel I'm where I'm supposed to be.'

The Rose of Tralee extends well beyond the 500,000-plus viewers who watch it every year on national broadcaster RTÉ. It is a uniquely international, Irish event open to all women of Irish birth and heritage from all over the world.

Every August, over the course of one week, dozens of women from around the world descend on Tralee, Co Kerry to represent

their region or country and compete to be named that particular year's Rose of Tralee.

The Rose of Tralee festival's definition changes depending on who you ask. Some say it's a more wholesome version of a traditional beauty pageant or the somehow more demeaning 'lovely girls competition', while others will say it's a celebration of women. Certainly, over the last twenty years, the latter is a more accurate description, representing contemporary Ireland and contemporary Irish identity. In 1998, Irish-Filipino Luzveminda O'Sullivan was the first mixed race winner to take home the title; Irish-Indian Dr Clare Kambamettu won in 2010; and Tara Talbot, who is Filipino-Irish, won in 2011.

The Rose of Tralee winners also includes individuals such as Dr Aoibhinn Ní Shúilleabháin (2005), a mathematics and statistics professor and RTÉ broadcaster, and Maria Walsh (2014), the first openly gay Rose, who ran a successful campaign to be elected a Member of the European Parliament (MEP) for Ireland in 2019.

In 2018, when Kirsten entered, she was at a point in her life when so many young people ask themselves, what do I want to do for the rest of my life? She explains:

'There are two days that changed my life I suppose – one being when I realised it was okay not to go to college and the other when I won the Rose of Tralee in August 2018.'

Modern Ireland, like much of the Western world, tends to dictate that third level education is essential for professional growth. Throughout secondary school, students are encouraged to pursue university at all costs – the ultimate victory after completing their final exams. According to the Central Statistics Office, 56.2 per cent of people aged fifteen to thirty-nine have a third level qualification,

in comparison to 18.9 per cent of those aged sixty-five and over (as shown in the 2016 census).

But – what if your dream job doesn't require additional education? Or what if – gasp! – you don't even know what your dream job is yet?

'Like a lot of people, I was waiting for a moment for it to hit me what I want to do and it never happened,' Kirsten reflects. It wasn't until she sat down with her father, Kwalo Mate, an army officer from Zambia and her mother, Jacinta – who told her they would support her decision to postpone college if she still studied hard and got a full-time job when she finished school – that she realised she would have the luxury of time.

'One day, we had a career guidance class in school in sixth year and my teacher said, "Hands up who thinks they're going to go to college." I remember not knowing what I was going to do, but I stuck up my hand anyway because there were only two others who didn't and they were two troublemakers. I looked around at everyone knowing what they wanted to do, knowing I didn't feel the same. When it came time to do my Leaving Cert, my parents sat me down and said they'd understand if I didn't want to go to college, but I still had to put the hard work in and get good results. They would support me, but I needed to get a job and earn my keep.

'That conversation with my parents changed my life. My dad went to college, he was in the army, he studied business and speaks a number of different languages – and I really liked styling women and riding ponies! Their support changed my life because after that day a lot of other opportunities popped up.'

After finishing her Leaving Certificate, she followed through on her promise and began working in fashion retail to support herself. She was content, but wasn't convinced it was a job she wanted for the rest of her days. Kirsten then became an A-grade student at the school of life, learning self-sufficiency, financial independence and how to accurately assess any new people in her life.

'It was a little intimidating, but, with my time off from academia, I learned more about life than I would have at college. College nights out and college life is a mystery to me, but I know how to work hard and put my mind to anything,' she explains. 'The older I get, the more I realise college mightn't be the best idea for a lot of people. A lot of friends have dropped out of their initial course and re-enrolled in something else, but I can't help but think how their lives might have been different if they had taken just one year off.'

During what had originally began as a year off and a college deferral – a time during which she could work and figure out what it was she wanted to do and how to get there – the opportunity to enter the local heat of the Rose of Tralee came up. Kirsten had always been a solid student, but never an academic. She worked hard, but it didn't come as easily to her as others and she never had the impulse to fully immerse herself in education.

'I never had that drive for academia, not in the same way as my sister, Danielle, who wants to be an English teacher. I loved studying Irish growing up; I've always had a *grá* for it. But I didn't want to be a teacher and I knew I'd end up ruining the language for myself if I pursued it. I'm not that strong academically – I did fine in my Leaving Cert – but then I quickly figured out it doesn't really matter what you get in your Leaving Cert. I don't want to be a doctor or a lawyer but I'm grateful there are people in the world who do, because we need them!'

Kirsten had come to the realisation it takes most people more than twenty-one years to realise: knowing what you don't want to do is half the battle. If not for the support of her parents, Kirsten might have been deterred from education entirely.

~

Kirsten entered the Rose of Tralee competition on a whim, but it initially took some coaxing from her friend Jenny Walsh, the 2016 Waterford Rose. Kirsten didn't feel quite ready, but a year later, she was convinced. She was approaching the end of her year off and saw the potential in it.

'The most nerve-wracking moment is sending in the application,' she says. 'At that stage, I hadn't ruled out college forever and felt that when the time is right, I will know. If I had gone that first year after finishing school, I know I would have dropped out. It was only supposed to be a year break, and then it turned into two years when I went travelling. Then I decided to do the Rose of Tralee and that's how it turned into a third year – now I don't know what I want to do! I'm realising the hardest thing in life is making decisions. If I could tell anybody anything in a secondary school, I would encourage students to take a year out if they're not certain what they want to do.'

Kirsten intended on her deferral to college to be just that, a deferral, but the best laid plans often go awry. The night she won the Rose of Tralee in 2018, she found out the following morning she had been accepted into a course to study multimedia and application development at the Waterford Institute of Technology (WIT). She declined, declaring it would be 'ridiculous' not to embrace 'with both hands' the opportunity she had just been given as Rose.

And so her decision was postponed another year; during which time, she would remain laser focused on her work and family. Her family and friends had always been integral to her life, but during that time, she was also mourning the loss of a close friend who took his own life in May 2018.

'It made the year bittersweet,' she says. 'In between being selected as Waterford Rose and Rose of Tralee, I had to deal with his death and that entire time is a bit of a blur. I learned to deal with that and put on a brave face if I had to go to an event.'

Kirsten found out about her friend's death on a Tuesday night, went to work on Wednesday morning ('I don't know why') and her mother collected her almost instantly at the insistence of her manager who knew something was wrong. 'I was in a state of shock for about two weeks after that.'

When the conversation shifts towards life lessons and highlights from her year as Rose, Kirsten can't help but remember her lost friend and remains emotional speaking about him.

'It was a bit strange, learning to deal with that,' she says. 'I find it hard when people ask if this year has been amazing: one half of the year has been fantastic and people don't realise you have a personal life as well as being Rose of Tralee. You don't want to say, "Well actually, it was the worst year ever, but the best thing in the world happened to me." For every bad thing that happens, something good also will. I'd never had to deal with something so close to me. It's meant that now I work with Pieta House [an Irish charity which provides free therapy for those in suicidal distress] and I've met people along the way, which has definitely helped.'

For three months, while preparing to take to the stage at the Rose of Tralee Dome, she was privately grieving, but had been holding it together publicly as much as possible. However, when she walked off stage after her interview with host Dáithí Ó Sé, the tears began flowing – and they wouldn't stop.

'It was like a release after such an intense experience. You just cry and cry. This entire year has been very overwhelming and learning to deal with his death has been something . . . I'm really proud of myself for holding it together for the year, but it was hard.'

Perhaps the biggest life lesson she's learned is to be kind to herself and to know not to push herself too far. When it came to an appearance at the Galway Races, she left as early as possible in order to spend time reflecting in her hotel room alone. She had often gone horse riding together with the friend she'd lost and the memories were too strong – and too soon – to bear at the time.

> It was like a relief after such an intense experience.

'It's starting to become a part of life,' she says. 'It never really goes away but you learn to deal with it better, even though when I talk about it, I start crying straight away. I had one month of being comfortable and getting used to what was coming with the competition and then, there was this other thing happening. You have to learn to keep Rose of Tralee and a personal life separate. It cast a shadow on the year.'

During her reign, Kirsten was also caring for her beloved grandfather Charlie, who has Parkinson's and wasn't expected to survive after a difficult diagnosis in March 2018. He is now home in Waterford with her grandmother Margaret Bridget, or M.B. (both of whom were particularly thrilled with Kirsten's victory in Tralee). Charlie's illness has, however, brought her family closer together; it has meant that his children, and grandchildren, are spending more time with one another.

'At the end of the day, my family have never had a reason to be close,' she says. 'Everyone always did their own thing. We always met at family events, but since my grandfather's diagnosis we're always together now. Even with Tralee, my whole family came down together – to the point where I had nowhere to leave my dog Fluffy, a fourteen-year-old Border Collie, so even she was there with me.'

Since the day that changed her life, Kirsten has matured well beyond the expectations you might have of the average early twenty-something. In fact, she seems to clearly understand her own best qualities, the ones which extend well beyond academia.

'I always thought I wouldn't be smart enough for media interviews, but I've realised I'm smart in my own way. I might not be the most academic and I definitely wasn't an A1 student, but I was happy enough being a low B or high C student and I don't think there's anything wrong with that. I'm not as stupid as I thought I was. I used to think I was a fairy but after this year, I've learned that I'm not. In fact, I'm quite good at judging people. I learned to trust myself and listen to my instincts. It's always good to ask someone's opinion, but now I know that anything I say I can really stick by it.'

While it takes more people a few decades to reap the benefits of hindsight, Kirsten came to the realisation that even the nasty people we encounter have something to teach us.

'Everyone deserves a second chance,' she says, 'but usually my gut is right. I've come across some of the most amazing people this year, but I've also met the worst people in the world. Those people really teach you something. You learn something from everyone. Just because you don't like someone doesn't mean you have the right to be nasty. Not everyone sees eye to eye, and it would be a boring world if we did.'

She created change
through sheer grit.

Louise O'Reilly

Model and body positivity campaigner

'The day my modelling career began ...
after learning to love my body.'

~

When it comes to the modelling industry in Ireland, few can say they've achieved as much as Louise O'Reilly. She's a thirty-year-old from Dublin who has spent much of her career – one which might traditionally be rooted in the superficiality of external appearance – becoming an agent of change. I first interviewed Louise in 2010 when we were both still new to our respective fields and she was, even then, gaining attention for her determination to revolutionise an industry which sees its customers as a problem instead of a solution.

~

Just a few short years ago, before supermodels like Ashley Graham appeared on the cover of *Sports Illustrated*; before ASOS stopped airbrushing any stretch marks from their models and before certain corners of Instagram became a mecca of self-acceptance and body positivity, the international modelling industry was working off an old-school business archetype that only skinny women would ever be considered beautiful, be considered *worthy* of high fashion. In particular, skinny white women.

There were, of course, the exceptions. There was *Vogue Italia*, which featured three plus-size models on the cover and subsequently propelled the movement in a positive direction back in 2011. But the bulk of the advancements has been through the sheer grit of women like Louise, who are campaigning, boots on the ground, on a daily basis.

The day that changed Louise's life was in 2011, when, still new to modelling, she got her big break – one which would pave the way for the path she finds herself on today.

'Going back ten years, when I started modelling, there was only one other curvy model working in Ireland so we split a lot of jobs. I was getting a lot of work on television and balancing it with studying International Relations and Politics at University College Dublin (UCD) and working at a DVD store for money,' she recalls.

'I started to wonder what else I could do. With the greatest respect to Ireland – as much as I love my country – it had limitations for me. Back then, being taken seriously as a curvy model was very difficult. I had to do a lot to persuade people to work with me, which is why I started taking trips to London where, at the time, only one or two boutique agencies catered to curve modelling, but it was a start.'

If a 'straight sized' model works hard, Louise had to work much harder, just to be considered for the same calibre of job. She practised her posing by cutting out pictures from magazines and recreating them in the mirror and became her own best publicist, convincing casting directors to be open to her and brands to see the value she could add to their business. She was extremely effective.

Louise took inspiration from women such as Candice Huffman and Crystal Renn, supermodels who forged a path even earlier, in the early 2000s, with the aim of applying their mantras to a reluctant Irish market.

'I always found it very difficult,' Louise says, 'because I had to prove myself and show I could do what any other model could do. I was almost turning into a saleswoman. I wanted to be the same standard as the other models while at the same time breaking the mould and the preconceived idea that a bigger model couldn't be like everyone else.'

After a hat campaign for an Irish designer in London, Louise's portfolio finally had enough gravitas to take her to the next level of her career. She was an early adopter of social media networks such as Facebook and Instagram and when a friend asked if he could share her information with a friend of his, someone who was looking for new plus-size models for the brand which he was overseeing . . . That friend turned out to be Tim Walker, the former creative director of Shop Direct (the company behind Littlewoods) and, within two days, Louise was on a plane for a casting in Liverpool.

They took one look at her and booked her on the spot. Littlewoods, a major brand in the UK and Ireland, with millions of shoppers and huge reach, wanted her to front a campaign for them which would take ten days to shoot.

'It was a really big deal for someone like me who was trying to work internationally. Until then, I had done some catalogue jobs in Germany but I really wanted to do more in the British and American markets, which are much more difficult to break.'

The saying 'when it rains it pours' has merit in the case of Louise. After her first job with Littlewoods, Louise was suddenly up to her neck in opportunities. That one job led to her securing an agent – one of the biggest in London – who also saw her potential in what was just a grainy mobile phone photo.

'I was finding it difficult to find an agent because of my size,' Louise remembers, 'and work had been going through my Dublin-based agency Morgan until then. Chase Aston, a celebrity makeup artist, was doing the makeup on the Littlewoods' set and asked to take a picture of me. He sent the photograph to a friend of his who happened to be heading up the yet-to-be-launched curve division at Models 1.

'At the time, they were one of the biggest agencies in Europe, representing models such as Naomi Campbell and Olivia Palermo, and they wanted to work with me! Karen Diamond, the agency's director, called me after I finished the shoot . . . I remember walking outside into the car park – we were shooting in an industrial estate – and I got that phone call which changed everything.

'She asked me to come to London as soon as possible, offering me a contract on the spot! I can still remember how much my voice and body were shaking. I was trying to play it cool, while also trying to be appreciative and grateful for the opportunity, which is a hard balance to find.

'Later that day, I was on a train from Liverpool to London. And that was it. As the industry was moving forward, people were seeing the need to use curvy models. After that, I got representation in South Africa, Sweden, Australia . . . it was a snowball effect.'

By 2011, Louise had established herself as an influencer in the fashion industry – before the term became so divisive – building a global network of contacts and clients. But, with each country came a different standard of accepted beauty. This defined the self-confident and barrier-breaking signatures that make up much of Louise's personality.

Nowadays, calls for diversity are reflected in the increase in an inclusive mindset within the fashion industry, but just eight years ago, a plus-size model would only ever be just that: a plus-size model. A 'curvy' model would rarely walk in the same fashion show as what we now call a 'straight-size' one (but which was then simply called 'normal'), and they definitely wouldn't appear in the same campaign or work together to normalise acceptance of different body types. You were either one or the other – and the two were kept apart.

That's not to say that any model gets off easily when it comes to an over-analysis or scrutiny of their physique by casting agents, clients or anyone in a position of influence. 'Back then,' Louise says, 'you had to stay in your box, which I didn't think was right. In some places, I'm considered an 'in-between', but then in Greece, for example, I'm considered a super-size model.

'I remember going to a beauty casting. On these types of casting, they look at every single part of you. One person commented that they thought my earlobes were too big. I burst out laughing, but they were deadly serious. In New York, they're more cutting, more incisive, but it all goes back to the need to process the discourse insofar as understanding that you are supposed to be a blank canvas and, as such, you may not be suitable for the job. You can't try and make sense of this in personal way.

'On one occasion, I flew in early on a 4 a.m. flight (I honestly can't remember which country) and I had queued up for several hours hoping to make a good impression. They took one look at me, looked at one page of my book and thanked me for coming. I had to go straight back to the airport.

'They know as soon as they see you if you're right for the job or not. There are all these elements within fashion and modelling that can be quite hurtful to a person's body image if you're not strong enough in yourself.

'In Milan, I'm considered quite big – too big even for plus-size brands. I did Madrid Fashion Week and it was one of the most exciting fashion shows I've possibly ever done. We were doing a fitting and they told me they didn't anticipate my hips to be as curvy as they are. They had to get the dress altered a few hours before the show. In the end, the designer was happy because I made his clothes look good, but there are some instances where if that happened you'd be sent home.'

The examples are endless: a systematic chipping away at one's self-worth through judgements about one's appearance. But for Louise, these practices simply would not do; and if she was going to work in an industry that expects models to be seen and not heard, then she would defy expectation – and loudly. That's where her wildly successful blog and online brand Style Me Curvy (SMC) was born. Invention, being as it is the mother of necessity, facilitated her growth from a relatively unknown model to a legitimate industry powerhouse.

Louise loves her industry, but loving something and thinking it's perfect are not the same thing. Here she was, a girl from Dublin's Northside seaside town of Malahide, travelling around the world working as a model, giving her followers an insight into what really happens behind the velvet rope, years before social media wielded the power it holds today.

'I wanted somewhere where I could talk about fashion for all sizes and try to eliminate this whole mindset of putting everybody in boxes,' she asserts. 'The more I got into it, the more I loved it – even though there were some very bad days.

'I reached a point where I couldn't believe I was modelling, but I still wanted more. There was an emptiness in me. I loved my work and never thought I would even get to do it, let alone for as long as I did, but I wanted something else. That's where Style Me Curvy came in.'

SMC originally began as a blog intended to remove the mystery from a famously tough-to-crack industry and, ten years later, Louise is still fighting the same fights. Having cut her teeth in an environment which values appearances above all, she felt compelled to share her insider knowledge that nothing is as glamorous as it looks from the outside.

> Before the current trend of body positivity, body acceptance and even body neutrality … we weren't aware that ordinary aspects of a woman's body were photoshopped out.

'Before the current trend of body positivity, body acceptance and even body neutrality, from a consumer point of view, we weren't aware that ordinary aspects of a woman's body – stretch marks, for example – were photoshopped out. I knew this, and more, from my work in the industry and I felt a responsibility to share it with the outside world in some capacity,' she says.

'We are in a culture where "influencer" has become a dirty word and I was sensitive to that. I didn't want to be painted as someone who doesn't add value to their readers' lives. For the first five years of my blog, I didn't go out at the weekend or see my friends; I was glued to my laptop and I spent a lot of time writing back to people individually.'

As Louise's career continues to take off, her correspondence has suffered, something she admits to with great disappointment. Her demographic is broad, from ages seventeen to sixty-five, and is comprised predominantly of women – of all sizes – but their commonality is that none of them feel included in the mainstream consumer experience.

'It goes back to the conversation that the scope of body image covers all ages. I try to do things in a seamless way without shoving it down people's throats. I've changed my approach now because I see people talking about body image and it upsets me because I feel there isn't an authentic thread behind it.'

Authenticity is the name of Louise's game as she recalls the road-blocks to the self-assuredness she now possesses. This self-imposed need to be a force for good comes from her childhood, one which was marred by body image issues, and something she never wants anyone else to carry.

As a child, Louise was always big, but her issues with her size became exacerbated after twice breaking her kneecap. She was, at her peak, a size 22 to 24. The mental affects her weight had on her self-esteem permeated every aspect of her life. In the 1990s, there were no plus-size ranges from which she could shop; no high-profile women to emulate and all that was available in bigger sizes was that kind of too-casual clothing that does little for one's self-esteem at the best of times.

'Growing up for me was really difficult. I am the youngest and I have two brothers, my mum was always very petite, so I had no one curvy who was into fashion who I could associate with. The only woman in the public eye I could relate to at my size was Oprah Winfrey,' she says.

'Back then, online shopping wasn't a thing so I was wearing cartoon T-shirts, sports shirts and tracksuit pants because they were the only things that fitted me. I look back at my friendships and I see that I isolated myself because my body image was so bad; I spent a lot of my childhood in a very low place.

'I couldn't participate in a lot of activities. When I was around nine or ten, I broke my left kneecap and I ended up in a full cast from my ankle to my hip for weeks. Then I went to a physiotherapist and tripped over something, and within a few days, I had re-broken the kneecap all over again. I ended up spending an entire summer in a plaster cast and on crutches.

'The weight just piled on. As a kid, being that size was very difficult. In my first year of secondary school, my uniform had to be specially made because they didn't have skirts that accommodated my size. I tried every diet from Weight Watchers to Atkins, and eventually by the second year, the weight started to come off.'

Nowadays, Louise might seem the pinnacle of self-acceptance and the proud curator of a community which encourages unashamed self-love, but it's hard for anyone to heal the scars of their past. As part of her on-going healing, she is taking on fashion – and she's doing it in style.

'Even when you lose weight, those body image issues still stay with you. You always think you're not good enough or you shouldn't do something because of your size. A big part of it always went back to fashion. I wanted to look like my friends but I couldn't and I didn't really know how to dress. I lived outside of the city so I couldn't go into the fashionable stores and I was limited in my shopping destinations.

'But by the time I turned eighteen, my confidence began to grow. When I went to university, I was exposed to all different people – people who looked like me, people of all different sizes, and that's how my journey to loving, and appreciating my body, really started. I was definitely a late bloomer in terms of my confidence. I look back and it makes me sad looking at parts of my childhood and teenage years, because I remember that feeling of how awful I felt. That feeling of being so lost, of not even knowing what pair of jeans to buy and the fear factor that comes with that.

'There are still women out there now – of any age – who have that exact same feeling. I'm grateful in many ways because I feel that in some capacity I am able to help other people in the same boat, people who are feeling low about themselves. If I have even a one per cent chance of helping someone's confidence and self-acceptance, then I'm very happy to do it.'

SURVIVAL

~

STRENGTH
COURAGE
CONVICTION

'I'd lived this perfect life.'

Georgie Crawford

Broadcaster and wellness advocate

'The day I was diagnosed with breast cancer
aged thirty-one'

~

As far as life-changing days go, Georgie Crawford, a radio news-reader from Dublin, thought she'd experienced hers when she gave birth to her daughter in February, 2017. Little Pia was the start of a family she and her husband Jamie so desperately wanted.

~

But when Pia was seven months old and Georgie was in the throes of the highs and lows that can accompany being a new mother, she found a lump on her breast. It was three days after her daughter's christening and two weeks before she was due to return to work after maternity leave.

'I'd lived this perfect life so far: I had a gorgeous husband, we'd just bought our dream home, and we had a gorgeous, healthy baby. We had our daughter, which is what I'd wanted my whole life because I never had any sisters,' Georgie says. 'Everything was just absolutely perfect.'

Then, the unimaginable happened. It was a Wednesday night, it had been just like any ordinary day, and Georgie had asked her husband to feed their daughter because she was feeling especially tired.

'Pia was still sleeping beside me and Jamie was putting her back into my crib . . . I was a first-time mum so I was always so nervous about everything and I'd jumped up to see if she was okay in there. I leaned over and my left hand fell against my chest and I felt something I'd never felt before on my body.

'I got such a fright. It was like a bone or thumb sticking out of my chest. I felt it again and I was completely terrified. In that moment, I knew. *This is bad.*

'I called Jamie over to feel it and I knew by the way he looked at me that he felt the same way I did.

'At that moment, I got on my hands and knees in the bed. I was trying to breathe and I began bawling, silently. Jamie was trying to calm me and I said, "This is it. This is bad." I'd never felt anything like this in my life.'

Georgie and Jamie sat on their couch, mesmerised in silence and they both spent the evening thinking of plausible explanations for this lump that didn't involve cancer. He suggested it might have been a blocked milk duct because she'd just finished breastfeeding, or it could have been the result of something hormonal.

'But I knew my body,' Georgie said. 'The lump was so hard and I couldn't move it.'

She went to bed; still exhausted from caring for an infant full-time and unaware of the illness that lay in wait for her and her family. The next morning, she woke up early to text their GP. The GP asked Georgie to attend her clinic at 8 a.m., so Georgie dropped Pia at her mother's house. Georgie remembers that when she told her mother, she 'had the same look on her face that Jamie had.'

So began the first of many doctor's appointments, over the course of nearly a year. Georgie's GP gave her a referral letter to St Vincent's Hospital in order to be assessed as quickly as possible, but the wait was long.

'I couldn't wait five minutes, let alone weeks,' she remembers. 'I went home and I called every hospital in Dublin – Beaumont Hospital said I could come in the next day.

'Within two minutes of my consultation, they ruled out a cyst and then the tears came. I was inconsolable. I had planned on going to the IMRO Radio Awards the following night in what was supposed to be my first night out since I had my baby. I hadn't seen my friends from work in so long and I was really looking forward to it. The doctors told me to cancel my plans.

'Straight away, I went for a mammogram and biopsy, and the following Tuesday I was told I had cancer. I remember being very anxious so they sped everything up for me as much as they could. They understood I was a first-time mum and, honestly, I couldn't bear to exist during those few days of waiting. On the Tuesday morning, they rang me at 10 a.m. and said, "Georgie we want you to come in at 4.30 p.m. and we want you to bring someone."

'My brain immediately went to the darkest place. I thought, *They're going to tell me I'm dying.* But then I thought maybe it was a benign tumour and some people faint when they hear the word tumour so they're just being cautious. At this point in my head, I still had a two per cent chance that this wasn't cancer and I was clinging on to it.

'That afternoon, I had a lymph node biopsy and I still didn't know what was going on. I was bawling my eyes out. They pulled me into a room with a surgeon and a cancer liaison nurse, both of whom were holding leaflets.

'I met this amazing man called Professor Arnold Hill [Arnie] and he told me I had cancer. During that meeting, he gave me so much reassurance that I left without that same fear I'd had for five days.'

Georgie says her diagnosis gave her a sense of peace. If knowledge is power, then Georgie felt more powerful in that room than she had in days.

Professor Hill didn't sugar-coat the road ahead for her, but, with a sense of directness, he also delivered positive news: her chances of recovery were promising. He said that most women with her type of cancer survived and some went on to have more children. Most importantly he told her, 'This is not a death sentence.'

During difficult moments in her life, Georgie would often tell herself that whatever she was going through was just another mountain to climb and that gave her the attitude she needed to pull strength from within to conquer it.

'I said, "Professor Hill is this just a mountain I have to climb?" He said, "This isn't even a mountain. This is a bump in the road for you."'

A few days later, Georgie arrived at Beaumont to have the cancerous tissue from her breast removed. She was then told that the tumour was bigger than they'd initially thought. It was stage two, which means the cancer was growing but was still contained in her breast and had only extended to the nearby lymph nodes. She asked for a mastectomy as she believed it would bring her peace of mind, but the medical team recommended a lumpectomy and she followed their advice with vigour.

'Whatever these guys told me, I was going to do. At that point, I would have chopped off my right arm to live.'

Despite the haze of those weeks, Georgie remembers every

minute detail. The night before she went in for her first surgery, she recalled a mantra she'd heard once, from a motivational speaker.

'He said, "Life doesn't happen to you, it happens for you." And I thought how that was exactly what I needed to hear at that time. I kept telling myself that over and over again. While the doctors prepare you for surgery, you feel like a puppet – they're pulling you up and sitting you down, sticking things in your arm, and you just surrender.'

> This isn't even a mountain. This is a bump in the road for you.

The next week, the results showed that her margins, the rim of tissue around the removal area to be sure it's clear of cancer cells, weren't clear enough; but the good news was that her lymph nodes were 100 per cent clear, meaning the cancer hadn't spread.

'After the second surgery, I had a very bad reaction. That's when reality hit me. They brought me out in a wheelchair and I completely fell apart with my husband for about half an hour.

'I was so emotional with the compassion people had for me. People treat you differently when you have surgery for cancer. That made me really sad because I felt more vulnerable. Do these people think I'm dying? People feel sorry for you when you have cancer and that's what I found really hard, but also lovely. I have to say the staff at Beaumont carried me through that time.'

Georgie was also facing yet another obstacle, one which she is still affected by: her fertility. At thirty-two and a new mother, she had hoped for a busy house filled with more children, siblings for her beloved daughter, a plan which has been paused for now, and possibly forever.

'I found my lump on October 15th and within two weeks I had my first surgery. Within ten days, I had my second surgery and then, two weeks after that, I was pulled in to meet an oncologist for the first time. They recommended I go straight into IVF to try to save my eggs on time, because after that, I was facing five months of chemotherapy, followed by four weeks of radiotherapy. I was told I had to go on a drug called Tamoxifen for up to five years, and I can't have another baby as long as I'm on that.

'I could cope with the chemo, radiotherapy and the surgeries, but I took the fertility aspect really badly. They said they may reduce my medication time to two to three years to give me a chance at having another baby, but I'm only thirty-four and this is not the life I had planned for myself.

'I want my baby to have a sibling and in so many ways, I wish this happened to me after my babies had been born because then I wouldn't worry so much about little Pia.'

Even so, her daughter was Georgie's source of inner strength, which she drew from during dark days. As time went on, her thoughts wandered to the deepest corners of her mind and, when she was faced with her own mortality, her only concern was for her daughter's wellbeing.

'I was very worried that I would die. You think of everything... if I died, would Jamie go on to have more kids with someone else? Would Pia feel like an outsider? I knew he wouldn't let that happen of course... I wanted her to have a happy childhood where she didn't have to worry. I didn't want people to ask her where her mum was.

'That was the hardest part. I could have coped with the idea of dying if it wasn't for Pia. She gave me the strength to get up and fight every day because I had to, I had no other option.

'The first thing I did was accept help from my family and they were there for me every single minute of every single day. Pia needed to get out and that was the best medicine for me. I think if I had gone to bed for a year, I would have been really depressed, but I had to get up and face each day.

'Pia's face was the first face I saw every morning and she smiled at me every single morning. It's weird because, when I was sick, I still felt happiness and I still felt joy. Even though I was down in a dark hole I could see the light.'

After her diagnosis, her surgeries and the emotional rollercoaster that accompanies it, now it was time for the hard part: the gruelling reality of her treatments.

'My husband kept me on track by telling me it was only temporary. He kept going over the facts and telling me what the doctors said. He was great during that time because he would do all the research I was too scared to look at.

'I cried every single day, but getting up and getting fresh air and daylight did wonders for me.

'I felt like I set the tone for my family. I felt strong on the inside, so they felt strong. I'd say to my mum that she shouldn't worry when she gets home at night. I knew deep down that I'd survive. Even now, I have moments where I worry about the cancer coming back and I'm trying to get help to live in the moment, but even then, I wasn't a complete mess.

'I was surprised by my own positivity,' Georgie tells me. 'I wouldn't have described myself as being a particularly positive person before the cancer, but being faced with life and death changed that. I thought, Oh no, this is not going to happen to me.

'I was determined that it wasn't going to take my family or my child's happiness away. I didn't want to look back at the first year of

Pia's life and think of cancer. I want to think of her beautiful life and her happiness.'

According to Breast Cancer Ireland (BCI), an organisation for which Georgie is now an ambassador, thirty per cent of people diagnosed with cancer in Ireland are under the age of fifty. She still doesn't know why she 'got it' beyond it just being bad luck. During her treatment, she sought counselling and BCI introduced her to other young women in similar situations.

'I didn't want to go to a cancer support group because I thought everyone would be old, but on my first day of chemo, when I sat in the chair and looked around, it was like a line of people you'd see at a Spar – all ages. Cancer doesn't discriminate.'

The recommendation is that we don't use language like 'cancer free', 'all clear' or 'remission', but these days Georgie is healthy and healing. Cancer is no longer present in her body. The disease may be gone, but its lasting effects on her are still visible. She says she has become an entirely different person as a result of her experience – someone who is self-assured, confident, appreciates the little things and values her health more than ever.

'It absolutely sucked in some ways, but in others, I feel it was almost meant to be this way. I struggle with that a little bit. When I'm in counselling now, I say that if I had a choice I don't know if I'd change it. Every second of my life has changed. Everything. A lot of people think that after you've had cancer, you're back to normal after some really bad thing happened to you, but there's not one part of me that's the same as it was. Every thought in my brain is different; every choice I make is different. I really like this version of myself.

'Cancer allowed me to be my true self. It gives you confidence and a sense that I deserve to be here, I deserve to live. I was a bit of an apologetic person before and a little bit self-conscious, but not anymore.

'The clichés are all true! I live my life for my family now and I absolutely adore my job. I have more respect for myself. I need to go to the gym for myself and for my family. I need to just take five minutes. I was always so far down my own to-do list and now I feature pretty high at the top. No one thanks you for being super-woman. I don't know what I was trying to prove.

'When you're in a little tiny room in a hospital and you don't know if you're going to live or die, you think, "You know what? Mondays really aren't that bad."

'I start work at 5.30 a.m. every day and it's not easy getting up at 4.30 a.m., but I thank God every day that I have the energy to get out of bed. Believing that I'm a messenger for breast cancer in young people helps and the awareness that I've created through my own cancer helps.'

Now that she is of a healthier body and mind, how will she tell Pia, the centre of her universe, about how tough those first few years were – when the time is right for them as mother and daughter?

'When I was younger, my mum was my world,' Georgie says. 'When you're young, we think our mums are invincible and when I felt like there was a chance I could die . . . what I've learned in the last year is how differently I live my life. If I die next year, I have taught her more than I ever would have been able to. Hopefully she'll look at me and think I'll be fit, healthy, look after myself and be breast aware. My cancer will hopefully help her live a happier, healthier life and help her make the right decisions.

'We will have to sit her down and tell her and we have all the photos. She was my angel getting through it. She's my best friend. I always say to my husband that no one's ever looked at me the way Pia looks at me.'

There is still an arduous journey ahead as Georgie waits to hear when she can come off Tamoxifen and hopefully begin the journey to have more children, but, like everything, Georgie is staying positive.

'Our IVF was really successful. They took twenty-seven eggs and fifteen of those were successfully fertilised – so we have fifteen embryos. It was a great bit of good news in the middle of an absolute storm.

'The thought of starting that journey again is pretty terrifying. My husband is four years older than me, and of course he also wants another baby. This has taken his dreams away as well. But I believe that everything is happening for a reason and I really trust that whatever is meant to be will be.

'I think we'll go on to have another baby. I believe in medicine and I trust my doctors and I know they wouldn't let me become pregnant again if it was a danger. I'll cross that bridge when I come to it. I just have faith.'

It all comes back to kindness.

Kathy Ryan

Alzheimer's activist

'The day I was diagnosed with younger onset Alzheimer's'

~

Civil rights activist Dolores Huert said, 'Every moment is an organising opportunity, every person a potential activist, every minute a chance to change the world.'

~

Kathy Ryan, one of the five per cent of Alzheimer's sufferers in Ireland with younger onset Alzheimer's, is an activist right down to her core. When she was diagnosed with the rare condition in 2014 at the age of fifty-two, her world was turned upside down. Her brain had betrayed her and no aspect of her life would ever be the same again.

'Looking back, there are three days that changed my life – the two days my sons were born, those were joyous moments; but ultimately, the day that changed my entire life, and really rocked my world, was 23 January 2014.

'It's as clear in my head today as it was then.'

At the time of her diagnosis, her father, Ted, had been diagnosed with vascular dementia and Kathy had signed up to a course at a local branch of the Alzheimer Society of Ireland in order to educate herself on the best ways to help him and improve his quality of life. Before his passing in early 2019, he would often visit the home she shared with her sons Andrew and Matthew (whom she affectionately refers to as 'the guys') in Clonmel, Co Tipperary.

While taking the course, Kathy noticed that she too had some of the same identifying characteristics of Alzheimer's disease, but had been subconsciously incorporating coping techniques into her life for many years to offset the symptoms. For example, on occasion, she might forget the word for dinner and would demonstrate eating with her hands to her sons instead, something she always put down to the stress of being a busy single mother.

Kathy sought medical help, but was initially misdiagnosed, making the day that changed her life all the more traumatic.

'For me, it was a little bit more shocking [when I was finally diagnosed] because I had been led to believe that whatever was medically wrong with me wasn't Alzheimer's,' she recalls. 'I had spent about two months celebrating. And so it came as a real, real shock.

'It was a freezing cold, windy day when I was finally told I had Alzheimer's, but it didn't really hit me until the specialist nurse walked me out into the car park after my appointment to ask if I was okay.'

Discussing the cruel blow of her devastating diagnosis in a car park – with little time to digest the information as she was in a hurry to pick up her son – was not the most ideal of circumstances for Kathy. But she didn't have time to dwell on that.

'I was leaving the hospital on my way to pick up my son Andrew and immediately I went into "mom mode". I knew I'd be collecting him within ten or fifteen minutes and I couldn't have a meltdown. He would have been able to tell if I'd been upset.'

In the car, she received a phone call from her doctor, letting her know the name of her prescription medication. When she looked up its name, she learned it was to treat Alzheimer's.

'Then it was very real. I remember thinking, "How do I deal with this? How do I face the guys and tell them this?"'

'The nurse that told me the news asked if we could meet for coffee the next week and we did. She told me there was a day care centre in Clonmel.

'I had such a negative view of Alzheimer's because I knew there was no cure. Everything in my life was now a question: How do I tell the guys? How do I stay well?'

Kathy had, somewhat ironically, time to decide how she wanted to tell her sons. In particular, she wanted to protect her son, Andrew, who was repeating his Leaving Certificate at the time.

'He deserved a chance to have a really good go at it,' she says. 'That was in January and after his Leaving [Cert] around June and I was glad to have had that time to decide how I was going to handle it. What did I want for the guys? What information did I need to gather for them and myself?'

After the diagnosis, Kathy grappled with what can only be described as grief for her past and future self.

'I would get up some days and think, "This is crazy, I'm fine," but in the midst of that thought there were a lot of negative feelings – the anger, sadness and devastation.

'There was a relief in some ways too because, until then, I hadn't been able to do some things that my friends were able to do, things that you would normally expect someone to be able to do in their early fifties. Now I had a reason why I couldn't.

'Although I had Alzheimer's, I knew I wasn't going mad.'

There were times when Kathy would pick up a toothbrush and

couldn't remember its function; other times she would turn the tap on, leave it running and forget to turn it off, causing the sink to overflow and the kitchen to flood. All things she recognises now as being early indicators of Alzheimer's.

'I couldn't seem to hold on to the most recent of details. I watched the news and I could recount what happened, but not where it happened. I could be at my kitchen table and ask if you wanted tea or coffee, you'd answer, and by the time I turned around to the kettle, I would have no recollection of what you said.

'At Mass, even though the Responsorial Psalm was one line, I couldn't hold onto it. If things weren't in their place, it was very frustrating for me.

'I couldn't follow a book if there were characters operating parallel to one another. One evening, I was flicking through the channels on TV and told my son I couldn't remember the end of the film, only to realise we hadn't watched a film.

'It sounds silly but all of those things add up. And it's a big part of why I try and create awareness and advocacy around Alzheimer's from the moment of diagnosis, because that's when the grieving starts.

'This is one of the most devastating illnesses, not just for the person but for their family. I'm only one side of the coin.'

Kathy is at pains to distinguish the difference between the natural parts of depleted cognition with age such as sporadic forgetfulness in comparison to a degenerative condition like Alzheimer's. In fact, it's this common misconception that has prompted criticism from some who misunderstand the distinction between the two and, thus, have issues with her high-profile advocacy work.

'Many people will say, "I'm sure you know, our brains gets slower," but it wasn't just about my brain getting slow. I couldn't remember individual words and I would often use my hands to describe them. The guys always knew this and it was part of who we were.'

At the time, she was 'stone broke' and availing herself of disability wasn't a realistic financial option. A psychologist advised her to pursue something that excited her and so her work with the Alzheimer Society of Ireland and the Irish Dementia Working Group began.

Since her diagnosis, Kathy has appeared on every major radio and television programme in the country and travels to mainland Europe to deliver speeches at conferences focused on Alzheimer's, offering human insight from her personal experience. She has had to become pragmatic regarding her future care and is adamant that she doesn't wish for her sons to care for her, citing information about the long-term effects on carers who devote their time fully to loved ones.

'The last gift I can give to them is the freedom to live their lives – they are still so young.'

Her sons, now twenty-two and twenty-four, have yet to agree to this arrangement, of course, wanting to care for their 'kick ass' mother who has raised them so devotedly their entire lives.

When Kathy eventually sat 'the guys' down in September 2014 to tell them she had Alzheimer's, she also began her public journey with the disease.

For her, she knew she would be okay. 'Life hasn't always been easy,' she says. 'I was sexually abused as a child and my mom was an alcoholic. So the idea of making life work and getting on with it is in my DNA.'

But some people in her life stopped speaking to her, either too uncomfortable or ignorant to pursue a conversation. Others were fearful of facing their own worst fears at seeing a vibrant, intelligent and strong 52-year-old woman with an Alzheimer's diagnosis.

'People who I knew quite well ignored me. They would see me shopping in Tesco and turn around. It's very hard to deal with that when you're questioning everything else in your life,' she recalls.

'Some people cry every time you see them and you have to just tell people that's not who I am. At the time, we didn't have dementia advisers, so I was really going it alone. I went to see a psychiatrist who was asking me, "Are you depressed? It's okay to be depressed. You know, it's okay, take medication." But I wasn't depressed.

'As a younger on-setter, I was referred back to my primary caregiver, who says to this day that I am teaching him more about it than he does me. When you're that young facing Alzheimer's, it's a very tough place to make sense of it all.

'All your friends are still working and, in some cases, you have to stop working. What do you do with your time? If you're rich, you can go traveling or socialise and try new things;, but if you're poor, then you don't have the money to spend. So what can you really do to fill in your time?

'And that's where, for me, the dementia working group came in. The minute I stepped into that room, it turned my life in a completely different direction.'

~

The Irish Dementia Working Group is a group of people living with dementia who advocate for better services, supports and policies in Ireland. They function with the support of the Alzheimer Society of Ireland (ASI) and work to improve life for people living with dementia – and their families – throughout the country.

'I would credit the work I have done in keeping me as well as I am five years on. I have made the most incredible friends. You become very close very quickly sharing the same challenges.'

Early on, Kathy's devotion to educating herself and improving the quality of life for those around her became a catalyst for positive change. She was asked by the ASI to do a video with her sons detailing her experience, which was released on social media and soon went viral.

'I was asking the boys how okay they are with me sharing and Andrew just said, "Mum, go kick ass. Share what you need to share and say what you need to say. We're proud of you and we love you."

> Mum, go kick ass. Share what you need to share and say what you need to say. We're proud of you and we love you.

'People around the country, even some doctors, have said to me that they wouldn't want to tell people that a loved one in their family had dementia, as they believe it would bring shame to their family. And that makes me angry.

'There are families who keep their loved one kind of locked away. I'd like to say it's not common, that it's rare, but sadly it isn't.'

Some days are harder than others, but helping those in need helps pull her through. Having known what little information was – and is – out there for those experiencing early onset Alzheimer's galvanises Kathy.

Most recently, a neighbour of hers was diagnosed with the same condition at the age of fifty-five.

'She was told to stop driving, stop working, go home and write her will. She has a fourteen-year-old at home. I don't have the right to sit back when I have the lived experience and information that I can give to this woman whose rug has been pulled out from under her.'

Similarly, Kathy met with another woman in Killarney who was diagnosed last September and her adult children got in touch with Kathy to thank her. 'They said, "In September, somebody switched off the light in my mum. Her soul was gone. You switched it on last week. We are so grateful to you,"' she remembers.

'All that visit cost me was a coffee and a little bit of diesel. Now their mother is back out hill-walking and thinking, "If Kathy can do this four years on, I can live, too."

'You can still partake, you can still contribute to your community, you can still be a part of your community, and you can still take joy in experiences. There are so many people around the country who are not told that. You need to look outside of yourself. Kindness costs nothing, so if I can be there for one person, then why wouldn't I?'

Kathy has always given back to her community and takes pride in a life devoted to volunteer work, but now that desire to help has shifted into a feeling of responsibility.

'I believe people have a right to information. It's going to take rocket science to develop a cure, but it isn't rocket science to give people information.'

In Ireland, early onset Alzheimer's is defined under mental health and, as such, people with the condition are not guaranteed affordable, accessible healthcare specific to their circumstances until the age of sixty-five. This often leaves people out of pocket as they are usually not working and relying on their savings to carry them through financially in order to visit doctors and explore paths towards better brain health.

Despite her extraordinary efforts, Kathy's condition is progressing and still she fights the fight because of the responsibility she feels, because she's seen too many people's lights go out at diagnosis.

'I have so many strategies in my life to stay well, but sometimes, those strategies don't work. I'm falling downstairs now. If I was to lift a cup of coffee now, I'd have to focus or else I'd spill it. That's not normal and people don't expect it at my age. So, I think, who better to explain it to those who aren't living it and to bring comfort to those who are?

'At fifty-eight, I'm frightened of spiders, daddy longlegs and mice, but somehow, being frightened of four steps of stairs is . . . a fear of fear itself.

'Sometimes, I use a disabled bathroom. It isn't that I necessarily need to go in there, but with a bank of mirrors and doors in the other bathroom, I can get confused and disoriented and I don't know how to get out.

'I've sat on a train parched and my hands were too weak, I couldn't open a water bottle. Everyone had headphones in or weren't making eye contact. I've gotten sarcastic responses double-checking that I'm on the right train. It all goes back to kindness.

'On a good day, I try to explain I have Alzheimer's. On other days, I feel exhausted and tired and I need to walk away.'

Tired she may be, but she will never stop.

'What's tiredness compared to speaking in Europe? Exhaustion is part of my life now. I'm not going away. I'm not shutting up. No matter how difficult it is and how much it makes me feel sick to my stomach, as long as I have power to give information to people, I will keep doing this.'

Hope in the aftermath of grief.

Sarah Tobin

Businesswoman

'The day my daughter Alice was born.'

~

Washington Irving, the 19th-century American writer, wrote about grief: 'There is sacredness in tears. They are not the mark of weakness, but of power. They speak more eloquently than ten thousand tongues. They are the messengers of overwhelming grief, of deep contrition, and of unspeakable love.'

~

His words, 150 years later, remain as powerful as ever and appropriate for Sarah Tobin's story. Originally from Kingswood in Dublin, she has been living in the UK for the past twelve years with her husband Dave. They had, for their eight years together before starting a family, something of a picture perfect life.

But, as is often the case, they felt there was something missing; a void which could only be filled with the child they desperately yearned for. After eighteen months of trying, their dreams came true and Sarah became pregnant with their first child. But then they were dealt a crushing blow when their daughter Alice died when she was just five days old.

'I always knew her name would be Alice before she was even conceived. It just came to me, and I began to notice a lot of things like *Alice in Wonderland* popping up in my life in ways it never had before, so when we found out she was a girl, I knew straight away that was her name.'

In November 2014, Sarah went into labour five days before her due date, the only hiccup throughout an otherwise seamless pregnancy. What then followed was a traumatic and life-changing experience. When she realised she was in labour, she stayed home as long as possible, incorporating her long-practised hypnobirthing techniques, before the couple made their way to hospital in Brighton, England to begin the next stage of the delivery process, which would go on to last a number of excruciating hours.

'They admitted us to the triage room, but I wanted to be in water so they moved me to a birthing pool around 3 a.m.,' she recalls. 'They noticed around 6 a.m. that there was some deceleration and the baby's heart rate was dropping more than usual. Also, at this point, there was a shift change with the midwives. The new midwife, who I hadn't met with before, decided to get me out of the birthing pool and move me into a labour ward so they could monitor the birth.

'At this point, I was eight or nine centimetres dilated. When we were in the labour room, it took three different machines and two attempts by the midwife to finally monitor my baby's pulse properly. Only now do we know that, at this time, it is standard practice to check the maternal pulse so there is a baseline for my heart rate. By the time I was ten centimetres dilated, I had been pushing for two hours and was completely exhausted.

'I remember my arms shaking for days after as I'd been squeezing so tightly on to the bed or Dave. Eventually the medical staff realised they could feel the baby's head but she wasn't in the correct position to come out.'

By this point, unbeknown to the medical staff, Alice had been in distress for some time as they had been monitoring Sarah's heart rate and not Alice's.

'Her heart rate continued to decelerate, all the while, mine was going up because it was so physical, and when hers dropped to sixty beats per minute, alarm bells went off. That was when they gave me an episiotomy so she'd come out after one push. At this point, I was on the bed and, because of the episiotomy, I couldn't stand or really move.

'She was born floppy and lifeless and they tried to resuscitate her on a table near me. Her heart was beating, but she wasn't breathing so they were giving her oxygen.'

The gravity of the situation had yet to set in for Sarah as she was in an 'oxytocin Zen mode' post-birth, which protected her from the immediacy of the tragedy that awaited them. Her husband, on the other hand, came close to fainting after seeing his daughter and wife's frail condition.

'They brought her to me so I could hold her for just a few seconds and then they took her upstairs to the Neonatal Intensive Care Unit (NICU). I leaned over, touched her chest and said, "I love you." Then she was gone.

'For the next two to three hours, we stayed in that room. I was still bleeding and we were waiting for a theatre to open up so I could have surgery because of the episiotomy. I didn't know much of what was going on.'

Doctors had put Alice on 'cooling', which involves placing

newborn babies on a special mat to be cooled at 33°C. This is standard practice for a newborn after a difficult birth and is often used to prevent brain injury. It can help with recovery from a lack of oxygen, but Sarah says only now do they realise that at the right time this can be a life-saving treatment, but it does reach a point where it is no longer effective; a point, which, sadly, Alice had reached.

'I couldn't grasp what they were telling me,' Sarah recalls. 'After her birth at 9.50 a.m., I didn't see her again until 6 p.m., after my own surgery. I was under a local anaesthetic and I remember bawling after that because it hit me all at once that what I'd just gone through. Before then, I was on a birth high, but between the surgery, drugs and being sewn back up, I was just lying there and all I had was my thoughts, sitting in a blood-stained bed without my daughter.'

During her surgery, Dave contacted his parents, who live locally, and they travelled to the hospital immediately, and also his in-laws, who booked the earliest flights from Dublin the following morning. Sarah's uncle, a paediatric specialist for metabolic disorders at a hospital in Texas, explained the seriousness of the situation in layman's terms – and with genuine compassion.

'The next few days I was in recovery. I had a catheter and I was walking up to see Alice every time I could, hobbling along the corridors. My mother sent my uncle Alice's Apgar scores [a test taken one and five minutes after a baby's birth to monitor the baby's condition outside the womb] and he made me realise the seriousness of the situation. He said, "You have an opportunity to do the right thing over the next few days."'

In this case, the right thing was allowing their daughter to die peacefully in their arms.

'We didn't want to do anything until we got the MRI results and a brain scan. We had to wait a few days to have that done because it's so early in brain development that it's a specialist practice and there's only one person in the country who can do it. She confirmed on day five that Alice's brain was not responding, which made our decision a little bit easier. There was no hope, no prognosis and no alternative.'

Throughout those five days, Sarah and Dave lived in a room at the hospital so they could have easy access to their daughter during her short life.

'We had her christened by an Irish priest and she was given three godparents. We got to wash her hair and put nappies on her and dress her and hold her.

'After the cooling pads, we had some physical contact with her. Then when we made the decision that it was time to let her go, and we sent our families away so we could do it.

'It involved taking off all the life support, bringing her into a family room with a double bed and then just waiting for hours. Waiting for someone to die is really hard. The body's natural instinct is to gasp for breath. They didn't tell us that would happen and it was horrific. In the end I was willing her to pass, I was calling in all sorts of angels and loved ones to come and ease her transition.'

After the trauma of her birth and tragic death, Sarah and Dave had to return home – but how does one ever return to normal after such a tragic injustice?

'Your breasts are still producing milk,' Sarah says, 'and it's a constant reminder of what you don't have. Seeing the baby car seat in our car as we made our way home was devastating. We brought the car seat into the hospital with the intention of taking her home in it, so coming home with it empty was horrible.'

In the immediate aftermath, their days were consumed with preparing funeral arrangements. This time confirmed Sarah's sense of spirituality.

'Initially, it was about organising a funeral, which, in a way, was a good thing to occupy your brain. We kept busy. The day itself was very difficult, but it was lovely because over one hundred people came – including my granddad, though my grandmother was too sick to travel and then, sadly, she died three months later. So when I think of Alice and my grandmother, I see them together. Going through all this, how could I not believe that Alice's spirit survives or that something of her exists? I'd hate to not have that belief.'

For the first session of tapping, I cried for the full hour and a half, but I felt so much relief afterwards.

Early on after losing Alice, Sarah and Dave realised that being at home would be too painful, so they planned a trip to Thailand for an escape, funded by the money she had saved for her maternity leave. 'It was like a light at the end of the tunnel that kept us going. The heat, the time alone, the time not talking, that was all great – we probably drank too much. I kept drinking for about three months – every night, I was numbing the pain with a few glasses of wine. After a while, I realised I couldn't do it forever.'

On their return home to Brighton, Sarah said she gave herself opportunities to immerse herself in depression. 'I tried to see what really wallowing would be like – if I didn't get dressed or have a slow day – just to see what it felt like, and quickly I realised it wouldn't help me move forward.'

She and Dave, together in an 'invisible cave' built on the fortitude of their bond, found strength in one another when things turned bad. In the hospital, they made a pact that they were stronger together and would lean on each other whenever the other needed support;

it's a decision which carried them through the most testing time of their marriage.

They knew soon after how much they still wanted to be parents and decided to try for another baby. Sarah became pregnant for the second time.

'It was a good excuse to look after myself – no alcohol or caffeine – but pregnancy was harder this time around. I fainted a lot and felt more ill, but I look back now and realise my body wasn't ready to be pregnant again. My first pregnancy and my grief had massively depleted its resources.

'I was more nervous throughout the nine months than I had been while I was pregnant with Alice. I was well looked after by my midwife because of what we'd been through. I was more anxious about the labour than the actual development of the baby and pregnancy. I decided early on I wasn't going to try a "natural" labour and I'd have a C-section instead.'

What helped renew her happiness and vigour for life was tapping, a method of Emotional Freedom Technique (EFT) therapy, which involves physically tapping parts of your body with your fingers with the aim of stimulating the release of painful emotions. Her sister recommended the method to her and Sarah was acutely aware of not wanting to pass on any anxieties to her yet-to-be-born son.

'Birth trauma links hugely with postnatal depression and trauma is different for everybody. I was conscious of the baby growing inside me and I didn't want to pass on anxiety and negative emotion to him. For the first session of tapping, I cried for the full hour and a half, but I felt so much relief afterwards. At this point, I had already done counselling and Reiki, but nothing had been as effective as those first ninety minutes.

'They changed my life in a way. The technique gave me the ability to look back but experience the trauma of Alice's birth. I can talk about it without feeling that pain. Over those five days of Alice's life, there were so many different aspects of pain . . .'

Sarah gave birth to her son Casper, now three, saying, 'I was happy he was a boy because it felt like, if it was a girl it would be too close too soon.' Soon after, she became pregnant again, this time with her son Josh, now one, and she felt confident in her ability to have a vaginal birth.

'The C-section recovery was really hard and I didn't want to not be there for Casper. I wanted to be a guinea pig for the tools I had learned,' she says. 'Josh's birth went how I planned. I felt empowered. Finally, I have this birth story that everyone around me has and I've always wanted. It was a good, full circle conclusion to having my children. If I hadn't had that, I'd be missing out on that joy and the bonding I had with him as a result.'

After her baby daughter's death, it was hard to see a deeper meaning in life, but she knew there could be comfort in something altruistic, which is what Sarah does now, through her Tapping for Mums workshops around Ireland and the UK.

Firstly, though, the couple launched a case of medical negligence against the hospital and received a formal apology for the care they provided the morning of Alice's birth, after a nearly four-year legal process and some process changes on the maternity ward, which will help prevent others from experiencing the same.

Reliving the pain of the worst day of her life wasn't easy, but Sarah takes comfort in knowing she's prevented another woman – and another Alice – from suffering the same tragedy.

'When Alice passed on, I asked myself how could I go back to living life like normal? How can I carry on like nothing has happened? Deciding to take our experience of loss, and recover, and then learn how to help others in similar and different situations has empowered me, and helped me on the journey of healing. It has also helped me find happiness because I know I am going to spend my future years helping as many women as I physically can to clear the traumas and pain of the past so we can all look forward to a happier future.

'I am proud of myself for how I've coped and I look forward to a continued happy future with my gorgeous boys (my husband included!), all while connected to my daughter by my side.'

'And here you are living
despite it all.' – Rupi Kaur.

Christina Noble

Humanitarian

'The day I left my abusive marriage and
began my life's work as a humanitarian.'

~

The Christina Noble story has been woefully under-told. Nowadays, there is an exceptional amount of national pride taken when anyone of Irish descent does well abroad; but Christina, a 74-year-old from the Liberties in Dublin, is from an era that didn't champion individual successes in the way we do today.

As a result, many know of the life-changing work she has done in Vietnam and Mongolia, but few know the story of Christina Noble, the woman.

~

Christina is, above all else, a survivor. A survivor of domestic abuse, of having her son sent for adoption without her consent at a Mother and Baby Home, of childhood sexual abuse, of a gang rape, of being forced to live on the streets, of industrial schools, of being the child of an alcoholic – of injustice after injustice, that seem to culminate in more than any one person should ever have to endure.

With so many life-altering days, Christina credits the day that changed her life as the day she left her abusive first marriage, during which she was beaten nearly every day.

'My life has changed direction several times, but I think the day that most changed my life was the day I left my ex-husband. The day I decided I couldn't take anymore. It was either that or under a train,' she says.

Her ex-husband, whose name Christina has asked not be published, was a philanderer who would often bring women to their home; she walked in on him having sex with them more than once. The physical abuse in Christina's marriage was so severe that some of her wounds still necessitate medical attention: her nose was broken twice and she required surgery in order to breathe properly; her then-husband banged her head against their wardrobe so many times it broke the wood and she was often bruised black and blue.

Christina also miscarried three times during that marriage. During the last miscarriage, she began bleeding heavily in the kitchen, but was so concerned that he would be upset with the mess, she didn't tell him. She says she didn't fully grasp the severity of what had happened to her body until she went to the hospital the following day.

Christina went to a number of psychiatric institutions around Birmingham, England, where she lived during her marriage and throughout her late teens and twenties, but doctors failed to grasp the psychological impact that the beatings and emotional abuse had on her. They also failed to accurately diagnose the crippling depression she was experiencing; instead blaming it on other psychological conditions such as schizophrenia, claiming she inherited it from her father, despite him not having any symptoms.

After each of these times in institutions, she would go home and live with a man who would beat her mercilessly for the slightest perceived error on her part.

Christina has three children with her ex-husband – Helen, Androula and Nicolas – and she did her best to protect them from the misery of her marriage. She tried leaving her ex-husband a number of times and, on one occasion, successfully made it back to Ireland, but he always found her – because of the children. She knew if she was going to leave for good, divorce him and get custody of her children, she would need to make the heart-breaking decision to leave him without taking her children with her.

'I worked extremely hard and no matter what I did, it didn't seem to make any difference. If he was in a bad mood, I got it. I was in and out of hospital. I hated waking up in the morning. My heart would pound not knowing what was ahead of me each day.

'He beat me very badly. On one occasion, I had to go to the dentist because he had broken some of my teeth and, when I came back, he was screaming at me about why it had taken so long.'

Despite the fact that they were both working at a fish and chip shop, Christina's ex-husband withheld all the money she earned and she was forced to give her wages to him every week. In return, he gave her just £1 a day to survive on. She decided to save the family allowance (known as child benefit in Ireland) as an alternative means to gather the money for a bus ticket out of the city.

Christina had no formal education. She left her industrial school – St Joseph's in Connemara, Co Galway, one of the many institutions set up in Ireland in the late 19th century to care for orphaned children – at the age of sixteen; after years of living on the streets and at the school, and dealing with the psychological damage of being sexually abused as a child and the trauma of being separated from her siblings. She attempted to enrol in night school at one point during her marriage, but she only attended two classes before her ex-husband 'dragged me out of it, so there was no way I could better myself'.

'I just left,' she says of her life-changing day. 'I left in the evening and I left the children because every time I took them, it didn't work. He always found us.

'When I decided to go, I went down to Digbeth coach station in Birmingham; I was terrified and broken hearted from leaving the children. I got on the bus to London, then I got another coach to my sister Catherine in Surrey.'

On one occasion, Catherine had visited Christina in hospital but hadn't recognised her because she was so severely beaten from head to toe. Christina says, 'Catherine and I didn't really know each other well, because we were split up and sent to different institutions, but she'd been to see me in Birmingham before, so I knew she cared about me.

'I decided to go. I never came back.'

Christina hopped on a bus, dreaming of a life without fear, with just £20 in her pocket.

~

Although Christina credits leaving her first husband as the day that truly changed her life, we must first rewind a little to her childhood, to fully understand her extraordinary life and what spurred her on to become Ireland's most devoted humanitarian.

Growing up in the Liberties, then a severely impoverished neighbourhood and now a thriving area enjoying the benefits of gentrification, Christina lived in unfathomable poverty. Her mother, Annie Gross, died when Christina was ten years old and her father, Thomas Byrne, was an alcoholic whom she loved, but with whom she had a complicated relationship as a result of his addiction.

Thomas lived in a home for down-and-out men and, after Annie's death, Christina and her siblings were sent to live with relatives. There, all of the siblings were severely neglected, and Christina was sexually and physically abused.

On one occasion, Christina was taken to visit a doctor. Upon seeing she was severely malnourished and had lice, the doctor called the authorities and the police came and took her and her siblings into care. They were then placed in separate orphanages and industrial schools, whereby each sibling was cruelly told that all their siblings had died, only to find out the truth much later when they were eventually reunited.

'We were children whose only crime was that our mother had died, our father was an alcoholic and our relatives beat us and abused us, but we were treated like criminals,' she says. 'I had eight brothers and sisters, but two brothers died and there were six left: three boys and three girls. I was the eldest girl so I tried to look after them.'

For a period, Christina ran away from the industrial school she'd been placed in, and ended up living on streets of Dublin city from the age of twelve to thirteen; sometimes she was unable to sleep because of the cold, and had to survive on whatever sustenance she could find – mostly comprising of leaves and honeysuckle and rummaging through bins for people's scraps.

It was this inconceivable hardship that later gave her a unique insight into the plight of the street children in Vietnam; her commitment to helping them would later become her life's work.

In her autobiography *Bridge Across My Sorrows*, Christina writes, 'I needed just one person who would not see me as dust, or barely more than an animal . . . my sense of being cut off from the rest of the world increased.'

As a child, Christina was denied the basic rights of food, shelter and safety for so many years. It informed every consideration of her life thereafter, including her truly life-altering decision to help desperately needy children halfway across the world.

~

When Christina left her husband, she demanded she be treated with the dignity and respect she had been so deprived of during her life. She got a job at British Olivetti, a typewriter company, working in the kitchen. She asked her boss if she could change her name in case her husband tried to look for her. She went on to befriend her boss and his wife, who helped her with setting up what she needed for this new part of her life, including finding a solicitor.

'They allowed me to operate under a different name and I was delighted. I couldn't believe that people could care so much for me.

'I knew there were three things I felt compelled to do: I had to get a divorce and regain custody of my children, I had to have therapy in order to work through my issues and, someday, I had to go to Vietnam.'

Christina's need to go to Vietnam came about through a dream she'd had one day, while still working at the fish and chip shop and while still married. She had dreamed about the country, not understanding where – or what – it was, but knew that she must go there. By the time she escaped her husband, visiting Vietnam and helping the children there had become a part of Christina's daily mindset.

'I filed for a divorce and I wanted the children as well. I didn't want to stop him [her ex-husband] seeing the children, but to cut a long story short, a clean break was never going to happen with him. He was always going to get me.'

The case was sent to the High Court in London and when the judge saw the hospital records of extensive abuse, she was granted a decree nisi. She was also granted full custody of the children, although she would allow them to see their father if and whenever they wanted. She would send them to see him via train, and she began renting a house in Surrey and continuing with her work.

> Someday, I had to go to Vietnam.

But Christina's ex-husband eventually tracked the family down, with the intention of taking their son. A physical fight erupted as Christina's protective instincts took over and she attacked both her ex-husband and his new wife in order to buy her son time to escape to a pre-arranged spot she had told her children about in case this exact situation arose.

'They would only take him over my dead body. They had him in their hands and I bashed the door in and screamed, "Run Nico, you know where to go." My ex-husband threw me from wall to wall and I ended up in hospital needing seven pints of blood.'

After that, life for Christina went back to business as normal – or the closest she could have to normal after the hardships she'd had to endure. Eventually, she set up her own catering company, successful by any metrics you might use, and was at last relaxing and enjoying her new life.

But she could no longer ignore her need to visit Vietnam. So, after receiving the blessings of her three children, who had all finished school by this time, she hopped on a plane.

'I didn't have much money or anything. My dream was that I had to go and help the children of Vietnam, so that's what I did. I didn't think about setting anything up. I didn't even know how to go about doing so.'

In the 1970s, Vietnam was still ravaged by the aftermath of war, it had been subject to a trade embargo by the United States (which was only lifted in 1995) and, at the time, humanitarian aid was a virtually non-existent concept.

'I remember the plane landing in Vietnam and I was the only foreigner alongside an American gynaecologist seated next to me,' Christina recalls. 'It was a sad country that had been obliterated by war.'

On landing in Ho Chi Minh City, she was overcome. Her senses were overwhelmed by the sight of thousands of men, women and children living in the streets; the smells of a non-functioning public waste system; by everyone speaking a language she didn't understand.

'I had never seen so many people on the streets; never seen the amount of children, and mothers and fathers sitting there, lying on the roads with nowhere to go. There was nothing. There was, in the atmosphere, a taste of fear, loss and abandonment.

'I remember tears rolling down my face. There were thousands and thousands of people and I didn't know what I could do.'

Christina didn't speak Vietnamese, but she had a willingness to provide some semblance of comfort to the people suffering on the street. And so she communicated through the universal language of music.

'I sang at the Ben Thanh Market, it's all I knew how to do. I remember crying . . . sobbing,' she says. 'When I started singing and a man came along with a little guitar. I sang *One Day at a Time*. I sang so loudly I felt like I was letting something out for me as well.

'My face was wet from the sticky heat and my tears. I was feeling everything at once, including a sense of helplessness and hopelessness. I remember going back to where I was staying in this tiny little room and I remember thinking, "Who am I to give up? Who am I to feel sorry for myself?" I remember thinking: I'll find a way. Whatever it takes. I'm not going to give up.'

So, Christina went for a walk to assess what she could do for the people of Vietnam with what little she had. She was all too familiar with life on the streets and understood the experience from a truly visceral level.

'I went for a walk and I came across two little kids who were digging up ants to eat. I went right down to their eye level and they stared at me. They were two little sisters, called Houng and Hang.

'I asked the word "Mama" because I was trying ask where their mama or papa was. I said, "My name Christina." Of course, they didn't understand.

'I said, "I am a mama. Don't be afraid." When I spoke to them they heard "Tina". That's where the name Mama Tina came from.'

The children she helps through the Christina Noble Foundation affectionately refer to her by the name of 'Mama Tina'.

'I searched the city and I found out that those two sisters had a mother and father, who were blind and deaf. I signed as best I could, trying to describe asking if I could buy clothes for the children.

'I got them two beautiful frocks. I wanted them to feel like princesses and it didn't matter if it was for an hour, or a day or a month. It's very important that children's dignity is always protected at all times.'

Christina was staying at the Rex Hotel, a venue only open to non-Vietnamese, which she says was mainly occupied by Russians, and she managed to sneak Houng and Hang into her small room so that she could bathe and feed them.

Soon, word got out that there was a generous Irish woman in town who wanted to help children and people began lining up outside her hotel in search of food and love, both of which she was happy to offer by the bucketload.

To date, the Christina Noble Foundation has helped nearly one million children in the poorest regions of the world. Christina's formidable strength comes from a life of sorrow and pain that has been manifested into a work of awe-inspiring altruism; she works tirelessly every day so that no woman or child should ever endure what she has.

As the Indian poet Rupi Kaur wrote, '*And here you are living despite it all.*'

She is devoted to
supporting women.

Norah Casey

Broadcaster and Businesswoman

'The day I left my abusive first marriage.'

~

When Norah Casey speaks, and recalls in painstaking detail, the darkest period of her life, it is from the depths of her soul. The day that changed her life is one she describes as having a 'cataclysmic' effect on her; one which changed the entire trajectory of life as she knew it.

~

At the age of seventeen, Norah was working as a student nurse at Scotland's Vale of Leven Hospital and then she moved to London to retrain as a journalist. She was still new to the city, far away from the well-established friends she had made throughout her past life as a nurse, when she met her now ex-husband, whom I will identify as 'P.' He was a wealthy man who dazzled her with lavish gifts, declarations of undying love and a promise to introduce her to a world of wealth and privilege she otherwise had no experience of. But that life came at a cost: P was abusive, both physically and mentally, and remained so throughout their five-year marriage.

When they first met, P., at forty, was nearly twice Norah's age and, looking back, she realises that, at least subconsciously, he targeted her for that very reason.

'He was very sophisticated and he was introducing me to a whole way of life I'd never had before in London,' she recalls. 'In the early part of that relationship, before we got married, I was living in a bedsit in Hammersmith. Suddenly I was living in this beautiful house that he owned – and he was taking me around the world.'

One night, when they were driving home from dinner, he hit her for the first time. The next day, they were due to depart on an around-the-world trip, for which he was paying. 'When we were coming up the drive, he suddenly slammed his hand on the steering wheel. He got out of his side of the car to open my door – I thought he was going to open the door for me – and he slammed my head across the top of the car. I was stunned. Afterwards, he walked up to the house and went up to bed.'

Until then, there had been 'moments of clenched fists and stern warnings', but it was the first time he had turned physically violent. Norah's first thought was, 'What did I do to make him do that to me?' It was the beginning of a psychologically imposing cycle of self-blame, a trait prevalent among domestic violence survivors.

'I was shocked that somebody who loved me would do something like that to me. And then, to my shame, I started working out what kind of makeup I could use to mask the bruising that was coming up on the side of my face. It was 3 a.m. P. had fallen asleep without bother and my ear was swollen. All I was thinking of were ways to cover up my bruise before getting on our flight the next day.'

Norah says their relationship wasn't all bad – outwardly, P. was charming – and her parents, who didn't know about the abuse, loved him; her father, Harry, died not knowing the truth of what really happened in their marriage. ('It would have killed him,' she says.)

'After that particular incident, we got up the next day and without saying a word to each other, went to Heathrow Airport,' Norah says. 'He, of course, had all the passports, money and flight tickets. An hour into the flight, he leaned over and I could see he was crying. He kept saying over and over it was the stress of the holiday and he had worked too hard, if I hadn't said this or that . . . then he wouldn't have done it. Now I know that if a man hits you, he's never going to stop. But then I wanted to believe that the person who loved me most in the world, who was prepared to whisk me around the world, was never going to do that to me again.

'I ended up marrying him of course.'

Norah says the most common question asked of domestic abuse survivors is, 'Why did you stay?' But she knows from personal experience, we should be asking, 'How did you leave?' She stayed in her marriage for five years, the last two of which she tried to leave many times only to return later when he would threaten suicide or throw her clothes out the window and, having been desensitised to this behaviour over the years, she had accepted his coercion as normal.

'People on the outside don't understand why it is you stay in a relationship with the complexity of loving and living with somebody who exerts that kind of control over you . . . it's something that becomes the norm and you increasingly tolerate more and more coercive and abusive behaviour,' she says.

However, there is one particular moment that stands out for her and sent alarm bells ringing in her mind. She knew that if she wanted to live, she would have to leave him.

'One day we were having lunch with friends,' Norah explains. 'As usual, he didn't get along with someone at the table and he left in the car, but as he'd been drinking I wouldn't get into the car with him.

So, when I arrived at the house later, I had no keys and I was trying to wake him – I was hammering the door, the window, ringing the phone constantly. Eventually I heard him coming to the door and thought, "At last!"

'When he got to the door, he grabbed me by the hair, pulled me inside and began beating me and kicking me while I was on the ground. He broke two of my ribs and a bone inside of my face . . . I still don't smile properly on one side . . . he rained blows at me and I curled up on the hallway floor.'

Then he went into the kitchen and grabbed a large knife, telling her he was going to end it all. She mustered up all her strength and moved to the sitting room where she barricaded herself in with furniture, eventually falling asleep on the couch which she was using as a barrier.

'I woke up at about 3 a.m. and he was standing over with me with that knife in his hand,' she says. 'He fell to his knees and began sobbing and crying. By now, I could barely see out of my eyes they were so black and blue. I was completely beaten to a pulp. I couldn't even speak, I couldn't talk to him, and even if I could I didn't know what to say.'

After waiting a few hours, she asked him to take her to the hospital. He said no. He agreed to let her see a doctor (not her usual) on the other side of the city. The doctor was suspicious and questioned both of them separately about her story about falling down the stairs. His questions caused more trouble on the way home as P. had berated her about whether or not she had told the doctor what happened. He was placing the blame on her for ruining their relationship.

That was the moment that broke his spell over her.

'For me, it wasn't so much that he beat the hell out of me, but rather that his remorse lasted for about four hours before he was back to blaming me for the injuries I had,' she asserts. 'During that time, I had to go back to that doctor a few times and I was unable to drive. At that time, they strapped your ribs if they were broken, and if I cringed getting into the car, he would say, "Seriously, are you going to make me pay for this the rest of my life?"

'I knew in my heart of hearts I couldn't stay with him. After that, it took me two years before I managed to leave him.'

When Norah recovered physically, she threw herself into her work and enrolled in any course that would keep her out of the house. She did what she could to avoid socialising with him publicly.

'I filled my life with as many things as I could,' she says. 'I stopped drinking alcohol completely for a long time. I don't think it's enough to say that alcohol blurred his decisions because he was just as aggressive sober as he was with drink, but I didn't trust myself. I stopped going out with him. I would make excuses and try not to be in a situation where he was drinking alcohol.'

Towards the latter part of their marriage, he no longer tried to hide his emotional abuse in the company of others who saw the way he was treating her. By that time, on the occasions they did socialise as a couple, it was always with his friends and never hers.

'I didn't really have any friends at that point,' she says. 'I used to tell people, "The marriage isn't great but we're good friends." The truth is he wasn't a good friend to me – ever – but I convinced myself that all relationships were terrible and you had to accept some downsides.'

One day, her parents were visiting from Ireland and they had gone to the pub after lunch. Her mother was sitting behind her and her father was at the bar, so P. and Norah had only each other in their shared line of sight when she told him he had too much to drink.

'He lifted his hand and slapped me across me the face and then he casually walked to the bathroom,' she remembers. 'My dad thought I'd had an allergic reaction because the side of my face was so red, yet I still couldn't tell them. In my heart, that really was a steely moment of knowing I had to get out.'

Norah knew she had to leave, but she was still financially dependent on him; despite reaching dizzying professional heights at a young age. She was working full-time in a role that paid well, but she was left shouldering the responsibility for their finances, while he controlled the money relative to their lifestyle.

'Somehow, I ended up with the bills and he ended up with all the money,' she says.

Her name wasn't on the deed of their home or any of their assets, so she believed she would have to start from scratch after closing that door for the final time.

'I didn't have a cent to my name. In order to leave him, I had to accept I wasn't going to have anywhere to live.'

That weekend, she flew home to Ireland and told her mother the truth. It was the first time she had ever let anyone know the horrors of what had been happening behind closed doors for so many years. Her mother promised to keep her secret, but said she had to leave for good or else they would intervene.

'The following week, on a midweek morning, I woke up at around 4 a.m., ready to finally leave him. I had a shower and packed the smallest bag I could. I woke him and said I'm leaving you. He started to laugh. I made a little speech that I had rehearsed thousands of times about how I couldn't stay because of his abuse and, as I was coming towards the end of my speech, I could hear him snoring. I got into my car and drove away. It felt like I was driving off a cliff. I had no money and nowhere to stay.

'I'll never experience anything as frightening or terrifying as driving away that day. It was like a terrifying out-of-body ordeal. Physically, I was in a state of absolute adrenaline, my stomach was in a knot... I can't describe it.'

That morning, Norah went to work and pretended it was business as usual to the outside world (although she remembers wearing her top back to front the entire day) and looked up the cheapest hotel room she could find anywhere in London. It wound up being the Ibis at Heathrow Airport 'for something like £49.99'.

Once she was there, it felt particularly distressing as she could hear the excitement of boisterous children in neighbouring rooms excited about their impending holidays; joy which was juxtaposed with her sitting on the floor of her hotel room having overcome the biggest hurdle of her life. It was sad, yes, but, 'At the same time, I was free.'

> " Part of my overwhelming workaholic drive comes from the need to feel secure and I still have it, I can't let go of it.

She says, 'In the first few weeks, the hardest part was not going back to P. because he tried everything. He was carted off in an ambulance three days after I left because he drank an entire bottle of vodka. He told all his friends he was going to kill himself, without telling them the truth. It was like free-falling. It wasn't a comfortable feeling.'

He had exerted such control over her for so many years, she couldn't digest the seismic shift that was happening to her. He called her non-stop, using every trick in the book to try to convince her to return. 'I knew it was different this time. I had never managed to get to stay somewhere else overnight before. I had some really good friends from my old nursing days and, to try and find places to stay, I started calling people I knew.'

Her circle of friends went above and beyond – all without knowing the truth behind the marriage breakdown – to support her. She couch-surfed with friends for several weeks and the financial director of her former employer welcomed her to stay in the home he shared with his brother for several weeks. A former colleague's friend (a doctor) had an apartment in London which he only required two days a week and so Norah moved in there, while he stayed elsewhere. She would regularly volunteer for out-of-town events in order to have a guaranteed roof over her head with some semblance of independence.

During this harrowing period, she confided in one other person – the late Richard Hannaford – whom she later went on to marry. They met through their respective media work and Norah felt a sense of calm when speaking with him. It wasn't love at first sight, but it was clear there was something special between them. After one year of close friendship, they became romantically involved and within a few months, they were married.

'Whether he understood it or not, he made me feel good,' she says. 'I airbrushed my whole marriage with P. and continued to airbrush those nine years we were together out of my life – there are good friends in my life now who never even knew I was married before. Richard made me feel okay with myself. He made me believe it wasn't my fault.'

After they had their son, Dara, Norah was finally living the happy family life she had always deserved. But P.'s shadow would haunt her once more. After her father's death in 1999, P. travelled to attend the funeral.

'Dara was tiny, not even six months old. And P. came into my sitting room, within two days of my dad dying. I always describe that day as the worst possible day: I was dealing with the death of my father and my abusive ex-husband walks into the room,' she says.

Then, after P.'s death some time later, he left everything to Norah in his will, despite the fact they had been divorced for several years. For a sense of closure, she attended his funeral. 'Legally, I had to allow the money to go through my account, but I sent it straight out twenty-four hours later. I didn't want a single cent from him. I walked away from that marriage with nothing and I didn't want anything now.'

I ask Norah if she felt a sense of peace after his death, knowing this 'super monster' could never hurt her again. 'It was the biggest relief that he was gone. It's a terrible thing to say. Who would wish anybody to die, but I knew he could do nothing to me now. My world was better because he wasn't in it.'

It was her experience with P. that informed the making of Norah Casey as we know her now: formidable businesswoman, savvy investor, women's advocate and, above all, devoted mother.

'I was dependent on a man in my twenties as I never earned a lot,' she says. 'I went back and started studying again at aged twenty-three and I got to the end of my twenties with no savings but in a reasonable position. I swore I would never allow anybody else to control my life. I would make enough to sustain myself, even if it killed me, and never rely on anyone else again. Part of my over-whelming workaholic drive comes from need to feel secure and I still have it, I can't let go of it.'

She rarely talks about this troubled period in her life and, like all painful memories, she feels it is best left in the past. In 2017, she spoke on the *Late Late Show* about her experience with domestic violence and, afterwards, was inundated with requests for interviews. She began working with Women's Aid, where she still continues her advocacy, but has recently chosen to adopt a less public role. Not long after that television interview, Norah vowed not to speak about her experience again but, such is her devotion to supporting women, she made an exception in the case of this book.

'They say what doesn't kill you makes you stronger and I did come out of that relationship stronger. I was more resilient, I had grit inside me,' she says. 'Everyone in business is always talking about failure and saying that failure is nature's best teacher, but they tend to sanitise it for business life. In your personal life, failure is probably the biggest lesson you'll ever get.

'Your entire character changes when you go through something like that. It's not that it was my failure that I chose him or that he was so abusive to me but, when you face massive adversity like that, your character develops in a way you never thought possible.'

When art imitates life.

Tara Flynn

Actress, Comedian and Repeal the 8th Campaigner

'The day I made the decision to have an abortion.'

~

I'll begin this chapter by being frank: nobody actually enjoys talking about abortion. There is always room for both sides of a story to be heard, and in Ireland much of the political landscape has been dominated by this unpopular conversation topic for years, but it's a story worth telling the truth of.

~

In 2015, the Repeal the 8th campaign grew from a whisper to a roar, empowered by the historic 'Yes' vote for marriage equality.

Grassroots campaigners, many of whom were involved in the Yes equality campaign, knew they had another fight ahead, arguably an ever harder one. Until then, the Eighth Amendment had been something of an accepted, but ugly, truth about the Irish healthcare system. It was considered political suicide to attempt to repeal it. For years, Ireland would 'send its problems to England' – its problems being women in crisis pregnancies seeking abortions. In December 2017, that would change when Taoiseach Leo Varadkar called for a vote to repeal the amendment. What ensued was six months of deeply upsetting news coverage, no matter what side of the fence you sat on. The movement had been bubbling for years, gaining enough momentum to prompt Mr Varadkar to declare a personal change of heart and encourage citizens to go the polls and vote yes.

Tara felt it a dereliction of her personal duty not to tell her story. Until 2015, she was best known for her comedic talents; she was well-established as a writer and actor and had worked the comedy circuit in the UK and Ireland for years. Privately, she had been contending with an internal struggle to share her experience with abortion.

She broke that silence at the Amnesty International tent at Electric Picnic where she was speaking on behalf of Amnesty International Ireland's 'She's Not A Criminal' project, which was looking specifically at developed countries such as Ireland in which abortion was illegal. In a field in Stradbally, Co Laois, Tara told her story in front of a crowd for the first time.

'My role is that I'm a storyteller. I have a communications skill; that's my superpower. Otherwise there's no need for me to have been part of this campaign. I have nothing to do with politics.'

Over the course of three and a half years, she became the unofficial face of the Yes campaign, sharing her most personal secret with the entire world as she immersed herself headfirst into activism, a path she'd never foreseen for herself.

Tara's story is that, in 2006, she had consensual sex with a man and the next morning she was prescribed the morning after pill. She took it. It didn't work. She said previously that 'my body knew before my brain did' and after consultation with a counsellor, she made the decision to travel to the Netherlands for an abortion. It was not an easy decision, but it was the right one for her.

At that time, she was thirty-seven and her counsellor, informing her of all possibilities, told her it could be her last chance to have a baby. But in her heart of hearts, she knew it wasn't right for her. She wanted to be left alone to contemplate this life-altering decision until it was over.

In the immediate aftermath, it changed her life in ways she now only recognises through the lens of time as being correlated to Ireland's attitude towards abortion. The law at the time made her feel unwelcome.

> My role is that I'm a storyteller. I have a communication skill; that's my superpower.

'Very soon after that, I moved to Britain. Retrospectively I'm certain that influenced everything,' she explains to me.

'I wanted a big change. Subconsciously, I think one of the reasons the move was easy to make – leaving all my friends and family behind – was because I wanted to be out of Ireland. While I was in Britain, I got better at my work, I developed a great relationship with my agent who I'm still with and I met my husband. I got married in London. In a way, everything flowed from there. Although I was already doing well on the work track, now I was upping my game and taking risks.

'I think when you make a big life-changing decision for yourself, it's very hard to feel that everything needs to stay the same. Before you make that choice, you ask, "What are my priorities? What do I want? Can I be a parent? If I can't, what then do I do? What is my productivity in the world?" I couldn't just fritter away the rest of my days. I became hyper productive!

'I became more driven in a way that I never had been before. Of all the many life-changing days – moving to Dublin in 1990 changed my life, doing my first voice demo changed my life – that's the thing I suppose that motivated me not to waste a day.

'It taught me not to waste time and to realise there are important things you have to say. It's not a conversation I'd ever had with myself, but I realise now that the decision to move and to pursue different work are connected.

'Then, in terms of activism and truth-telling, that became a huge motivator. When I started seeing my LGBT pals on the road to the Marriage Equality Referendum, sharing their truths that made the other people in their lives uncomfortable, but knowing they had to do that in order to help other people ... I knew I had a story that could, if not change anything, at least make other people feel better. I started to feel like fraud.'

After nearly ten years of deliberately keeping her medical history private, Tara made a conscious decision to insert herself into what would become the most divisive referendum in modern Irish history. The road to Repeal success was paved by women like Tara, who put their personal and professional lives on hold because they believed at their core that it was the right thing to do.

In Nelson Mandela's *A Long Walk to Freedom*, he writes about how no passion is to be found playing small – in settling for a life less than the one you are capable of living.

This mantra is something of a calling card for Repeal campaigners like Tara, who sacrificed both her mental and physical health for what she believed to be the greater good of the nation.

Before that talk at the Amnesty tent, she told her story to *Irish Times* journalist Kathy Sheridan, but she says there was little effect afterwards specifically because many stories in that particular series were – like hers – anonymously told. And it's easy to overlook someone's personal tale if you don't know who they are, especially stories which had been largely swept under the carpet at that point.

'Some very kind, feminist writers in various publications were sharing stories periodically and running them to remind people that these everyday stories were out there. The headline grabbers were always the exceptions – the cases of rape, fatal foetal abnormalities, wanted pregnancies going tragically wrong, the so-called "sympathetic' stories",' she says. 'They were often there and they were rarely anonymous. Those women were exceptionally brave to share their stories because no one else was, yet.

'Kathy didn't share anyone's identity, as she had promised, but then of course, they are faceless stories on a page. They're all valid; they're all full of weight and empathy and sorrow and reality, but people just read them and turn the page.'

It wasn't until Colm O'Gorman, the executive director of Amnesty International Ireland, asked Tara to be part of that talk at Electric Picnic that she shared her story with anyone outside of her inner circle. She was originally asked to moderate the discussion, but she told Colm of her experience and said she might have something to contribute on a more personal level.

'And of course we became very close after that.'

With the help of the organisation she began considering the best way to share her story. She didn't know who was in the audience – were they friends or foes?

They were, for the most part, friends.

'Women started sharing their own stories and we all got so emotional in that tent. It made me think, as a random straw poll of the country, it was probably a good barometer for the fact that people aren't speaking but they are ready to . . . hope is what I came away with that day,' she shares, admitting she still gets choked up when speaking about the intensity of feeling in that tent.

'I knew the papers would cover it the next day and I was going away to Cork with my husband for a week. I also knew that Roisin Ingle would be sharing her story that same week in the *Irish Times* and we couldn't have planned that. I didn't book Electric Picnic and her book publisher had picked that date months before.'

The timing was serendipitous.

Until then, Tara had confided in only a handful of people – her husband and some close friends – when one night, on her birthday, she felt an overwhelming need to share it. There was a table of seven and she knew she was risking friendships by opening up as there was a possibility not everyone present would agree with the decision she'd made.

'For some people, it's a deal-breaker and that's absolutely fine, I utterly respect them. But it happens to people and it had happened to me and I know in my heart I did the right thing. I'm not a criminal; I'm not a murderer, according to my own beliefs. I understand people's views differ but I knew my conscience was clear. I knew in my friendship group there might be people who disagreed, but that was the risk I had to take.'

Then came Tara's one-woman show *Not a Funny Word*. In May 2018, she travelled around Ireland telling her own story in the best way she knew – through comedy. She never set out to become the face of the Repeal campaign, but here she was, empowered with the tools of influence, and she would use them as a cause for good. The first half of the show was filled with jokes, until it reached the point where she realises she's pregnant and the production comes to a screeching halt. It was a literal representation of art imitating life.

'I've become recognisable for an issue-driven thing, which is very strange when you want to tell jokes. It was also one of the reasons why it was important for me to put my story into my work and put it in that comedy frame. Parts of that show are very, very serious. Being pregnant when you can't cope isn't funny.

'Then I talked a bit about the abuse I got when I told my story and what people call you . . . how you feel like you're in a pit and the whole country is standing on the edge above you with their opinions. So, on top of your own personal decisions, when you're grappling with your own moral stance . . .

'At the end of the show, I beg people to be safe and not wind up on stage telling the world about your hoo-ha.'

The show was critically praised, but also offered an alternative insight into what campaigners like Tara, and so many others, were fighting for – which was the humanity of it.

'I shared the despair, the quandary, the grappling with, *how do I feel about this?* Do I think it's murder? I don't, but should I? It was within my comfort zone to do that through comedy. It also helped take away some of the pain. Even when you're very clear morally – and you know what your beliefs are – it's still a big decision. It may be straightforward but it's not easy.'

It also proved a useful tool in sharing a 360-degree view of her experience, something you can't convey in a 1,200-word newspaper or radio interview. It was lengthy. It was immersive. It was heart-wrenching.

'I've had people who saw me in the show and felt comfortable to contact me in the time afterwards and say thank you because they no longer felt alone. It's okay to ask all the questions that need to be asked and it's okay to come up with these answers that I'm not a bad person. I felt really touched by that.'

By that point in summer 2018, Tara had become accustomed to women reaching out to her to share their stories. 'I think busting stigma is one of the main things we need to continue as this goes on, because allowing people to robustly talk about this and not be silenced by shame or misinformation is the only way we'll hold on to these rights.

'Sharing our stories – removing the stigma around and demystifying abortion – is a really powerful tool that's often overlooked and I think that's something I can help with in an ongoing way.'

After 25 May 2018, when Ireland voted 66.4 per cent in favour of repealing the eighth amendment and legalising abortion, it was a culmination of three and a half years of work for Tara. It was also the moment she finally allowed herself to take a breath.

In the early days of her campaigning, work had become quiet and so she found herself time-rich which allowed her to say yes to every event she was asked to be part of. This meant, after three and a half years, she had burned herself out.

She started going to counselling to quell her growing anxiety, which had risen to the point where her hands were constantly shaking and, she says, she was 'very ill' for months afterwards.

After this time, when the Yes vote was passed, she became a 'lightning rod for abuse'. Not long after, she deleted her social media accounts. She goes to great lengths in our conversation to emphasise that, despite what people think – or thought – that she has no political affiliations and was never even part of Together For Yes. She only went in occasionally to say hi or buy buttons and offer moral support to the volunteers; Tara clarifyies that she remains 'in awe' of their work and doesn't want to take 'even a fraction of their credit'.

She was, however, uniquely equipped in the skills of storytelling. It was her superpower, after all.

Soon after, she and her husband went on a week-long holiday, which she spent reading books, going on long walks and watching

Real Housewives. 'Last year, not only could I not write, I couldn't read. Thank God for the *Real Housewives*! One day I will write Nene Leakes [*Real Housewives of Atlanta* star] a letter! Thank heavens for shows like that; they got me through the summer. Not only could I not create, I couldn't take in rich creative projects.'

The last twelve months have been a journey of self-rediscovery, which sounds great on paper, but Tara's devotion to the cause crippled her financially and she soon hopes to get back on stage, in front of the camera or behind a microphone. She is working on a podcast, she hired a new agent and is constantly writing down notes for jokes and productions and aims to have her next show at Dublin Fringe Festival 2020.

'I am voraciously reading again,' she says. 'I am hungry to start writing, but I'm not quite back there yet.' The experience took its toll on Tara, who still asks her husband if she's back to her pre-Repeal self yet. 'At the time, he said 60 per cent. Now it's more 89 per cent. Then something happens to rattle me and I have no resources to deal with it. That's where I notice I'm not quite 100 per cent yet.

'Everyone keeps asking what I'm working on next. I reply "Me" – for now.'

FAMILY MATTERS

~

LOVE, LOSS AND
EVERYTHING IN BETWEEN.

Ireland's most impressive teenager.

Terry Prone

Chairwoman of The Communications Clinic

'The day I first appeared on television . . .
which led to meeting the love of my life.'

~

At seventy years old, Terry Prone knows a thing or two about life. She has spent nearly all of her seven decades working in media in Ireland, having made her first appearance on television at thirteen years old. This appearance led to countless work projects in broadcasting in RTÉ, publishing thirty-four books (including eight novels) and a prominent career which would explore several avenues of success. This wealth of experience eventually prompted her to set up The Communications Clinic – a crisis, media training and PR business, which she runs from Dublin's Adelaide Road.

~

From an early age, Terry's potential was obvious: in her adolescence, she was interviewed by Barbara Walters as 'Ireland's Most Impressive Teenager' and, by twenty-one, she edited a national magazine. Now, in 2019, she is one of the most respected women in business, media and politics. She knows everyone who's anyone and has an inside line with decision-makers at the highest level in Ireland. If you want things done in any of the above fields, you go first to Terry Prone.

Terry's experience, like so many others', has been a colourful one littered with highs and lows, but through the chaos there remained one constant: her late husband Tom Savage, the love of her life. He had the biggest influence on her and, two years after his death in 2017, the gap left in her life is palpable. She credits the day she first appeared on television as the day that changed her life not because it started her successful career (though, incidentally, it did), but because it led her to meet Tom, ten years later.

'The day that changed my life was when I first appeared on television at the age of thirteen,' Terry says. 'I was a student at the Holy Faith in Clontarf and one of the nuns, Sr Annunciata, came into my class saying she had two tickets to *Teen Talk* [a teenage discussion programme which aired on RTÉ in the 1960s] the following Friday and the class went berserk,' she recalls.

'I was mystified because we didn't have a television as my parents didn't believe in it and I had no idea what they were talking about. This was 1964 and the programme had electrified Ireland.'

There was a catch, though – you needed to be sixteen to appear on the show. But, with Sr Annunciata's help in allowing her to wear the 'high heels she thinks I don't know she has', she bluffed her way through.

The show's premise was simple – it featured topics relevant to teenagers, with input from young people in the audience, but its panel was comprised exclusively of adults. It became a springboard for broadcasting talent in Ireland, where a young Vincent Browne first cut his teeth in television, and it was among the earliest type of panel format that remains so popular even now. You might say it wasn't a fair fight to put teenagers against experienced adults on live television, but Terry, already a formidable young woman, was up to the challenge.

She arrived at RTÉ's studios in Donnybrook and, for the first time, walked through the hallowed halls of Montrose, the first of what would be countless visits there over five decades. The show's premise was rooted in interactivity, so the producers did what producers do and sought to find any vocal audience members before filming began. She remembers the questions as being 'very solemn' and dull.

'There was a handsome man with a clipboard taking questions from the participants. Questions like, "If you were to make a time capsule, what would you put in it?"' Having never watched television before, Terry was unfamiliar with what would excite viewers and it was also long before an established trope of fiery exchanges was the norm for television. It made her appearance all the more empowering. It was genuine.

'I asked, "Why do parents stop their babies from sucking their thumbs? It doesn't give you cancer, it doesn't make you fat and it's free." He looked at me as if I was some different species.'

It was the closest thing to controversy they had seen and it was, as expected, a producer's dream. Her natural charisma and intelligence was displayed for the entire country to see and she became the episode's undeniable star. Her question caused a ruckus both with the panellists and the audience. During her thirty-minute appearance, Terry found herself fending off criticism with adrenaline-fuelled aplomb, for, in her words, 'lowering the tone of the show'. But controversy means ratings, and for a bold and intelligent teenage girl like herself, there was no better place to make her mark than on *Teen Talk*.

That day, she learned a valuable lesson about the merits of television, which she carries with her still. 'It was this wonderful epiphany,' she says, 'that for television you don't have to be good-looking or terribly well-educated as long as you cause a fight.'

Her appearance went down a treat and Denis O'Grady, a veteran television producer, asked her to become a regular panellist. 'From then on, I was a regular on that programme. A couple of months later, when I was fourteen, I started to do the *Late Late Show*.'

And so a career was born.

The late Bunny Carr, who presented the show then, was something of an RTÉ institution and as his career evolved across programmes, he would always find a job for his protégé. By the time Terry was twenty, she was well-versed in television and all its trappings and she was asked, for the first time, to help in media training. Bunny was now the director of the Catholic Communications Centre, which was teaching nuns and priests how to communicate on radio and television. In order to best assess their performances, Terry was asked to analyse the priests' sermons.

For her task, she was joined by a senior priest, whom she didn't know, who could complement her analysis from a different angle.

'Just before the coffee break, the priest stood up and walked out. I said to Bunny, "Listen your man disappeared, what did he say about me?" And he said you were grand but he didn't need to be there.

'What's the phrase from *Jane Eyre*? "Reader I married him." It was Tom.'

Within three weeks of meeting him, Terry knew he was The One, although it was a bittersweet realisation as he was, as far as she knew, still devoted to the priesthood. 'I knew that I loved this man and admired him as I had never ever loved or admired anyone, but it was with a great sense of sadness because he was a priest,' she says.

'I didn't know that, at the time, he'd decided to leave the priesthood because of an episode involving a bishop who, Tom believed, had not acted in the right way in response to a case Tom had brought to him. I just happened to be lucky in that way.'

So, a number of years later, Tom left the priesthood and they were married, but their union wasn't without its difficulties as he had, for many years, been a high profile figure in the church at a time when the Catholic Church's grip on Ireland was ironclad. But, rather than disappearing into the abyss to appease critics, they both maintained their public jobs and eventually everyone moved on. When it came to their wedding, Fr Gerry Reynolds and Fr Brian D'Arcy, well-known priests, officiated the ceremony, D'Arcy 'because he was so fond of Tom and believed he needed to make a statement' and show support for their union.

> What's the phrase from *Jane Eyre*? Reader, I married him. It was Tom.

When speaking with Terry, I'm reminded of a sense of romantic grandeur that seems so rare these days, a sense of love so pure at heart it's like poetry when she speaks of him. She is someone for whom falling in love was a privilege, one she remains grateful for. And it continues on, two years after his death.

Inspired by their love story, I came across a love letter from French philosopher Denis Diderot, written to his beloved Sophie Volland in 1719. It says, 'My affection for you is ardent and sincere. I would love you even more than I do, if I knew how.'

Terry's adoration for her late husband is ever-present and remains all-consuming; I feel sure that if she could love him more, she would.

Tom's passing was a notable news story, thanks to a combination of his political work (he was a former chairman of the RTÉ board and an advisor to former Taoiseach Albert Reynolds), his marriage and their son, the equally well-known broadcaster Anton Savage. This, paired with the fact that he was unusually vocal about his decision to leave the priesthood in the 1970s, made his death a national news topic. At the time, controversies were swept under the carpet, but Tom wouldn't be silenced and thus he earned the respect of his peers and, perhaps most importantly, the increased respect of his wife.

The happiness of their marriage was no secret. It is with such affection and admiration that Terry speaks of Tom that it's as if they had just met yesterday. He was her ultimate supporter, her champion, her raison d'être.

'I always find myself quoting him,' she says. 'I get really irritated when I'm dealing with women on how to pick a husband or a mate as they say, "You want someone who's supportive." I think you want somebody who, perhaps wrongly, as in my case, thinks you are cleverer than them, you are more talented than them, that you are the person who needs to be freed up to do everything you want to do. That's what you really want.'

History hasn't always been kind to women and, in particular, it isn't forgiving of women at the forefront of their industry. Tom believed it was his job to support his wife; he understood the complexities her gender added to her work.

'Any business that puts a woman out front in television and writing... there are days when you go home crushed. Somebody asked Tom about our relationship in an interview and he said, "You have to understand the job. My job... Tess [Terry] comes home to me usually on a Friday like a collapsed football and it's my job over the weekend to inflate her again."'

It's clear Tom was a kind and generous man, a devoted husband and father, but he was also an academic with fierce intelligence who could add nuance to any debate; a man whose desire to learn – and to listen – informed Terry's day-to-day decisions both in business and in life.

'He had this fantastically different, funny and witty way of addressing things,' Terry says. 'Whenever we'd be talking in a group, someone would ask a question and I would think, "I know the answer," and then, hang on a second, he'd be putting on a much bigger framework around it. People would become fascinated by him. Even now, people write to me saying, "Tom changed my life." It may be forty years after the event.'

In 2008, Terry, Tom and their son, Anton, set up The Communications Clinic together. Whenever she had the chance, Terry would sit in on one of Tom's consultations, 'because I would always learn something from him'.

I note that Tom was, by all accounts, not a man reflective of the era in which he lived: he had the courage to leave the priesthood, the conviction to follow his heart and the gallantry and generosity to encourage his wife's work. Theirs was a marriage of equals at a time when, just a few years earlier, so many women in Ireland were forced to resign from their jobs upon getting wed. Terry credits Tom's mother's own work ethic with his trailblazing approach to equality between the sexes and in same sex relationships.

'His mother had worked all her life. She had five children and she educated all of them way beyond what they could have expected – she was a strong country woman – so he had no notion that women were different or lesser,' Terry says.

Tom was also the first Roman Catholic priest in Queen's University, Belfast. 'He was the sort of priest who got called in when things got peculiar,' she says. 'What does peculiar mean?' I ask.

'I remember a nun ringing him in panic to say that two of the sixth-year girls were in love with each other,' she says before proudly sharing his heart-warming response. 'He said, "Love comes in such rare instances that you don't need to question it that much."'

He remained patient and considerate until the end and had a sense of forgiveness that even Terry couldn't understand at times.

'When he left the priesthood, the level of abuse that he suffered was just unbelievable – in the media because he was well known and in person because people sent him letters,' she recalls. 'He had merciful amnesia. I remember every nasty comment made, but he would quite happily greet and work with somebody knowing they had been horrible to him.'

For most of Terry's life, the influence of her husband was enduring and, instead of shouting about her own myriad accomplishments, she shifts focus to Tom, a man in whom she remained awe-struck until the very end. If not for that moment – that first television appearance – she never would have met her precious Tom, and Terry as she is simply would not be.

Meeting Tom boosted her already unwavering self-confidence and gave her a different option for a career path, one different to what she had planned; more specifically, as a teenager, she was determined she was going to be the greatest Abbey [Theatre] actress of [her] generation'.

'I was already winning awards and stuff which is why Annunciata picked me because she knew I could stand up and pretend to be confident,' she explains. 'I never would have thought of media training, ever.'

Then, when she was sixteen, she was fired from the Abbey Theatre because of her weight, a blessing in disguise. 'The artistic director called me in one day and sat me down and told me I was the most talented actress of my generation . . . and that I was grossly overweight,' she says. 'He suggested that I do something about my weight pretty quickly. So I did. I got into radio where they can't see you.

'Even so, that very first programme at thirteen shaped almost everything that I've done since,' she asserts. 'It was just magical meeting somebody like Bunny who was such a genius, exploring something I'd never come across – television – meeting wonderful people and just having a great time.'

For Terry, all the good in her life – her happy marriage, her son, her thriving business – can be traced back to that day.

'We were meant to
meet each other.'

Katherine Zappone

Minister for Children and Youth Affairs

'The day I married the love of my life,
Ann Louise Gilligan.'

~

Everyone loves a love story. For some, the pleasure is in hearing it; for many, it's the desire to live it; in this chapter, I hope it's in reading it.

~

For thirty-six years, Katherine Zappone, Ireland's Minister for Children and Youth Affairs was in a loving relationship with Dr Ann Louise Gilligan, an academic whom she described as an 'educator extraordinaire' after Ann's passing in 2015.

Theirs was a tale of romance that not only spanned decades, but was of the type that inspires Shakespearean sonnets in its almost otherworldly quality.

But, as two women who wished to marry in Ireland at a time when it was illegal, they faced endless complications which would challenge not only societal expectations, but legal ones, too.

Katherine and Ann Louise were instrumental in bringing attention to the Marriage Equality Referendum (which passed with a majority

62 per cent) in 2015, having spent years fighting on the battleground for equal rights, culminating in a glorious, sunny day at Dublin Castle when Ireland celebrated voting a resounding Yes.

What was the day that changed her life?

'Without a doubt, it was the day I married Ann Louise Gilligan,' Minister Zappone shares with me from her office at Leinster House. 'It was 13 September 2003, exactly sixteen years ago.

'However, it was really hard to identify the day that changed my life. In around 1999 or 2000, we had made a decision that we were going to look for some legal recognition of our life partnership – which was a momentous decision for us.

'We brought together a legal team and started to develop a strategy and, one day, my youngest brother, Mark, phoned me and mentioned he was heading to Canada for a wedding. Ann Louise was there separately for work.'

Mark was en route to a wedding between two men in Victoria, British Columbia, the second province to legalise same-sex marriage in Canada. At that time, the Netherlands was the only country in the world which recognised same-sex marriage. Other Western countries had begun to recognise civil partnerships while others had taken an opposing turn in definitively banning the concept altogether.

You could argue that this phone call was fate: unlike other jurisdictions, like Vermont in the United States and Toronto, Canada, it wasn't a requirement to be a resident to marry there, or even register for a civil partnership. The law was brought into effect on 8 July 2003 and, two months later, Katherine and Ann Louise would legally formalise their 21-year relationship.

'Ann Louise phoned me and said, "There's a possibility we could actually marry here." That was in July and by 13 September, we were married.

'At the time we had to think, "What does that involve? Do we really want to get married? We'd rather do it here, but should we do it there?" There were issues – we were very strong feminists and some of our friends and quite a few lesbians would not have been keen on the institution of marriage from a feminist perspective [as some feminist theory argues that marriage is the cornerstone institution of a patriarchal structure].

'I understood all of that analysis, of course, but thought if we had the opportunity to get married, isn't that ultimately what we want – and then to be able to change the institution from within?'

And so the couple travelled nearly 5,000 miles to begin their marriage; although it wasn't exactly an impossible distance for Minister Zappone who grew up in Seattle, Washington – 'Vancouver was only three hours from my hometown.'

They contacted the same marriage commissioner who had wed the male couple just a few months earlier, a woman called Anne Moore, who performed the ceremony at her stately home on the charming Granville Island.

'We flew to Seattle first and then drove with my parents, both of whom were in their early eighties, to Canada. I have four siblings and they came with their families.

'When we got there, we had to get a marriage license and then bring it to the marriage commissioner.

'We got on a little boat across the water and we were a bit nervous about that – it was fifteen years ago, we were in a different country, and we were concerned about what the marriage commissioner would say when we told her we were seeking our marriage license. But we were so taken with her response and how normally she treated us that we remembered her name – Ivy.'

The wedding was small and discreet, but breathtakingly beautiful:

a symbolism of two souls pledging their love for one another publicly in front of their loved ones.

'We had the most beautiful moment in Anne's home,' Katherine recalls. 'I had my close family, Ann Louise's sister [June Kelly] and brother [the late Arthur Gilligan] who happened to live nearby, came too. It was a fantastic moment.

'Ann Louise would often reminisce about the photographs being taken and our families, aged from thirteen into their eighth decade, beaming in their recognition of us.'

Once the marriage was official, they toasted with champagne flutes from Irish designer Louise Kennedy's collection, and Ann Louise's brother, a professional photographer, was on picture duty as they celebrated in Granville Island, a picturesque spot that overlooks the waterfront and downtown Vancouver.

Following the formalities, they returned to Seattle where Katherine's sister had a surprise for the couple.

'She had us come into their home blindfolded. Inside, there was a beautiful three-tiered wedding cake and other family and friends had gathered to celebrate with us. We were deeply moved by that.

'I never knew this until my own wedding, but when my sister got married in her early twenties, she was so upset to think that I would never have the experience of marrying the one I loved. I hadn't even shared my identity with her at that point. She adored me so much and wanted me to have what she had. As she toasted me and Ann Louise that afternoon in her home, she told us this. So here we were, in her house, celebrating this and her absolute belief and commitment that the right she had should be ours as well, which is so special. She and her daughter, Caitlin, very much participated in the wedding.

'That was the most important day of my life.'

Ann Louise and Katherine first met in 1981, when they were both studying theology and education at Boston College, a prestigious university in Massachusetts. They were the only two applicants approved for that specific doctorate programme that year.

'When I showed up for orientation, I saw her walk through the door and knew she was the "other one" to be have been given the same opportunity as me. We met in September. On 10 November, my father's birthday, we knew we wanted to spend the rest of our lives with each other.

'We decided to wait until the following October to have our life partnership ceremony. We would live with that commitment and those vows, but it was only recognised within a small group of people and ultimately not in law, not just in terms of recognition but also the practical supports that legality would provide.'

So, after falling in love at virtually first sight and a year together, they participated in a life partnership ceremony – 'Nobody even used that word then "life partnership" in 1981 in Rockport, Massachusetts!' – attended by just thirteen close friends and no family members.

'We wanted to commit to our lives together, that much we knew, and we wanted to celebrate a ritual around it with a ceremony and a dinner.

'We did that and it was absolutely spectacular. At that point, I don't think either of us imagined it would lead to marriage or that we would look to legal change. We just wanted to have our life partnership solemnised and we did that the best way we could.

'It was a very radical thing to do. We were both studying theology at a Jesuit university and we asked an Episcopalian priest, who was one of the first women ordained, to solemnise. There were prayers and rituals and blessings and rings – Ann Louise gave me one with her birthstone and I gave her one with mine.'

Soon after, they returned to live full-time in Ann Louise's native

Ireland where they were regularly reminded of the practical benefits of marriage they were being denied.

'I'm originally American and, when I moved here with Ann Louise, I came on a student visa. Then, when I finished my doctorate, I started to get some work at Trinity College and they gave me an employment permit. Every year, I would go to the alien section of Harcourt Street and get them to stamp my visa to say I'm permitted to reside for the next year because Trinity was giving me a job.

'It wasn't sustainable. And that's even though I had a much better time than everyone else standing in the queue because I was an American employed through Trinity College. I began the process of applying for my Irish citizenship and I eventually did get it ...'

This marks the turning point in Katherine and Ann Louise's next chapter: activism. They spoke for the voiceless, assembled the masses and, eventually, utilised their education and passion to mobilise a movement.

'Ann Louise and I were committed to improving human rights. We had a commitment to eradicate poverty, to working within disadvantaged communities, and we remained absolutely committed to women.

'We were strong feminists. When we made a decision to go to Chile to visit some friends, we got our affairs in order and wrote our wills for the first time.

'We'd bought a cottage in Co Kerry – we referred to it as my pension. However, when we went to a lawyer, we were told that when one of us dies, it will be sold and half will go to tax because our partnership was not legally recognised.'

This was the trigger that first brought Minister Zappone and her late wife to national prominence in 2006 when they sought to have their marriage recognised by the Irish authorities so – along with many other reasons – they could tackle the issues around tax. A High Court judge rejected their claim because, at the time, that right to inherit was confined to the union of a man and woman, according to the Irish Constitution.

'Ultimately, that's how our case became something that fought the Revenue Commissioners because we were looking for the same status as heterosexual married couples. That's all we wanted and they said they couldn't do that because we weren't married in the eyes of the Irish State.

> We had a commitment to eradicate poverty, to working within disadvantaged communities, and we remained absolutely committed to women.

'We were meant to meet each other. Fighting for our marriage was all part of that.

'In a very practical sense we experienced our own form of discrimination as we started to delve deeper into our wish to be married in Ireland. We had this incredible love, and we felt that if anyone is going to challenge the State, it could and should be us.

'Middle class, with good jobs, we looked like "normal" people and we believed we might be successful in achieving it.'

That aside, Katherine is acutely aware of just how special her relationship was. In 2008, she and Ann Louise wrote their memoir, *Our Lives Out Loud: In Pursuit Of Justice and Equality*, in a bid to explain it.

'We had an extraordinarily loving relationship. It was incredible: we worked together, we lived together, it was just magic most of the time.

'Ultimately though, we didn't think we could get married. Why was that day in Vancouver the best day? It began a marriage equality movement that led to the people of Ireland making a choice.'

Katherine and Ann Louise became integral figures in the marriage equality movement in Ireland, joining the thousands of campaigners who canvassed tirelessly and opened a dialogue on equality for all, which would result in a public referendum to legalise same-sex marriage in 2015.

Monumentally, it marked the first time a nation had legalised same-sex marriage through a popular vote. Lawmakers, politicians, LGBT advocates and citizens alike gathered at Dublin Castle on 23 May 2015 for a truly historic celebration the likes of which may not be seen again in our lifetime.

'The years until that point were really tough and difficult and lonely,' Katherine remembers. 'But our marriage in 2003 allowed us tell our story and it led to that extraordinary moment in Dublin Castle where tricolour and rainbow flags fluttered side by side and Ann Louise looked the happiest she'd ever been since the day we got married.'

Katherine and Ann Louise's relationship was further thrown into the public eye when Katherine, then a senator in her fourth year serving Seanad Éireann, got down on one knee and proposed to her love on live television. 'It was the best day.'

If not for their 2003 wedding and subsequent legal fight, Katherine never would have pursued a career in politics and spearheaded the movement from the inside.

'I don't know if it ever would have happened if I hadn't been appointed to the Seanad. When I was there, I learned everything about bringing about change from a human rights perspective in a civil society with an NGO context; how to raise money for it and how to develop strategies including legal, research, communication, everything,' she explains.

'In the earlier period, I put together a strategy for marriage equality and it blossomed, but we couldn't be seen to be doing that because we were in court. In the Seanad, I got to understand the politics and how to shape the debates around the subject – what language to use to achieve our end goal.'

She began regularly attending Citizen's Assembly gatherings and 'participating in shaping the language' that would be used to promote the Marriage Equality referendum.

'I never thought I would be able to do it – standing up and speaking personally about it in the Seanad. At that time, I don't think many people spoke about these legal issues from personal experience. I learned how to connect personal and legal issues in a way that would be persuasive.'

'I was still a senator when we won. We had a life partnership ceremony, we got married and then we "brought our marriage home" with our "Irish Wedding", in January 2016.

'We had a big renewal of vows and asked our friend Miriam O'Callaghan [the RTÉ broadcaster] to officiate and she was fantastic.'

Katherine was appointed the Minister for Children and Youth Affairs in 2016 after being nominated by Taoiseach Leo Varadkar. But one year later, Ann Louise tragically died after complications following a brain haemorrhage.

'We were together for 36 years. I loved her every single moment of it. I still love her of course, and she me.

'All that love for all those years was because of the incredible, loving relationship we had and the wedding we had in Vancouver. That's why that moment was so special.'

Motherhood breaks and remakes you.

Emma Donoghue

Author and Oscar-nominated screenwriter

'The day I gave birth to my first child.'

~

When it comes to female voices in Ireland, few are heard as loudly as Emma Donoghue's. The Dublin-born author is a force to be reckoned with in the world of literary fiction. She was already an established name when she got her big break in the form of her international best-selling novel, *Room*, in 2010. *Room*, inspired by the Josef Fritzl case in Austria, tells the devastating story of a woman and her five-year-old son – from whose perspective the story is told – who have been held captive in a windowless shed for years.

~

The book was – and is – as powerful as it sounds; it elevated Emma to the upper echelons of the literary world. *Room* was turned into a film in 2015, for which Emma was nominated for an Academy Award for Best Adapted Screenplay, while Brie Larson won the Best Actress Oscar for her performance.

But Emma is no flash-in-the-pan star – *Room* is her seventh novel, and its shift in tone, in comparison to her earlier books, reflects the biggest change to her personal life: she had become a mother for the first time.

Emma, who realised she was gay in her early teen years, had resigned herself to a life without marriage or children, despite having a deep yearning for both. She accepted that the world was not always built for everyone in it.

'I would argue that becoming a mother was a big deal for me for two main reasons – one personal and one professional,' she explains. 'If you grow up expecting to have children and then you do, then that's great and it's part of your plan. I didn't. At the age of twelve, I'm sure I thought I'd have children as most Irish women do, but when I realised I was gay, I thought it meant I wouldn't have kids. Remember this was in the 1980s.'

As time went on, however, attitudes evolved and so did the facilitation of 'non-traditional' births.

'I have friends in Ireland who tried it and it was hard; I have friends who have flown repeatedly to Denmark, but it's hard to time these things; I have another friend who flew to an American city to meet this guy who agreed to be her donor, he handed her the sperm and she had a baby nine months later. So it can work.

'I think the sheer logistical difficulty of it being in Ireland ... it could have gotten in the way. It might not have happened. I certainly have friends in each of these places who have managed to make families even in a same-sex relationship, so it's always possible.'

This was a welcome development, but it still seemed outside the realm of possibility as Emma wanted a partner with whom she could start her family.

Enter Christine Roulston.

'In my early twenties, I had accepted that I had simply chosen a different path. Around that time, I was starting to hear of women getting pregnant at clinics and I thought it might just be possible for me. Then I met my partner, Chris, and I was mad about her. I would see baby pictures of her and I would get this surge of emotion thinking how much I'd love a little baby version of Chris.'

But Chris hadn't factored children into her plans; in fact, she was ardently against the idea of becoming a mother.

'I continued working on her and, seven years of subtle nagging later, she finally caved. She said she realised it would cause me profound unhappiness if she kept saying no, so we decided we would have one baby and I would carry it.'

Now living in London, Ontario, Emma and Chris set about their journey to motherhood by visiting a fertility clinic and using an anonymous sperm donor; it's a process which resulted in successful implantation on the first try. The fact that they were in Canada rather than in Ireland meant it was an easier process, as Ireland still has relatively antiquated policies when it comes to fertility treatments in comparison to other countries.

'I've only encountered sperm twice in my life and a child has resulted each time! I have my mother's super fertility,' Emma laughs, referring to her mother, Frances, who gave birth to eight children.

While expecting son Finn (now fifteen), Emma enjoyed a rela-tively positive pregnancy, until he was born five weeks premature after a tree crushed the porch on their house and the excitement caused her to go into early labour.

'I felt smited by my own arrogance because I never read the bits in the book about early labour because I wasn't a high risk pregnancy. I had the impression that if you went into labour five weeks early it would be an absolute disaster.'

The midwives assured Emma that all would be fine and the labour itself was, until she experienced a retained placenta and her doctor was forced to remove it manually, an experience which would have had fatal results in a different place or at a different time. ('I remember once having a conversation with two of my editors,' Emma recalls, 'and each of us experienced difficulties giving birth that would have killed us. It was a moment where you realise: Thank God it's 2003 and I'm in Canada, because these things have – and still can – kill so many women worldwide.')

The drama of the birth aside, Emma and Chris fell instantly in love with their bouncing baby boy.

'As soon as Finn was born, I burst into tears of happiness that this little baby was here and healthy – this tiny little creature. His legs were folded up and his feet were under his chin, like this sort of frog prince. I think it was an extraordinary moment for Chris, more than me, because I'd always thought kids were a good idea but she hadn't. In that moment, when Finn was born, she fell in love with the sight of him.'

That moment of giving birth was the apex of a lifelong dream, a dream which Emma had locked away behind a closed door of her heart without daring to hope it could one day become a reality.

Chris, who had been so vocal in her desire to not start a family, later pushed for a second child.

'From a personal level, having a kid was amazing, given that, right through my twenties, I was thinking that because I was a lesbian, I wouldn't have a kid. So the feeling of having it all – following my heart, ending up with a woman and still having a kid – was amazing. She even said yes to a second one!

'I went away on a book tour when Finn was nine months old,' Emma remembers, 'and I left the two of them together. When I came back, Chris was high on love and said Finn needed a sibling.'

And so their daughter Una (now eleven) was born in 2008.

But Emma's life-changing experience of motherhood hadn't just affected her personally – turning her devil-may-care world upside down and introduced one filled with responsibilities, rules and schedules to deliver on – she now had a new world of inspiration to draw on, and this would transform her writing.

'Finn asked me, "Did you write books before us?"

'I said, "Yes! I've been making a living writing books since my early twenties." Finn asked what they were about and I suddenly couldn't remember.'

> So the feeling of having it all – following my heart, ending up with a woman and still having a kid – was amazing.

Emma has now not only written two children's books, but also all of her novels since becoming a mother feature interactions with children, influenced by how she now sees life through their eyes.

'For the last fifteen years, everything has had kids in it one way or another. It isn't always about motherhood, but there's some dynamic between children and adults,' Emma explains.

'It's been a massive new subject for me, which I didn't anticipate at all. I've written plenty of books before and motherhood sounds banal because it happens to everybody – like falling in love or having a parent – I didn't imagine I'd have anything new to say about it.

'I had no plans to monetise my experience of parenthood. Being a mother was personal – I thought I was lucky to have kids, but I never thought of it as a topic for my novels.'

The idea for *Room* struck her as she was listening to the radio in the car, driving down the highway. In 2008, Josef Fritzl was found to have kept his daughter Elisabeth captive in a soundproof basement beneath their family home for twenty-four years. He routinely raped Elisabeth, resulting in the birth of seven children: she raised three in captivity, one died after birth and three were brought up by Fritzl and his wife Rosemarie (Elisabeth's mother).

Emma was struck by the intensity of the case, and realised she had perceived it through the gaze of motherhood.

'Finn was about four and Una was one, when I heard about the Josef Fritzl case in Austria. One of Elisabeth's children, who lived in the basement with her, was five years old. I remember thinking that a small child would love having their mother physically there all the time – and I suddenly thought of the idea for *Room*, so I pulled over and wrote it all on a napkin.

'I'd been a mother for four years at this point, and I found parenting so interesting in terms of how it breaks and remakes you. Before having Finn, I'd been a carefree young woman and the youngest of eight siblings, so I wasn't a responsible big sister type. The writing life also isn't a very responsible one. At least with journalism, there are proper deadlines, but with fiction, they couldn't care less.

'There had been nothing in my life that needed me to turn up on time: I never had a 9-to-5 job, I worked briefly as a chambermaid and got sacked, and I had never done the responsible thing. Then suddenly I have this baby and he won't go to sleep at night and I'm totally accountable and responsible.

'You find this astonishing, urgent commitment to the child. It's exhausting and you're thinking, "Will no one let me go to sleep?" There's no break between night and day anymore. These are fairly obvious things, but because I had been carefree until I was thirty-three, it was a big shock to me.'

Emma had a newfound sense of purpose in her writing. She could now incorporate her own experiences as a parent into a rich tapestry of characters, including a long-suffering mother, a brave five-year-old boy and a real-life villain. She loved being a mother, but also recognised the complexities that come with it.

With *Room*, she found a way to apply all 'these universal and ordinary feelings and put them in this weird storyline of a child growing up in a locked room', and thus shine a new light on the so-called banal and universal feelings of parenthood.

'I thought, through this story, I could celebrate how amazingly committed parents are to their children, even on the bad days when they have to fake it,' she says.

'*Room* changed my career. It got me so many new readers – and got me into the film industry as well. All the books I've written since have children in them. I never would have expected this moment in my personal life would put me on a different train track in my professional life.

'Women writers are always warning you not to have children. They wait until you're pregnant and then they tell you that every baby costs you a book. I've heard some say every baby costs three books!'

Emma's career hasn't stalled like she was warned it might, but, like so many other working mothers, she is a master at prioritisation to the point of ruthlessness. Her children and partner come first, but her career is still of such importance to her and, since the big-screen success of *Room*, she has segued into a successful new screenwriting career.

'The permanent results of *Room* are that I get bigger contracts and more readers, so it has lifted all my work. Through the *Room* play, I had a show on in the Abbey Theatre for the first time ever.

The film opened the doors of film writing to me, which is a specialist training that tends to usually be done by a small cohort of men,' she explains.

'I've had loads of offers and I have six different television and film projects on the go; to suddenly be getting offers in the film world in your forties when you might expect your career to have tapered off a bit is brilliant.

'I don't have success at the level of *Room* with my other stuff, but it's given more oxygen to those projects.'

The success to which Emma refers is on another level: *Room* was shortlisted for the Man Booker Prize and Orange Fiction Award, it was an international bestseller and the film adaptation earned four Academy Award nominations, including Emma and Brie's afore-mentioned nods, and Best Director for Lenny Abrahamson and Best Picture.

The film was produced by Element Pictures, an Irish-based company, which encouraged a familial sense of camaraderie throughout the excitement of the 2015 awards season. Emma knew the strength of the work she was putting forward, but still hadn't expected to set the world alight in the way she did, but with a back-bone of literary excellence behind her, she kept her cool during an exceptionally exciting few months of her life.

'If you're going to have a big hit, it's good not to have it at the very start. I quite pity those who have a great book or album right away because it's all going to feel downhill from there,' she says. 'Nobody stays at that level of stardom.

'Because it was my seventh novel, I could tell it was so different to how things were usually done. My publishers would ring me up to share sales figures and normally they don't say a word! Publishers don't typically send you first class anywhere, but in the film world, we were sent business class and I got used to travelling on those full-length flat beds, which absolutely spoils you for real life.'

Emma's real life, however, is modelling her art and vice versa, transforming her writing style into a fresh level of ambition and reach, a constant reminder of the multi-layered joy her children have brought to her life.

'It was great fun for Finn and Una to visit the film set and see the excitement. And I loved how they were able to say, "All this happened because of us."'

Sport is her thing.

Evanne Ní Chuilinn

Sports broadcaster

'The day I became comfortable in my own skin.'

~

In the world of Irish sport broadcasting, there is one woman who is a constant. Currently sports news presenter on RTÉ News: Six One, meet Evanne Ní Chuilinn.

~

Evanne was adopted in 1982, a few months after she was born, by her parents, Catherine and Cathal, and raised at their home in Kilkenny. They would go on to adopt Cormac, from a different family, and then welcome their youngest daughter, Áine, who Catherine gave birth to.

Evanne is quick to emphasise that her adoption experience has been a positive one but is aware that others in Ireland have not been so fortunate. In recent years, the adoption process in Ireland has been marred by scandal, reflecting the country's darkest history. Recent findings have shown that many adoptions that took place in Ireland in the mid to late 20th century were falsely recorded, forced and took place under the radar. The children – now adults – affected by these illegal adoptions are on an ongoing quest for personal information, working in conjunction with the Adoption Authority of Ireland, the government and the individuals seeking to unlock the stories of their past.

Evanne does, however, see herself as something of an advocate for the adoption cause, thanks in no small part to the day that changed her life. She was sixteen years old when she felt a connection to where she came from, a connection which would inform much of the confidence she now possesses.

'When I was sixteen, like most teenagers, I felt very physically awkward. I've always been tall – I stand at 5 foot 10 now. My parents were a lot smaller than me, and I used to really struggle that I didn't look like them or my sister, Áine.

'I know that might not sound like it makes any sense unless you're adopted, but it used to bother me that I didn't look like the rest of the people in my family. Even some of my friends would get annoyed at me when I'd say they looked like their siblings, because they hated it!

'I felt insecure and I didn't know if it was because I was a teenager or something more, so I asked my dad to try and find out details about my birth mother and her family and whether they were tall.'

Over time, Evanne realised this yearning to know more about her genetic makeup wasn't just down to standard teenage hormones and, instead, was something unique to her circumstances. She knew she had an opportunity to put her curiosity at bay by reaching out to her birth mother, who was open to the concept. She knew this because, for many years, Evanne's father would write letters to Evanne's birth mother every January to keep her up to date on what interests Evanne had, how she was doing in school and so on.

Evanne never struggled with her somewhat non-traditional family makeup, but she did feel a persistent insecurity about her height and, she says, the size of her feet, which rather embarrassingly to her were several sizes bigger than her petite mother's. 'It was one of my biggest issues! I was a size seven which felt huge compared to Mam's size five. I used to try to squeeze my feet into a size six so they would look smaller. I was completely hung up on it.

'Looking back it sounds ludicrous, but I almost needed to justify my physical appearance. I knew I would feel better if I found out that my biological family were tall people. Every teenager feels awkward on some level, but I found a fix for it.

'Dad obligingly wrote a letter to be forwarded on to my birth mother, which we knew she would get. I cringe now when I think about that letter because my big focus was on the size of her feet and how tall she was!

'You probably take it for granted if you're not adopted that you have your mother's nose or your father's big feet, or you know why you're good at hurling because all your uncles played for Kilkenny . . . whatever the case is. If you don't know why you have certain physical attributes, it can really affect your confidence. Your identity can take a hit.'

Mary's – Evanne's biological mother – reply gave Evanne a sense of calming confidence that changed her life for ever.

'The letter went into great detail, not only about height and feet size, but about sport. I found out that Mary was a brilliant racquetball player and members of her family had played different sports. This resonated with me as I was already playing every different sport off my own bat. My parents weren't particularly into it, but I had a huge passion for sport. I learned how Mary is 5 foot 8 and her sister Aileen wore a size eight shoe and was 5 foot 10. I got all this detail about her height, her sporting prowess and her sister, and I remember thinking, "Now I know who I am."

'It made such a difference to me – a very subtle difference outwardly – but I was more accepting of who I was, including my strengths and weaknesses. I was more confident, quite literally, in my own skin.'

From that moment, Evanne, always a diligent student and natural athlete, flourished. She had finally found the missing piece of the puzzle and could look forward to her future, no longer consumed by questions about her past.

'I took that self-acceptance and ran with it. I started wearing high heels and no longer minded that I was towering over people. It was a big, big day. I remember reading and re-reading the letter. That particular letter told me it's okay to be who I am.

'I didn't realise quite how important that day was to me until years after the fact. In particular, learning about their interest in sport completely floored me. Since I was young, I played every sport I could – my parents were fantastic in their support and my dad was basically my taxi driver – but I was the only one in the family who had such an intense interest in it.

'Sport was my thing and I kept it going myself. Even in transition year in school, I took on extra classes and coaching where I could. I always drove myself to go further. When I found out there was a lot of sport in my background, it really impacted my opinion of the nature or nurture debate. It opened my eyes to the fact that nature is very strong.'

Evanne's natural knack for physical activity might be inherited, but her personality traits are down to her parents, whom she praises for their unwavering support in facilitating her inquisitiveness.

'I had a very caring upbringing; my parents were – and are – amazing, and so selfless. They never once wavered in their support of my meeting Mary.

'They supported me and continue to support me in every journey when it comes to anything to do with being adopted. It must have been difficult for my mother to see me so curious about my birth mother, but she never once let me feel like I was in any way hurting her. She never stood in my way and neither did my dad.

> I was more accepting of who I was, including my strengths and weaknesses, I was more confident, quite literally, in my own skin.

'I'm definitely who I am because of them. I wish I was more like Mam – she's so patient, non-judgemental and caring; kindness is her *modus operandi*. I must have gotten my interest in media work from my dad because he was really involved in pirate radio and I would go to the studio with him back in the 1980s. I caught the bug and specialised in radio when I went to college. But there's definitely a nature vs nurture argument to be had because I didn't pick up anything to do with sport from them.'

She's acutely aware of the positive circumstances around her own adoption story. Through her advocacy, she is familiar with others who haven't been so lucky in tracing their roots. The letters between her and Mary would eventually lead to an in-person meeting when Evanne was nineteen years old, where both of them were afforded the opportunity to ask the burning questions they'd built up over a lifetime.

'The curiosity is hard to put your finger on,' she explains. 'Other people I know who are adopted have different stories, but the one thing that runs through every adopted person's journey is this is innate curiosity. It was itching away at me for years, but I was lucky in that I knew Mary was willing to meet me and not everyone is that lucky.

'If you're not able to meet your birth mother or they don't want to meet you, that curiosity doesn't simply go away. You have to learn to close that part of you off because you'll never get the answers you're searching for.'

Because of the emotions at play, before she met face-to-face with Mary for the first time, both of them went to a social worker who would facilitate their introduction to ensure a smooth transition. One of the most powerful ice-breakers proved to be those letters that Cathal had been sending Mary for so long.

'When I met her, she knew so much about what I was doing at school and if you think about it, from her point of view, those letters probably filled a void as well. She gave a child up for adoption and most people who go through that don't know anything about where their child is and what their interests are, but my dad gave her that.

'When I first met her, I said how much that letter about her height and shoe size meant to me. I also jokingly apologised, but she understood.'

On that impactful day, Evanne and Mary met at a hotel in Clonmel, Co Tipperary. Their conversation went on for so long that Evanne missed her last bus home. ('I couldn't be in a car with someone ahead of the biggest meeting of my life,' she explains. 'I needed to be anonymous on a bus.')

Mary's sister Aileen – with her now infamous size eight feet – had been waiting outside the entire time and drove Evanne back to her family home in Kilkenny.

'I told her, too, about that moment of acceptance I felt when I got that letter. It's really hard to stay on the rails when you're sixteen, when you feel awkward and you've got hormones running through you. Being adopted doesn't help . . . but we look back at it now and laugh. My dad is something of a would-be Samaritan: he just loves helping people.'

As time went on, her relationship with her birth mother developed and now they are close friends; Evanne's children – Seímí, seven, and Peigí, four – have a third grandmother in Mary.

'Every family is different and for me my unit was perfect growing up. What's wonderful is my children have three grannies and they don't see anything strange about that. It's so beautiful because it's so pure. My mother is Mamó, Mary is Nana and Brian's mother is Gran. They have three totally separate relationships and every single one is absolutely adorable. They're so lucky.

'Seímí is starting to ask questions about whose tummy I was in, and it's not a taboo. I tell him that Mary was too young to mind me so Mamó and Daideo brought me up and he just completely accepts it as fact. That's a beautiful part of the story as well.'

When Evanne's brother Cormac died tragically in 2013, she sought counselling for her grief and unlocked a box containing her feelings about her adoption that she'd long since locked away.

'Cormac's death drove me to counselling, but what came out for me after a year was absolutely everything. I have a really positive story, but I had issues – I had vulnerabilities, weaknesses and struggles and they all came out.

'I emerged from that process even more comfortable in my own skin. Until then, I didn't even understand the full picture of my life myself. It's so complex and I'm grateful I have a good story to tell. The reason I picked the day I received Mary's letter as the most life-changing is to let people in the same boat know that the curiosity they have is so normal. It's like an itch you can't stop scratching. If there's no fix and you never get answers, that can be tough.

'Ireland being the way it is, and has been ... there are so many people experiencing this. I'm thirty-seven, I was born in 1981, and the last Mother and Baby home closed in 1996. I know dozens of people going through the conflicted identity crisis that adoption can give you – it's not just because I'm adopted, but just because that's how widespread it is.

'How many people have this really silent struggle? They can get on with their lives of course, but in their private lives, there's a sense of vulnerability around their identity.'

Since becoming a mother to two adorable children, Evanne now finds a new layer of appreciation in seeing her DNA in the next generation, reflective of a family unit she and husband, Brian Fitzsimons, worked so hard to create.

'I can't describe how that feels. Before I met Brian, all through my life, I used to worry I wouldn't be able to have my own kids. It was because I'd been through the process of being adopted and the complications that go with that, but I didn't want to have to go through it from another angle. I didn't want to have to adopt – obviously there's nothing wrong with it – but I just didn't think I would have the strength to go through what my mother did in helping my own children trace their birth mother.

'I don't have that in me. When I was pregnant, I was so sick, and at the same time, so happy. I was so grateful to be having a baby. Every time someone says Peigí looks like me, I scream "Yes!" inside. Seimí is more like his dad, but you'd know he's my son, and I get *such* a kick out of that. It probably sounds a bit obvious, but I'm so happy my kids look like me or Brian, and we have this unit we've created. It's a miracle.'

The complexities
of grief.

Helen McEntee

Minister for European Affairs

'The day my father passed away.'

~

C.S. Lewis, renowned author of *The Narnia Chronicles*, wrote, 'No one ever told me that grief felt so like fear.'

Grief is complicated. It's painful. It's enduring. It's omnipresent. But grief is also powerful. It's life affirming. It can be hopeful. It's a reminder of the love you once shared with someone and your responsibility to now tell their stories and ensure their legacy lives on.

~

Minister Helen McEntee is, at the age of thirty-three, one of the youngest women to ever hold such a high position in Irish government – ever. She is also someone who understands as well as anyone that death is a heart-breaking part of life.

Helen's late father, Shane, was a long-serving politician, with experience at local grassroots and national levels, in their shared Meath East constituency. Shane took his own life on 21 December 2012, two days after his fifty-sixth birthday. His funeral took place on Christmas Eve.

Helen worked alongside her father for two years before his death and the tragic circumstances around his passing complicated the already troubled road of grief. The day her father passed away proved to be the day that changed Helen's life in more ways than one – setting her professional and personal life on what became a marvellous course, but one she would take back in a moment if it meant seeing her father again.

'The day that changed my life is not a good day, it's probably the worst day I've had in my thirty-three years,' she says. 'It's a day that changed my life for many reasons: it changed our family setting and structure, I have an older brother and younger sister and we were always a very close family. We have a wide network, too: I have seven aunts and uncles either side, forty first cousins and I still have two grandmothers who are fit and well at ninety and ninety-three. To lose such an integral part of what is a wide family – and a very close family – it changes not only your relationships, but your outlook on life as well.

'The fact my father died by suicide changed the way I look at life. I wouldn't be here talking to you now, I wouldn't be in this depart-ment [at her office in Leinster House], I wouldn't be doing the work that I'm doing. It probably catapulted me forward to something I wanted to do previously, but I had been looking at it from a different way and approaching it at a different speed.

'Would I change it and take all this back? In a second – because the reason I'm here is not a positive one. Unfortunately, it wasn't a good thing, but it has set my life in a different direction.'

Shane was a national figure and was serving as Minister for State, Food and Agriculture at the time of his death. The immediate after-math was overshadowed by the collective goodwill of the community – the family's grief was felt across their hometown and beyond.

'I don't think it matters what age you are,' Helen says, 'if you lose a parent, especially in those circumstances, it has a huge impact on you.'

Helen's brother, Vincent, and her sister, Sally, grieved in their own ways, as did her mother Kathleen, who had known her husband since she was fourteen years old.

'It impacted not just my life, but everybody around me. The next couple of weeks after he died were a blur. We spent our time making tea and welcoming people to the house, constantly coming and going. It was very touching that there were so many people there and that first month or so seemed to blur into one day.'

> The fact my father died by suicide changed the way I look at life.

Shane's death prompted a by-election and Helen, inspired to continue her father's legacy, successfully inherited his seat in 2013. The result made her the youngest female elected in what became a landslide victory for her party, Fine Gael. Simon Harris, the Minister for Health, was the youngest sitting politician, pipping Helen to the post by just a few months. ('My birthday is June and his is October. I know this because I was asked so many times back then!')

Helen was only twenty-six at the time, but had already built an impressive CV: she held a degree in economics, politics and law from Dublin City University; a Master's in journalism and media communications from Griffith College, and had worked as her father's personal assistant during the last three years of his life. Her long-term plan had been to pursue a career in politics but, at the time of her father's death, she had moved back to her family home in Co Meath and intended to spend her twenties exploring adventure and opportunity before committing to a long-term career.

But Shane's death sparked a fresh determination in her; a sense of self-belief she never possessed before.

'Certain instances can change just your life, but others have ripples that go much further,' she explains. 'I had been working with my father for over two and a half years. I think I was very different to how I am now. I was the same person, but I didn't have the same determination. I wasn't as vocal and I don't think I was as outgoing in work. I had a different view of myself and what I could and couldn't achieve.

'I'm not a different person now, but, in putting myself forward in this role, I've certainly found an ability, strength and determination I didn't know I had. I spoke to my dad about running for local elections because, as far as I was concerned, he was going to be a TD for a long time, but even at that, I was nervous about putting myself forward and doing it – wondering whether I would get it or if I would be good enough.

'Then, things just clicked. It's as though any doubt around whether I should be doing this or whether I couldn't do it or I couldn't achieve what I wanted to achieve – they all just disappeared. I don't know how to explain it – I just decided life is too short to doubt yourself, to think you can't do it.'

Now, seven years on from Shane's death, Helen – and her family – is in a better place emotionally. There are the additional complications of mourning a death by suicide, with the particular struggle of the 'why', but she has reached a point of acceptance and with that, some sense of peace. She can only reflect now on the life-altering impact that moment had on her, changing the course of her entire life; to live not just without her beloved father, but to be led on a path towards public service.

'It would be very easy to be constantly angry, upset or annoyed

– and I have felt like that and sometimes still do. But I can't change it. There's no point sitting here thinking, "What if?" If I'd done things differently or if I'd been here instead of there, could I have changed it? I wouldn't have been able to get out of bed if I thought that way. I can't change it, but what I can do is try and make the most of what I have.

'The way I saw it, my whole world fell apart; it's not that it changed direction. As you come out of the cloud, or mist, you start to see things differently – and I had a new outlook on life.'

Helen inherited much of her devotion to public life from Shane and she is quick to pay tribute to him in the way only a daughter knows her father: the larger-than-life character, full of joy, and she speaks of how his family will remember him.

'He was somebody who loved life. I often look at the end of his life as you would with somebody getting sick with cancer. Something just happens and it's not anything they've done or you've done. Sometimes you can prevent it, and sometimes you can't. He loved people and I think that's why he loved politics. He loved having a laugh, he was good fun.

'There was always devilment, even though he was my dad, but we were good friends. He was very understanding. We all have to have boundaries when we're younger, but he let us make our own mistakes, he didn't judge us, he tried to help us.

'He was the last person in the world you ever would have expected to die this way. But his death is just a snapshot of his overall life. He was fifty-six; he'd had fifty-six years of a wonderful life. He was somebody who loved being around people and he got great joy out of helping people in his work.'

Helen takes significant pride in the fact that she has carried on some of her father's work locally. She is inspired by her late father's personable approach to constituents and remembering the human side to serious issues.

'My father felt – and was – human. When we grew up, he always had a beard and it made him look fiercer; people would often say he looks angry because of the beard, but if we watched the likes of *Children's Hospital* or *Pet Rescue* you'd look over and he'd be bawling. What he might have looked like was completely opposite to how he was.'

Helen's father's death not only led her down an extraordinary path as a government minister, but in the time afterwards, she found herself falling in love with her now-husband Paul Hickey.

In January 2013, a month after her father's death, her colleagues at Leinster House invited her to lunch. Paul, a former parliamentary assistant, whom she didn't know particularly well, was also invited and their relationship evolved from there.

'With the election – he was helping out, as everyone was – he was supportive. Paul's somebody who's engrossed in politics as well. He worked in Leinster House and he's since moved on and is working in a different area, but the fact that he understands and is supportive is a huge help.'

Soon after being elected a TD, Helen was appointed as a Junior Minister for Mental Health and Older People, a particularly poignant appointment given the circumstances around Shane's death. She could offer an intimate experience of the importance of mental health services in Ireland and effectively help to improve the system from the inside.

'There were quiet intakes of breath when that happened,' Helen recalls. 'It's something that I really enjoyed doing. It's difficult at the same time, though. It's hard not to take on board so much of what you're hearing and what you're engaging with and people's concerns and problems. You have to try and separate the two, which isn't always the easiest thing to do. I look back and I'm proud of what I've done in a relatively short space of time.

'Even at the time, a huge amount of my work was with young people. We established a youth task force and I'd like to think I wasn't that long out of school, which meant that I understood school is hard, when you're a teenager growing up; lots of things are going on and life is tough.

'I tried to come at it from my own personal point of view. We all have our own struggles and I had my own personal challenges in school, not just my history with Dad. I wasn't ever a doctor; I don't have a medical background or anything near it. Sometimes you need a different perspective and sometimes that perspective can be good as well.'

By the time the next election cycle came around in 2016, Helen was determined to prove any naysayers wrong; those who argued she won her local seat on the basis of legacy and sympathy. She won again. It allowed her to continue her government work and, in her role as Minister for European Affairs, she has become a key figure in the on-going Brexit discourse. ('It's completely opened my eyes to the rest of the world.')

'Being elected in the first instance was unusual because it was fantastic, but it was so close after my dad dying. He died in December and I was elected in March. At the same time, it was something I was very proud of,' she says.

'Being elected for the second time, that too was something I was extremely proud of. When I was first elected, people could say that I got in for certain reasons – riding on coattails, sympathy – or whatever reason and that's fine if people want to say that. My second election was different. While I didn't have a full five-year term, it was halfway through as a by-election, so I had three years of my work and engagement with people.

'This time I was elected on my own merit. That for me was an important point throughout the whole process to show that I can do the work.'

Writing about suicide isn't easy. Speaking about suicide isn't easy. Bringing up painful memories for those affected by suicide every day isn't easy. The most recent statistics by the Central Statistics Office (dated to 2017) show that almost four hundred suicides were registered in Ireland in 2017, with men accounting for roughly eight in ten deaths; the highest rates were observed among men aged forty-five to fifty-four.

Helen goes to great lengths to establish that she doesn't take a one-size-fits-all approach, but rather one based on her own personal experience. And she hopes that by speaking about it publicly, it can help others in pain.

'Everybody's experience is different. And the way I look at it might be different to the way someone else looks at it and the way I have gone through my own process might not necessarily work for somebody else,' she asserts.

'I'm always conscious that you have to be careful what you say and how you say it. It's always just from my point of view. It's a complex issue. I don't think dwelling on trying to change the past helps; it's about trying to prevent it from happening again.

'I genuinely believe that in some instances, you're not going to prevent suicide, and that's the sad fact of the matter. I don't know how we can eradicate it completely because it's so complex.

'I absolutely take criticism on board where services aren't in place and people could have been helped and weren't and so they fell through the cracks. They are very different stories to mine. I think me talking about mental health in general helps other people talk about it. It helps put it on the agenda, it generates money and puts services in place for people in difficult positions. It's all connected. It's about asking the question: how do we make good from something terrible that's happened?'

In the year 2019, arguably one of the best times to be a woman in history, Helen is a political dynamo, enjoying a seat rarely held by women at the top table. But she's all too aware of the devastation that brought her here:

'I would change it all in a second to change what happened.'

Questions of freedom.

Amy Huberman

Actress

'The day I visited Auschwitz with my father.'

~

With a career as illustrious as Amy Huberman's, I can pinpoint many life-changing days. There's the day she got her first acting role in 2001 (a small bit part in a psychological thriller called *Bad Karma*); the day she won her first IFTA (Irish Film and Television Academy) award; the day she was commissioned to write her first television series *Finding Joy*; the day she wrote her first bestselling book; the day she met – and subsequently married – Brian O'Driscoll and, of course, the days when she became a mother to Sadie, six, and Billy, four.

~

I've learned from this book just how difficult it can be to determine one life-changing day – and for Amy, this day was one she shared with her father, Harold Huberman, whose Jewish heritage made her visit to Auschwitz with him in 2003 all the more impactful.

'I found it really difficult to think of "The Day". But when I visited Auschwitz with my dad, that's something that stood out to me for so many obvious reasons.

'I went with my cousins, who I didn't know very well at the time, and my Uncle Alf, who's older than my dad and a veteran of the Second World War; it was a very emotional day for everyone. Uncle Alf was a rear gunner [a crewman on military aircrafts who protects the tail of the plane] and went on something like seventy-two missions. Only one out of every three men would return alive from those missions – my uncle went on seventy-two and he's still going strong!'

The Huberman family left Poland in 1910 and joined millions of disenfranchised Jews around the world, before settling in London, England, effectively as refugees. In the early 1970s, Amy's father decided to move to Dublin 'on a whim', then met and married her mother, Sandra, in 1975. In 1979, when Amy was born, they settled in Cabinteely, south county Dublin.

"The Rabbi said, If you have Jewish blood, you're a survivor.

Like most Irish families of the day, the Hubermans went to Mass every Sunday, during which time her father would visit the closest bretzel bakery to buy bagels, making Polish recipes that had been passed down through generations of the Huberman family. Her father wasn't particularly religious, but he understood the value of expressing his Jewish culture in their home and in particular with Amy and her brothers, Mark and Paul.

Sixteen years ago, Amy was living in London trying to make it as an actress and there she reconnected with the other side of her family, who had remained in England and who now lived in Golders Green. There seemed no more appropriate time to visit Auschwitz, the former concentration camp in Oswiecim, Poland, where at least one million Jews were murdered under the Nazi regime. It stands as one of history's bleakest landmarks and a stark reminder of the depths humanity can sink to.

'The trip to Auschwitz was incredibly poignant for my father and uncle because they're from a Jewish family – their father came to England from Poland in the years leading up to the First World War when Jewish communities were being persecuted. I'd never been to Poland before.'

They flew together alongside other members of London's Jewish community, including a Rabbi, who led the group in prayer and consultation – which proved helpful for Amy when she was struck by a sort of guilt for not embracing her Jewish heritage.

'The Rabbi was a survivor of the camp; that was incredible. I had a moment where I was speaking with him and I felt like a fraud,' she said. 'I told the Rabbi, "I feel like I'm looking at this through the eyes of my father," and he said, "Not really. If you have Jewish blood, you're a survivor."

'I was felt almost numb for the whole day we were there. It was so important to see Auschwitz through the eyes of my dad and my uncle; it was such a big moment for me and my dad, and our family. When we arrived at the gas chambers, the Rabbi led a prayer service around tea lights.'

Visiting one of history's most sombre memorials alongside the descendants of one of history's most oppressed peoples was a sobering moment for Amy, who was in her twenties and living the carefree life of so many young people.

'I was enjoying my hedonistic, wild and free days in London, and so that day at Auschwitz was pivotal for me for so many reasons. Not only to share that with my dad, but I fully recognised the privilege of growing up in Ireland and not questioning my freedom, because I'd never had to.

'I think my dad was really proud to share the experience with me.

He was born in London in a tight-knit Jewish community. He isn't particularly religious even now, but for him being Jewish is more of a cultural expression. As he came to Ireland and because we were raised there, we were a bit removed from our cousins and from the Jewish community. For him to share his Jewish identity and be allowed to explore it in the comfort of a group of people, to whom it also meant so much, was special.'

Visiting Auschwitz reignited the value Amy places on her personal history and heritage; she understood the importance of recognising the impact her father's Jewish upbringing had on her own.

'My Jewish heritage was something I knew very little about – it was always the other side of me. I didn't know many other Jewish people when I was a kid,' she recalls. 'It was always this "other thing" in my life, but visiting Auschwitz brought my history closer to me.'

After visiting Auschwitz, Amy connected with her Jewish cousins and felt closer to the Jewish side of the family. She began joining them for Friday night Shabbat.

Growing up, her parents wanted their children to experience both sides of their heritage and the family celebrated Hanukkah and Christmas. Now aged forty, through the lens of wisdom and age – and while also being a mother – she can truly understand her parents' decision-making and appreciates the impact her father's personal history has had on her family.

'We moved so many times when we were kids. My mum said dad could just sell a house and move and it didn't ever bother him,' she says. 'I asked him recently if it was because of his history, and the history of Jewish people being displaced, that he didn't feel an emotional attachment to places. He agreed.

'I think being Jewish shaped his entire life and outlook. And his approach has definitely had an effect on mine. He worked for himself – that creative and artistic freedom was a massive part of him – and he wasn't afraid to take risks. For him, when you experience something so close to home – when people's freedom is taken from them – that made him always brave in his choices. I love his lack of fear, his commitment in just trying.

'A lot of that was because he felt really grateful for personal freedom. When I realised the true value of that, it was a big game-changer for me. When I came back from Auschwitz, I went home and let the enormity of the experience sink in – and what my Jewish heritage meant in my life.'

All these years later, she finds her family's history particularly relevant as xenophobia is rising again in much of the Western world.

'You can dismiss things so easily by saying it was in the past, but only two generations stand between the Holocaust and the present day – it really is just two chapters ago,' she says.

Her father Harold has a book's worth of stories about their family members trying to survive in any way they could during the Second World War. One of their cousin's uncles was forced to flee Poland on his own at the age of eight because his parents were too old to travel. He had to make his own passage to Manchester – a journey which took him three years on foot. In 1942, when he was four years old, Harold was evacuated to Doncaster, Yorkshire. He spent seven months in the relative safety of the countryside, away from his parents and two brothers.

'He says he will never forget the moment his mother had to leave him,' Amy tells me. 'A few months later, she returned to bring him home when London was safer, saying that whatever happened, at least they would all be together. I find it heart-breaking, overwhelming.'

~

When we spoke, Amy felt compelled to discuss the day she visited Auschwitz because of the racially motivated rhetoric informing much of today's political discourse and news.

'In some regards, it's like we're taking a step back and that's terrifying,' she says. 'During the Holocaust, some people at least didn't know what was going on; now, in 2019, we know nearly everything that's going on and that's the scary thing. I felt I'd lived a sheltered life in Ireland until I visited Auschwitz. I was living in a bubble, in a country that's effectively neutral in the broader, international sense of politics.

'It reminds you of all the things you take for granted. I grew up in Dublin in the 1980s and 1990s and I felt safe and nothing in my world made me feel under threat. Now, I feel really proud to be Irish and have Jewish heritage. In both of those representations, you've had to fight to be heard and that makes me feel even prouder.

'Every time I read about anti-Semitism, I ask, "How?" It's not just the horror of what was done to Jews in the Second World War, it's all that came before and after. There are so many peoples around the world being marginalised and persecuted. Sometimes, it feels we've taken steps forward and in other ways, we've taken so many steps back.'

Amy has felt compelled to trace her family tree, in part to honour her father and uncle, and that whole side of her identity; she's enjoyed the newfound intrigue about where she comes from that often comes with age – and having a family of one's own.

'My dad is now eighty-one and not particularly well, and my uncle is ninety-seven. I'm trying to get to know as much as I can before their stories are gone. When I read about survivors dying, I feel they represent the last living memories of their generation,' she says.

The harrowing history her family has endured resonated with Amy because of her Jewish genealogy and her perspective as a storyteller. She finally understood certain characteristics and aspects of her personality; many of which she believes she's inherited from her father's side of the family.

'Their stories of hope and resilience put my life into perspective,' she says. 'You realise how fleeting and short the time we have in the world is. We trip ourselves up so much with our own fears and failings – with a tunnel-view of what we think we should and should not do.

'If you lift your head up, you see what people have shouldered with such hope and resilience.

'Maybe this endurance is inherited, maybe it is imprinted on your DNA. I feel that I definitely have inherited some of these traits from my dad. I love to take risks and I'm not afraid of adventure. His family are expressive and they're artists – they are really funny and have a strong sense of goodwill. I feel more fortunate than ever that they are my family – and so grateful for things I had previously taken for granted.

'Learning your history can put into perspective how fragile and short your life can be. It feels fleeting. I know it sounds clichéd, but my dad always says, "Just try." I fully believe in that.

'Before I went to Auschwitz, I was more afraid of failure and now – maybe it's with age as well – I want to have as many experiences as I can. I feel very lucky to be able make choices.'

~

That risk-taking trait inherited from her father led Amy down her career path as an actor, a notoriously unstable job. But she never lived in fear of her parents' judgement, knowing she always had their unwavering support, even when the rejections were rolling in.

'I grew up in a household where we were encouraged to pursue our passions. We never had to be the best, but we were always taught to try. It was a house where education was encouraged and I know that's a privileged position to be in and I'm particularly grateful for it now.'

After graduating with a degree in Social Science from University College Dublin (UCD) and a Master's in Media Studies from Dublin Institute of Technology (DIT), she began work on *On Home Ground*, which would prove be to her big break.

'Acting unfolded naturally for me,' Amy explains. 'Because I never studied drama full-time, I always felt like I was on the outside and never realised it was the beginning of a career I would pursue. You can't decide to be an actor, can you?

'Once I started acting, I realised that was it for me. I loved it so much and I really hoped it would love me back. What I love about acting is that I feel free in it. It's a permanent sense of expectation that something good could happen and I still haven't lost that. You'd think sometimes life may have beaten it out of you, but in a weird way, there's that feeling of expectation of not knowing what's going to happen that I love the most. When an audition comes through, I don't think I'm definitely going to get it, but I think I'm in with a chance and I allow myself a mini-dream of it happening.

'I see my dad and cousins still exploring their artistic sides – maybe that comes from being part of a heritage where self-expression was forbidden and snuffed out – a sense of not being able to own your voice because if you did, you were in danger.'

Amy's father is now battling Parkinson's disease and has had to slow down as a result, but he still retains that same zest of life with which he raised her.

'He can't hold a pen to write, but he can paint watercolours in a way he never did before. He has the survival gene. When he comes up against a brick wall, he finds a way around it.

'I want to live with as much appetite for new things as my dad has. He has such a clear idea of the things he loves and the things he doesn't and I would love a bit more of that. His attitude and outlook on life has been a real influence on me.'

The result of that influence has seen Amy become one of Ireland's sweethearts and one of the most revered creative talents in the country. Her career has featured roles across national broadcasters RTÉ, BBC, ITV and Comedy Central and she has achieved the seemingly impossible balance of being famous without compromising her personal life.

'All the Hubermans I know have a sense of adventure. When you look at their history, you would think that what they've had to endure would nearly curtail them. I know I'm like my dad in the way I seek adventure and find positivity,' she reflects.

Amy is certainly more than a jobbing actress, but if you ask her, acting is just a job. Although she hasn't taken on any historical roles yet, she is interested in history and seeks to explore it in her private life.

Her new home, a Victorian townhouse built in south Dublin in 1870, has recently been restored to its former glory. She feels she's now carrying the torch as the next generation to call the house a home and is interested in its previous, distinguished owners.

'I'm a little obsessed with the history of places. I'm fascinated by our house's history. I find the blueprint of where people are from fascinating and I enjoy feeling a connection to my past.

'I'm not religious, but I feel spiritual and a connection to both my heritages.'

Heritage is an important hallmark to pass down to the next

generation of Huberman-O'Driscolls in the form of little Sadie and Billy, to whom Amy hopes to teach the importance of kindness, understanding and, of course, that *joie de vivre* she loves so much.

'I feel responsible as a gatekeeper for my kids in those formative years before they face the outside world; I feel I'm trying to block out the outside world but also managing it for them,' she says.

'Empathy is so vital and so many problems in the world are caused by a severe lack of it – people believing their own rhetoric and only seeing their own viewpoints. Sometimes, the most simple, honest values are those of truthfulness and kindness.'

LISTEN TO YOUR HEART

~

WHEN IT'S TOO HARD TO IGNORE YOUR GUT.

Sometimes the hardest thing
is accepting yourself.

Cassie Stokes

TV presenter

*'The day I moved to Canada and
gathered the courage to come out.'*

~

Cassie Stokes is one of the few openly gay women who features regularly on Irish television. An 'accidental trailblazer' in national broadcasting, she has fronted Virgin Media One's flagship entertainment show *Xposé* since 2016 – a programme that elevated her profile to that of household name-status, with all the social media following and influence that goes with it.

~

Her fanbase is comprised of equal parts entertainment followers who love the glitz and glamour of live TV and its trappings, and LGBT youths seeking advice on coming out. Her dichotomous appeal is part of the Cassie Stokes' success model: she is proof that the old adage that 'those who enjoy celebrity can't be serious' is false. When it comes to being a spokesperson for the LGBT community, particularly young people, Cassie is as serious as it gets.

Like most journeys, hers is paved with plenty of bumps along the road, most notably when she came out at the age of twenty-five. She is quick to say that coming out wasn't the day that changed her life ('I've always been gay, the choice was just to tell people'). Instead, it was the day she decided to move to Canada – a decision that would radically alter the trajectory of her life.

'When I was asked about the day, if any, that changed my life, it got me thinking,' Cassie says. 'Was it moving home to Ireland [from Canada] or was it coming out? It made me realise that everything in my life can be traced to my decision to leave Ireland in the first place.'

Until then, Cassie had, like many young Irish adults, remained living at home into her twenties, in order to avoid the burden of soaring rents. On the outside, she had it all: a career in television she had so desired, a happy home life and a close circle of friends. But privately she was developing a new hunger, one which extended beyond her already impressive professional accomplishments. In short, her feet were getting itchy.

Back in 2012, she was working in front of the camera on the now-defunct *fyi*, a youth-oriented news programme which aired on Virgin Media; in addition to being 'the girl who read out the tweets' on *Tonight with Vincent Browne*, a show which successfully ran for ten years. Both were respectable footholds in the industry, the latter of which had an average viewership of 120,000 per night.

At that time, the echoes of the recession could still be heard rather loudly in Irish media. Jobs in national media, in particular television, are hard to come by, even for the most experienced broadcasters, so Cassie's decision to up sticks and move 3,000 miles away wasn't one she made lightly.

She was still young, mortgage free and eager to take a bite out of life outside the Emerald Isle. Her confidence was also bolstered by the fact that she has dual Canadian citizenship after living there for ten years as a child. It seems Cassie might well be living proof of the saying that, 'If everyone thinks you're crazy, you're doing something right.'

'Some people asked me why I was leaving, especially because the recession was at its peak,' Cassie says. 'Most people were leaving Ireland in search of work, which thankfully I didn't need to do but I've always had a certain energy for exploring. I don't think having a good job has to define you. It shouldn't keep you from experiencing new things.

'One of my friends moved away and I started to think about moving, too. I wasn't particularly happy – back then, Dublin wasn't like how it is now. It was very quiet. But it was still hard to choose where to go. I thought, "If I move away, where will I go?" Choosing Toronto wound up being the biggest decision I ever made.'

And so she went, alone, to a city that she hadn't lived in for fifteen years. Without any job prospects lined up, she sent emails to any network she could find and began working at an Irish bar in the city's financial district to pay the bills.

Cassie was starting from scratch all over again and realised quickly that foreign markets aren't overly concerned with your previous work in your home country, or as she puts it, 'They don't care that you worked in TV in Ireland.' Those opportunities she worked so hard to create in Ireland didn't easily translate to opportunities in Canada.

While tending bar at P.J. O'Brien by night and taking improvisation classes by day – to 'help me get out of my shell even more' – she went through a colossal change.

Cassie's coming out story was more one of self-realisation than of discovery. She says it herself: she has always been gay, but living in a new city with new people allowed her to be completely herself.

'When I was in Canada, I was open to dating women whereas, before moving, I had only dated men. I can't explain it,' she reflects. 'I knew I was gay. When I was away and meeting new people, I got to be "Cassie in Toronto", who was the real me, not the person I moulded myself to be in Ireland. I wasn't trying to live up to anything. But eventually I could say it: "Actually I think I'm gay."

> "Coming out is a huge testament to anyone who's gay, because the strength it takes to even get that far is amazing.

'Because here [in Ireland], I didn't know how to be anyone but the person I was expected to be, or I had been up to then.'

After six months in Canada, she embarked on a serious relationship with her now ex-girlfriend, Kathleen Gauvin. When Cassie returned home to Dublin for Christmas that year, she carried the emotional baggage of knowing she had to have some serious conversations when she landed.

Her mother Deirdre was cooking cocktail sausages at the time, Cassie remembers in painstaking detail, and she took the news well, as did the rest of her family and close friends.

'They were surprised,' she says. 'You hear stories of people who say, "We knew all along," but that wasn't the case for me. My friends were really open to it. I think my family took a little bit of time to get used to it, but that's life.

'Everyone has a scenario or dream for people close to them and sometimes, when you have to change that, it can be a little difficult.

They were very open. It was hard at the time to change their dreams and hopes into other dreams and hopes, which, I think they're more excited about now.'

That experience taught her that she was made of tougher stuff than she had previously realised. Modern Ireland may have voted Yes in the Marriage Equality Referendum in 2015 but, like everywhere in the world there are still pockets – large and small – in society with homophobic tendencies. The fact that Cassie is out and proud with a high television profile has made her something of an agony aunt among LGBT youth.

'I am very proud of who I was – and am. You never know how people will react and you have to be strong in who you are. Coming out is a huge testament to anyone who's gay, because the strength it takes to even get that far is amazing. You're coming up against people who will either be okay with it or never talk to you again. That's the reality.

'I used to look online for coming out stories because I didn't know the best way to do it. It's like everything else – it will all be okay, you have to believe in yourself. At the end of the day, you're standing up for yourself and if you're gay, that's who you are. Sometimes the hardest thing can be accepting yourself.'

Emphasising the importance and benefits of self-acceptance is the closest Cassie gets to preaching, deservedly honouring her personal experience with a deep sense of empathy for others who haven't made it that far yet. Or, on the flip side, those who have been rejected for it.

'I didn't think I was a strong person, but now when I listen to stories, I realise I am. To be that certain about who I was. I take great pride in that.

'The biggest positive that came out of the move to Toronto was getting to know myself – there was a little someone inside me who wasn't being heard and, in Canada, I got to meet that person. Canada helped me become a more confident version of the person I'd always been. I'm not completely different, but I am much happier and more comfortable in my own skin. It was always there, I just didn't realise it.'

Over the course of nearly four years spent in Canada, that determination to achieve professional success abroad became a reality. Cassie was hired to do voiceover work, a lucrative side hustle which many on-air personalities appropriate to supplement their income, and she had landed reporting shifts with *Entertainment Tonight*, the Canadian offshoot of the American nightly celebrity news programme.

Though she had career success and a happy personal life – she was living with her girlfriend of two years and a new puppy – she found herself, once again, looking for more. In 2016, her sister Alex came to visit and so visceral was Cassie's reaction to her leaving, she knew it wasn't healthy for them to continue to live so far apart.

'My sister came over in my fourth year of living there and when I was saying goodbye to her, I cried for over a week. It was to the point where I couldn't even eat – it was like a bad break-up. I would cry from the moment I woke up to the minute I went to sleep – which would always be in the early hours of the next morning.

'I thought, "I don't think I can say goodbye to my sister like that ever again. I don't want to." I had already said too many goodbyes at Toronto Airport.'

Cassie had achieved what she had set out to when she moved to Canada – subconsciously or not – she was out and happy. Not everyone has a journey of their sexuality to contend with, but the experience of travelling and living abroad is always valuable, whatever the physical or emotional journey. Home might be where the heart is, but, as J.R.R. Tolkien wrote, 'Not all those who wander are lost.'

'I would always recommend people travel and experience new things, but you'll always crave home – and, a lot of the time, you will come back – but coming back with new experiences is what enriches you,' Cassie says. 'I missed out on a lot in Ireland when I was in Canada, which is why I wanted to come back. I missed out on a million little things like countless Sunday lunches with Grandma and Granddad, and I think that was the biggest downside for me. My granddad passed away while I was away, but that's what happens when you move country.'

So, just like that, the Canadian dream was over. That self-belief that carried her through her initial move and a thriving career in Toronto gave her the strength to return to Europe; a decision that would have dual benefits in spending more time with her family and, unknown to her at the time, landing her dream job. Two weeks after her sister Alex left, Cassie was on a flight to London, just a short flight away from Dublin, and had a brief stint working in digital media production. It was there that she received a direct message on Twitter – another life-changing moment – this time, from Daniel Readman, the series producer of *Xposé*, to gauge her interest in acting as cover for long-time host Karen Koster's maternity leave.

'Three days later, I flew to Dublin from London and auditioned. I was offered it the next day.

'I gained so much living in Canada, but I'm so happy I am now home. Family is the most important thing to me. I couldn't live without my sister by my side.'

Cassie was, to most on the outside, a wild card choice. She didn't have the same profile as her colleagues had when they were given the mantle, but one of the benefits was that meant she also didn't have to fight any preconceived notion of herself in the eyes of the public and press. She was the 'real Cassie', but this time she was at home for everyone to see.

She recognises that the four years spent honing her skills in a new, more competitive market in Canada, bolstered her position as a shoo-in for the role, which was one of the most coveted in Irish broadcasting, often resulting in presenters becoming household names almost overnight.

'Would I have ever gotten *Xposé* before the move? Absolutely not. I wasn't confident enough and I didn't have enough experience. Some 25-year-olds are capable at that age, but I wasn't one of them. At twenty-eight, however, I was ready for it.'

Her love of travel remains, but Ireland and its myriad charms will always hold a special place in her heart. In addition, by the time she moved back to the Dublin, the sleepy city had been transformed into a vibrant hub of activity.

'I always loved living in Ireland, but I appreciate everything so much more now. I love exploring and meeting new people,' she says.

'Moving to Canada gave me that first bit of independence. Until then, my only 'adult' decision had been buying a car at nineteen... and that wasn't a smart move. That leap, though, taught me how to be an adult, how to look after myself – then it led to the biggest love of my life. I'm so appreciative of that love. Although the relationship is over, that massive decision to move to Canada led to all that happiness which we shared together.

'It was the best decision I ever made. The move gave me strength to be back here doing the job I love. It helped me professionally and personally. It helped change me into the person I am now.

'It is still the best thing I ever did for myself.'

Feminist. Activist. Mother.

Ellen O'Malley Dunlop

Chairperson, National Women's Council of Ireland

'The day I decided to follow my heart
and pursue my dream job.'

~

It would be remiss of me to compile a book featuring inspirational Irish women and not include Ellen O'Malley Dunlop. She's the current Chairperson of the National Women's Council of Ireland, a role to which she was appointed in 2017, a culmination of the previous fifty years spent working to support women's rights in Ireland.

~

From an early age, Ellen was exposed to the inequalities between sexes – although it was never at home. Her parents always treated her and her brother equally, and both were afforded the same educational opportunities. But, like many other women, she was only faced with the additional mountains she would be required to climb on reaching adulthood, once she was free from her parents' unconditional support and encouragement.

'I grew up with the story of Grace O'Malley, the Pirate Queen,' she says. 'In those days, we [my brother and I] both had to go to boarding school because there no local school near us because I grew up in the countryside in Rathdowney, Co Laois. It was the same with university. Then, I started work and I discovered the man beside me was making more money because he was married. I couldn't believe it!

'There were personal things in my own life that pulled me up by the bootstraps that taught me how unequal things were for women. That really spurred me on. Anything I took up was motivated by my efforts to influence change so that we could get equal rights.'

> It was a huge turning point in my life … The counselling and psychotherapy opened up a whole other landscape.

Like many of those who live their lives well in pursuit of improving others', Ellen's is coloured with notable accomplishments both personally and professionally. She remembers one moment, however, that saw her debating which fork in the road her life should follow. Sitting in a car with her husband Sandy in 1982, she was fresh from a stint in London where she'd qualified in psychotherapy. The couple – not long married – had no confirmed job prospects. She was pregnant with her second child and the decision of what to do with her life was weighing heavy on her heart.

'There are lots of important days in your life – such as when your first child is born – but my most important life-changing moment landed on another day, that day sitting in the car with Sandy. At the time, I was a primary school teacher, which was my first profession. I worked in Tallaght in the late 1970s when people were being rehoused and I found myself often meeting with parents, listening to stories of their isolation and desolation,' she explains.

'I went to London to do a course in psychotherapy and, on my return, the school I was working with in Tallaght said there was a possibility of a vacancy coming up in a non-teaching role and I was given to think I had a very good chance of getting it. Miceal O Regan, a Dominican, had approached me because he wanted to set up a centre in Tallaght that was halfway between psychiatric waiting room and parochial house. He called it a pastoral care and counselling centre, and the job was mine if I wanted it.

'I'll never forget it – it was probably around May 1982, my baby was due in October so I was a good bit pregnant, and we were going to visit my parents in the country. At the time, my husband was setting up a company and my teaching job was twice the salary of what I would get in the counselling centre.

'As we were chatting, my husband said to me, "Where's your heart?" I said, "It's definitely in the Counselling Centre." And he said, "Let's go with that."'

And so Ellen went to work; work in which she earned half the wage she would have for the 'safe' teaching job. That moment she chose to follow her heart led her to the wealth of opportunities and influence she would pursue in her diverse careers from psychotherapy; group counselling, CEO of the Dublin Rape Crisis Centre (DRCC), her current position and not to mention her present ambition of running for Fine Gael in Dublin South West. She was exposed to a world she never knew possible.

'It was a huge turning point in my life. Had I gone back into teaching, I probably would have stayed there. The counselling and psychotherapy opened up a whole other landscape. I learned so much. It was an incredible experience.'

She was not only allowed, but encouraged, to identify areas for improvement in the services they provided in the area and where there was room for growth. She also happened to be a new mother, this time celebrating the arrival of her third child, and still breastfeeding. Having it all might be a debatable concept, but Ellen was getting pretty close to living it.

'In Tallaght, I was afforded the freedom to identify what was needed and I identified they needed more family therapy and so I trained with the Mater Hospital. I remember having my third child, breastfeeding at the training. You trained and worked as a team, so your family was on one side of the mirror and your team was on the other. I remember breastfeeding and handing the baby over to one of my colleagues, a man, who jokingly called out that the baby was rummaging and he had nothing for him! That was an amazing experience.'

It wasn't to last, though. After more than two years, they were shut down by the Archbishop, who Ellen says believed their work was conflicting with CMAC, which is now known as Accord. At the time, Tallaght was three parishes in one, but they were split and there was no room anywhere for a new counselling centre. It was a brief, but influential experience.

The O'Malley Dunlops needed to move to a bigger home because of their growing family. Ellen saw it as an opportunity to become self-employed and so she established a private practice from her home, which she ran twenty-three years. She still uses her office for professional purposes – such as this interview.

'I never saw myself as being redundant, funnily enough, so I simply began my own practice. We set up the Irish Council for Psychotherapy (she would eventually become the first female chair), we lobbied for statutory registration and set up a Masters training programme in Psychoanalytic Psychotherapy at Trinity College, which I worked on for fifteen years.

'In my twenty-three years of working in that profession, it's always been an amazing privilege to travel with people at times where they're at big junctures in their lives.'

Before there were mandatory reporting laws for healthcare professionals (introduced under the Children First Act 2015), and before the Ryan Report in 2009, which addressed past failings in protecting children from systematic sexual abuse, Ellen was meeting victims of child sexual abuse, many of whom never reported the crimes, on a face-to-face basis. These sessions stoked a fire within her to fight tirelessly for a change in legislation.

By 2006, she was a woman on a mission. When her last child was ready to attend third level at school, Ellen became CEO of the DRCC, which she ran for ten years. Through grit and determination, armed with facts and the right amount of finesse, she began lobbying politicians and the very top of the legislature for assistance in introducing a definition of consent into the Sexual Offences Act.

'The role gave me greater influence in terms of changes in legislation. I really used that to the fullest of my ability. I wouldn't have been able to do the things I did without being CEO of the DRCC. I'm good at using a role and getting into places.

'In Ireland, we have followed the UK in developing our common law,' she explains. 'The UK brought all their sexual offences acts under one act in 2003. That was something we needed to do here in Ireland. We had a rushed sexual offences act and, any time you bring in rushed legislation, it never works.

'Frances Fitzgerald, who was Minister for Justice at the time, did a huge amount of work on that. Under that bill, there were lots of changes. DRCC was part of Turn Off the Red Light, which changed the law to prosecute the punter instead of the sex worker. There was a lot of energy put into that and there needed to be because there was a lot of resistance. There was a lot of resistance to defining consent. The law very clearly states that rape is sex without consent, but there was no definition of consent in the law at the time.

'Defining terms is so important in terms of education,' Ellen clarifies. 'Doing this as early as possible, in programmes in secondary schools for example, means that there are no blurred lines as children grow up. Now that we have an official definition of what consent is, and what it isn't, a judge can clearly instruct the jury at the beginning of a trial on how to approach a case. By saying, "Someone who is unconscious or asleep can't give consent" – it eliminates the already irrelevant, yet horribly focused upon, interest in what a person might have been wearing when they abused, for example. Providing clear definitions addresses the myths that are out there in our society.

'A jury is comprised of twelve people coming into a courtroom. They could all potentially believe some of the myths around assault, but by having a judge define consent, it helps to challenge any thoughts they may have at the beginning of a trial. That way, then, when the trial is running, they're more educated and I would hope they would give a fairer judgement at the end of the process. That change has been wonderful.'

When it comes to consent, Ellen cites the viral Cup of Tea video, issued in 2015 by the Thames Valley Police Department, which explains in no uncertain times what qualifies as consent. She remarks that its simplicity was a key part of its effectiveness and was particularly relevant to the cause of establishing a clear definition of consent through metaphorical imagery.

The message reads as this:

> 'If you say "Hey, would you like a cup of tea?" and they're like,
> "Uh, you know, I'm not really sure," then you can make them
> a cup of tea, or not, but be aware that that they might not drink
> it,' the narrator says. 'And if they don't drink it, then – and this
> is the important bit – don't make them drink it. Just because
> you made it doesn't mean you're entitled to watch them drink
> it. And if they say, "No, thank you", then don't make them tea.
> At all.'

It may seem like a simplification, but when it comes to educating
people on consent there is no such thing as 'too straightforward'.
Ellen remains utterly clear-sighted and passionate about the quality
of the educational programmes in secondary schools now, many of
which can't grasp the tea analogy.

'When young people hear that, they get it. Everybody gets it,' she
asserts. 'Now the Department of Education are running programmes
that are twenty years old and they need to be revamped. Their
programmes should be property facilitated and run in small groups
to allow the young people to talk among themselves so they can
learn from each other.

'There's an unconscious bias there that we have to continually
knock on the door of. There was a piece of research done about
rape justice in Ireland which looked at juries, and would you
believe an all-female jury has never convicted a person accused
of rape. You have to look behind that research and figure out why
that is.'

Ellen is an ardent, committed and articulate feminist, who cites
influences from everyone from her mother to mythological stories

of women in power. She hopes the latter will become more common-
place in national discourse; she recognised the potential for equality
– even in stories – from a young age.

'We have been particularly focused on exploring the women in
our mythological stories. We all know the Fionn mac Cumhaills and
the Cú Chulainn but we rarely hear about Cessar, the first woman
to come to Ireland. She's mentioned in the *Book of Invasions* with
Fintan Mac Bochra and she came from Sudan and she travelled all
the known territory of the world at the time and she travelled to
the virgin territory of Ireland. She was supposed to be the grand-
daughter of Noah and she brought forty women with her. We don't
have an "in the beginning" story as such, but isn't that wonderful?'

It's hard not to be impressed by Ellen's career and, while the word
inspirational may be used a little too much these days, if you, or
anyone you know, is affected by any of the issues that I talked with
Ellen about, then you can be sure that this remarkable woman had a
hand in making your life a bit easier.

Ellen's personal life experiences helped inform her devotion to
seeking equality; in particular, how she was treated when she sought
a legal annulment from her first marriage, which she wasn't granted
for eighteen years. After her first marriage, she was determined to
make the most of life with her eldest son, whom she describes as
'wonderful'.

'I had a very bad relationship but I have wonderful son as a conse-
quence,' she tells me. 'My second husband's attitude when I met him
was – bear in mind this was 1976 and I had a four-year-old – that my
son was an asset. That will tell you the kind of man that Sandy is. I
wouldn't underestimate that. I met him when I'd come to a realisation
in myself that I was going to make our lives work, me with my son.
And we did.'

'And so I got a church annulment. I went to England and got an English divorce but it was pre-1986 and that meant an Irish married woman didn't have the right to her own domicile,' she recalls. 'I was "living in sin" in Ireland. The legal divorce had no standing because I went physically to England, but I was still domiciled in Ireland.'

Until the change in the law in 1986, Ellen and Sandy had to travel separately for fear of something – an accident, arrest or tragedy – happening to either one of them and leaving their children caught in 'no man's land' because their union wasn't legally recognised.

Sandy – they have been married for thirty-eight years – gets a lot of airtime throughout our interview. Ellen credits the 'support of a good man' for 'allowing' her to flourish with her work. And it is, thanks to the agency of this man, that Ellen can trace their lives back to that day in 1982, in the car, sitting at traffic lights, wondering what lay ahead for them.

'I remember the excitement of it and the relief when Sandy said *follow your heart*, because I knew it was the right thing to do. There are other times in my life when I had to make big decisions and I had to get in contact with that deep knowing within myself. Like anything, you take the decision but you don't know how it will turn out – but this turned out very well, thankfully.'

She followed her heart.

Áine Kerr

Journalist and entrepreneur

*'The day I left my job at Facebook in New York
to launch a start-up in Dublin.'*

~

If passion drives energy, then Áine Kerr is one of the most energetic women I've ever met. A former newspaper journalist, primary school teacher and manager at Facebook, Áine's career is full of real-life examples of feeling the fear and doing it anyway.

~

After working in journalism, Áine left the profession in 2013 to dip her toe into an emerging technology industry. She took on the role of political editor at start-up company Storyful – a social media verification agency founded by former RTÉ correspondent Mark Little – and, by her departure in 2016, she was managing editor. By then, the company had been sold to Rupert Murdoch's News Corporation and Áine had accepted the job of head of global journalism partnerships at Facebook's New York headquarters. A big job by anyone's standards.

While speaking with Áine, in a small conference room in Dublin's

Merrion Square, the new home of her latest company Kinzen (in which she reunites with Little as her business partner), her altruistic approach to the freedom of the press, and the ways in which we consume it in modern society, dominates much of our conversation.

Journalism, without sounding sanctimonious, is for many, a vocation. It's a calling to hone your craft or hold power to account through breaking news stories and investigations. Áine treats this responsibility with the greatest respect, earnestly advocating the power of truthful storytelling in an era where traditional media brands and newspaper journalists are fighting for survival.

But the day that changed Áine's life is not connected to her passion for journalism and news.

'At different points in my career, I'd come to a natural junction where I'd ask myself, "What would you do if you weren't afraid? What would it look like if you pushed yourself outside your comfort zone?"

'Hence, I went from being a school teacher to working in traditional journalism for seven years with the *Irish Times*, *Irish Independent* and *Irish Examiner*. From there, I worked at Storyful, a start-up – the first social media news agency in the world – for five years as managing editor and, from there, to Facebook, working for almost two years to lead global journalism partnerships.'

It was in 2017 that she left her start-up family at Storyful for Facebook. It was her shot at the big league, where she would lead a team focusing on building services and tools for journalists on Facebook; which was as tough a task as expected. This wasn't only because of the upward battle she faced in acting as an unofficial mediator between Facebook and news media, but also because her husband Aodhán Ó Ríordáin – the Labour Party Senator and former Minister of State for New Communities, Culture, Equality and Drugs Strategy, who was a crucial force in the passing of the Marriage Equality Referendum in 2015 – was still living in Dublin.

After nearly two years in New York, she decided to come home to Dublin, where she would go on to start a new business and also give birth to her first child. She came to this decision during a conversation with Karen Jordan-Markham, an executive coach working with Columbia University, where Áine was undertaking an executive leadership programme in order to maximise leadership potential for executive-level students.

'When I think about a fundamental day when things changed for me, I think of a day in summer 2017,' Áine recalls. 'I was sitting on a bench outside the Columbia University School of Journalism.

'It was a massive year of learning for me because I'd left Storyful, which had been my family for five years and very much in my DNA, to come to Facebook. Facebook has a tricky relationship with the news industry because, of course, it has perhaps unintentionally become one of the biggest distributors of journalism in the world, during a time where there's huge competition as to how best monetise it.

'Publishers are obviously aggrieved that they have to go and find their audiences on Facebook. It's very difficult to monetise once they've invested in the investigative journalism and day-to-day grind.

'My role at Facebook was that of a fire-fighter of sorts – that broker who could go out into the industry, see how we could help them and go back to Facebook and fight the good fight of the publishing industry. I did it with conviction and integrity. It also required moving to New York, my husband was still here [in Dublin], but I felt really strongly at the end of Storyful that working in New York was the right thing to do.'

But that conversation on that bench in New York City would stop her in her tracks and change the course of her life. Until then, she had at least a short-term roadmap for international success with impact to match. After the conversation, Áine decided then to leave her impressive, influential job at one of the biggest companies in the world and start over again.

'We were trying to get pregnant at that time. I had realised, that year, that starting a family was something I wanted to do. Mark [Little] and I had always said if we had the right idea and if it was of the right moment, we would come back together and do another start-up. I knew it had to connect to my new priorities.'

Karen directed Áine towards the Myers-Briggs personality test which analyses perception and judgement, and details distinct personality types determined through a series of different questions. Until she had taken the test, Áine had lived her life believing she was one kind of person, only to find out from an acquaintance on a park bench asking her seemingly random questions that she was in fact someone different. The sense of empowerment that came from those results emboldened her to follow her heart.

And her heart was in Dublin with her husband, her future family life and her soon-to-be-launched business.

'Your Myers-Briggs assesses your personality and allocates it into one of sixteen personality types, with associated spirit animals: for example, there are the improvisers in the eagles who swoop in and cause craziness; the owls are focused on data and science; the busy beavers who love getting s**t done, which I had always assumed I was,' Áine explains. 'Then there are dolphins. They are catalysts and harmonisers on teams who set the vision; they're about empowering people around them through a vision and strategy.

'Despite all my risks and decisions, I like having a routine and the process and protocols that come with it. After that conversation with Karen, I realised I'm a catalyst. It was an important moment for me because I had this assumption about myself that salary was the most important thing, but in fact it's having consistency and knowing what you're about . . . I realised I've always known I was a dolphin, but I've never been comfortable admitting it.'

> It's better to fail at something you love than win at something you don't believe in.

Áine understood then that there was a way to make her life even more gratifying and resorted to more practical tools in the form of the 'Job Venn Diagram', which is exactly as it sounds. At the centre of the diagram is your purpose and around that is information like your passions, salary, strengths, potential and what the world needs. It's about identifying the possibility of getting to that centre purpose when you're thinking of changing jobs.

'That was the day where I realised it was time to leave New York and return to Dublin,' she says. 'For me, in the industry, there was a massive moment of misinformation, mistrust, manipulation. I had a sense that I'd done a lot of good things in Facebook but now it was time to start again.

'If I hadn't had that moment with Karen, I wouldn't have had the courage weeks later with that Venn diagram to start a company with Mark and Paul [Watson], while starting a family and, ultimately, being okay with that.

'In the days and weeks after that bench exercise, my husband would say to me, "It's better to fail at something you love than win at something you don't believe in."

'I was leaving a comfortable, corporate, well-paid job with shares and perks, like maternity leave and baby bonuses and all that good stuff, to go back to Dublin. But I kept asking myself: what would our lives be like if we could start again in the news industry?'

Her two babies – her company Kinzen and the one growing in her womb – were the impetus behind what remains Áine's biggest life decision.

'I knew that being pregnant would influence a lot of the company's principles around time well spent, and family life. I knew I would need to change too. My sense of purpose would mean that I was going to be smarter with my time. I've followed that dual path of starting a family and starting a company. If I pinpoint why I'm sitting here today, it goes back to that bench with Karen.'

That summer turned out to be the biggest of her life in changing her perspective on how she wanted to live her life – and the world she could leave for her future daughter.

'Being happy in myself and being a happy mother would hopefully result in a happy baby. That was critical for me,' she says. 'I knew I could be happy with job security, but I think I'd be happier working on something based on my own principles, building a culture from the ground up, having control of something and a big, ambitious vision. When it came to the moment of making the decision to leave New York and Facebook, I made it knowing I was pregnant.

'People at the time thought I was crazy to leave what sounded like this wonderful job in New York, travelling the world and the financial security that came with it, to start a start-up. Months later, they thought I was even crazier when they grasped that I'd made that decision knowing I was pregnant with my first child.

'So, in September 2017, I left Facebook and in October, I started what is now Kinzen.'

After welcoming baby Anna last year, Áine's maternity leave was virtually non-existent, a standard fare for female company directors and business owners, and the balancing act of officially managing both began. Instead of 'mummy guilt', Áine looks at her situation through the prism of pragmatism: if she is going to be away from her daughter, it will be for good reason. And there is no greater reason than a sense of a larger purpose on a potentially infinite scale.

'I felt it's important I do this in this moment in time in this industry, and this company is in its early days and I want to be part of it,' Áine says.

'I want to be a good role model for my daughter. In years to come she will know her mother cared about the journalism industry and misinformation, and that she made sure people had news literacy skills and critical thinking skills in this massive moment when so many institutions were being questioned.

'Education is the great liberator: if we are given the skills, tools and techniques, we can all be critical, informed thinkers, but we need educators to empower us. Journalists are also educators who are trying to help us understand the world around us. I'm trying to build something that is exactly that.'

Áine's critical decision-making skills can be traced back to her teenage years when she was deciding her subjects for her Leaving Certificate, at the age of fifteen, which would carve out something of a rigid future for her.

'I took out an A4 pad and wrote "heart" on one side and "head" on the other. Under heart, I wanted to be a journalist and under head, I wanted to be a teacher. My uncle, who was working as a journalist, gave me good advice in saying, "If you have an interest in teaching, it's a vocation. It's a holistic degree, you'll learn every-thing you need from psychology to sociology and it's a degree that will ground you. You can have a life learning from teaching and working with children and you can have a passion which sustains your journalism." That, thankfully, broke it down for me. That was my springboard into journalism.'

Her passion for journalism – and more importantly, good, valuable, public-serving journalism – fills our conversation as it was the backdrop of so much pleasure in her professional life, but also personal joy as she met her husband on her first assignment for a local newspaper fifteen years ago.

Áine is filled with sage wisdom, acquired through international work, Ivy League education and just the right amount of motivational speaking, but she lives by the 'always be learning' model, which supports her self-belief and capability when she asks herself what she would do if she wasn't afraid.

'I've always had a longing to constantly be learning and challenging myself,' she says. 'The industry is so fast changing and evolving that if I'm going to serve this industry well, I need to make sure I'm doing the same. I need to make sure I have the tools and learnings to prepare me. It's all very well for me to sit here and say everyone should follow their sense of purpose, but you can only do that if you have the foundation to underpin it.

'I can tell my daughter, I got up from a bench at Columbia University and decided to do something I thought would matter. It matters to the world in which we live right now. I'm going to be happier for it, in trying to do good around me and you'll be better for having a mother who is trying to do some badass things. Hopefully my daughter will be able to see that I stood up to be counted and she and her generation will be bettered by the efforts of me along with so many other women in the industry.'

She explored the road
less travelled.

Joanne Byrne

Director of Presence PR and Presence People

'The day I received the best advice of my life.'

~

Much of this book is devoted to documenting moments in women's lives such as landmark events, diagnoses or a game-changing decision. In the case of Joanne Byrne, it was a stop-you-in-your-tracks moment of realisation when she was given the best advice of her life.

~

Joanne is undoubtedly one of Ireland's most revered publicists: she works with everyone from well-known Irish personalities such as Nicky Byrne and Louis Walsh to TV star Lucy Kennedy. In her daily life she works and represents some of the biggest names and brands around the country. As such, she is usually on the other side of the interview process, and our conversation only supported my belief that, oftentimes, the best stories are the ones rarely shared.

For nearly three decades, Joanne has been intermittently visiting Lough Derg in County Donegal, the 'sanctuary of Saint Patrick', a pilgrimage dating back to the fifth century. Over the course of one to three days, guests are guided through a programme of prayer, fasting, walking barefoot and a 24-hour vigil.

As she says, it's her space where she can take time away from everything, including her mobile phone. Her annual visits allow her a few days to take stock of the year and look forward to what's to come.

Joanne enjoys the spiritual awakening that comes from her annual visits, and it was at Lough Derg, over twenty years ago, that she experienced the day that would change the direction of her life by identifying her love of travel.

'It's less about the day itself and more about what somebody said to me on that day,' Joanne says.

'I see Lough Derg as a meditative and a wellness exercise. You stay up all day and all night, and you are quite literally begging dawn to come and with dawn comes the light.

'At the start of the day, you do a sort of reconciliation. It's less of a confession-type experience, but an opportunity to release anything that hinders you. One year, about twenty-five years ago or so, I spoke to a young priest who looked at me and said, "Are you the person you want to be? If not, what are you doing about it?"

'It really struck a chord. I asked myself, "Am I the person I want to be?"

'One of the things I knew I wanted to be was a traveller. So, I decided that's what I was going to do. I knew I couldn't say I'm the person I want to be without being brave enough to travel and see the world.'

Travel remains integral to Joanne's character; she's visited every corner of the globe, nearly always on her own, experiencing different cultures which in turn have enriched her life. Her nomadic desires have always been there, dating back to her first trip abroad as a teenager.

During her college years, while Joanne's peers were all mapping out their J1 trips, which would usually involve stuffing dozens of eager Irish teenagers into popular summer spots like the Hamptons in New York and San Francisco, California, she was making her dreams come to life.

> I knew I couldn't say I'm the person I want to be without being brave enough to travel and see the world.

Away from the aspiring actors in Los Angeles and the casinos of Las Vegas, Joanne was exploring the less-travelled route on the West Coast of the United States.

'I was definitely exploring the less travelled route. Instead of working in an Irish bar, I was in a Conestoga wagon retracing the famed Oregon Trail. All I was missing was the Laura Ingalls Wilder wide-brimmed bonnet!

'I ended up in Santa Fe, New Mexico, where I met an old Navajo woman in the famous square who was shocked that an Irish person knew so much about Native American culture. And she invited me to join them for a few days on their summer reservation. I was in the back of that Ute truck so quick and had the most memorable few days with her and her family.'

Joanne learned a valuable lesson that day about the joy of following her instincts. She is quick to assert the benefits of travel across every aspect of your life, in particular as a solo traveller. Her business partner, Sinéad Ryan, with whom she set up Presence PR in 2003, always laughs that Joanne insists on asking the same question every time they interview a potential new client or employee: 'Do you travel?'

'I think travel gives you an ability to think on your feet, to be resourceful; if you're travelling in South America, say, chances are half your travel plans will go out the window immediately: the train won't exist or the airline will go bust by the time you get there,' Joanne says.

'For example, at the end of 2018, I arrived in Ethiopia to catch a connecting flight. I landed in Addis, I had two hours between flights, and then was told the plane didn't exist. The next plane was in eight or nine hours' time – they weren't entirely sure! The airport is very close to the city, so I left my bag and headed off to explore.

'Travel has made me incredibly resourceful. And I believe it has made me very insightful. I will be in a train station, bus station or Tuk Tuk rank and I can pick out the person who will help me the most. You can read a person's body language from fifty paces away, even more so when you're travelling on your own.

'When you are travelling solo – like I do most of the time – you only have yourself to rely on. I always lose weight because I'm really careful what I eat because I have nobody to pull back my hair if I'm throwing up from food poisoning! Nobody will know if I get sunstroke. You become incredibly self-aware and resilient and, because of that, I nearly always can see a situation before it happens.

'For example, travelling through the Middle East, I will always travel with a black scarf. If I turn a corner and see there's a mosque or an area where it's clear they don't get many tourists, I will place that scarf over my head as a mark of respect. It's an immediate acknowledgement that, though I'm a tourist, I recognise that I'm in their country and respect it.'

Joanne's references are as fascinating as they are vast – no stone is left unturned and no corner of a city is left unwalked in her quest for deep exploration. Her tales are colourful and shared as nonchalantly as most of us might recall visiting a nearby shop for some milk.

'Somebody tried to kidnap me on Kenyatta Avenue in Nairobi,' she says, 'which is the equivalent of Grafton Street in Dublin. I had the East Africa edition of Lonely Planet with me and the minute I realised what was happening, I let out a scream only dogs and cats could hear and very strategically threw the East Africa Lonely Planet at his "hidden jewels". He let me go.

'Because I had done my research – actually in that specific book I hit him with – I knew to head for the nearest bank because every bank has armed guards. Though it was unexpected, I was prepared.'

When Joanne travels, she doesn't do so just for the Instagram 'likes', but for an opportunity to revisit the sense of happiness sparked from that throwaway comment by that priest at Lough Derg so many years ago. She knows what she wants and does her damndest to make it a reality; these are principles which can be applied to any aspect of one's life. Few who join her live to tell the tale; Joanne is so famously disciplined and structured in her travel regime that to call it a 'holiday' would be misleading.

'I have to be really careful because when I travel, it's in the most selfish way. I travel where I want, when I want, how I want and with whom I want,' she says. 'I want to be on the first bus out, if that means being at a train station at 4 a.m. somewhere in India, fighting for a place onto a second-class carriage, then I will. That's not everybody's idea of fun. I'm not prepared to compromise when I travel.'

One of Joanne's close friends and clients, Nadia Forde, the model and actress, lived in Tokyo, Japan for a brief spell in 2016. When Joanne visited, her itinerary extended beyond the filtered version many tourists share on social media, including a 3 a.m. wake-up call to visit the Tsukiji fish market. Nadia lived to tell the tale, but won't be joining Joanne on a trip abroad anytime soon.

(As Nadia says, 'Joanne had us staying in a capsule hotel in Tokyo and she thought nothing of hopping onto one of the bullet trains from Kyoto for *just* a few hours so we could experience the famous food vendor street in Osaka. I needed a holiday after the holiday.')

'I absolutely get my way is not for everybody,' Joanne says. 'When I travel like that, I come back invigorated, it's good for my soul. I know it is good for me. I come back maybe having had what other people would perceive to be an absolutely manic holiday, but for me, it gives me a boost. I like going off the beaten track.'

But, with that ability to see the world on one's own, comes the joy of friendship and fostering the often-endangered experience of forging a genuine human connection.

'Every time I travel, I embrace it. It is selfish. You do what you want, where you want. As you get older, it's harder to make friends and make a connection with random strangers, and yet, when you're travelling on your own, that is what you do every single day,' she explains.

It offers an opportunity for self-reflection and recognising one's place in the world, however small. If you allow it, it can humble you beyond measure.

'When I did the Inca Trail to Machu Picchu, I just clicked with the guide. I became incredibly friendly with Anna Marie and her boyfriend [now husband] Paddy and I was at their wedding. On a bus travelling between Jerusalem and Bethlehem, I befriended three Italian guys. I've since been to two of their weddings and I visit them in Bologna every year and they come to Ireland.

'In Egypt, I had to create an entire backstory about why I was travelling on my own because it was an anathema to them, they couldn't understand why I would be travelling on my own. I had a fake fiancé called John, who was a heart surgeon at a conference in

Cairo, and the minute I said it, they understood. For me to want to travel on my own was an unusual concept to some of the locals. Even I believed my fake story by the end!

Then there is of course the unsuspecting national pride which takes over as an Irish person. Stars of stage and sport act as informal ambassadors of the small island we call home; and there is nothing that will make an Irish person quote the land of saints and scholars more than leaving that home, even if just for a while.

'I don't think I ever appreciated being Irish as much as when I started travelling on my own,' Joanne says. 'Being Irish is a huge bonus. We are a nation that people accept. We are people who people accept. I remember being at the Zambia border about to cross the Zambezi into Botswana. There was a long queue, but the minute one of the border guards realised I was Irish I was moved to the front of the queue. Why? Because he was a huge Roy Keane fan. I love when I am way off the beaten track and on hearing I am Irish, someone will mention well-known Irish people and ask me if I know them. Which sometimes I do.

'Talking to random strangers is not as weird as it sounds. I always think that as adults we forget what it's like. If you're on a four-carriage train for twelve hours, invariably, you'll always try to talk to someone. And yet – just when you think the world is too big, on an overnight train in Vietnam from Sapa to Hanoi, I ran into someone I knew from Dublin who I hadn't seen since university. Of all the trains; of all the carriages – of all the rooms.'

The appeal of human connections moves well beyond simple conversation; it's about understanding our history as a species. Travel makes the world seem smaller and incomprehensibly larger all at once – a feeling that can come in the form of a visit to Lalibela in Ethiopia, for example.

'The Ethiopians of the 12th and 13th centuries built these amazing structures with a chisel and a hammer – and that's it. The day I was there, I was one of about seven visitors; I realised I was opening a door that's the same door that was there centuries ago. You get an incredible sense of the people who were there before you.

'Climbing Adam's Peak in Sri Lanka, often described as one of – if not *the* – most breathtaking sunrise settings on earth was a similar experience. Visitors begin the 7,359-foot ascent in the middle of the night so that they are at the top of the mountain by sunrise; welcoming the new day in all its glory. As the old day goes and the new day comes, you offer up what you've been through,' Joanne explains. 'I am so much more appreciative of my senses and I feel such amazing respect for all those people who travel who are in some way hindered by their physical attributes. One time, while climbing Sigiriya, known as the Lion's Rock, also in Sri Lanka, I witnessed true love.

'I saw a husband with his blind wife, helping her up the vertical climb, describing everything that he was seeing. You certainly felt she may not have been able to physically see it, but mentally, he was painting the most amazing picture. That's what love is.'

The world is changing around us; technology is distracting us and age diverts us, but Joanne is grateful for the grounding her navigation affords her.

'I remember reading *Lawrence of Arabia*, then being in Jordan and travelling by camel through Wadi Rum. I was in a mokoro [canoe] paddling through Botswana and Zambia while reading the biography of David Livingstone; I was reading Paul Theroux's books on South Africa as I was riding the train and, randomly, I actually met Paulo Coelho in his favourite book shop in Cusco.

'The older you get, the lazier you get and the lazier you get, the harder it is and the less effort you put in; then, I think the outcome is that your life gets smaller. We are on this planet for such a short space of time, anything that expands your horizons, you need to embrace. That can be places and it can also be people – it can be miles away or down the road. Still, one of the most memorable places I have ever visited is Irish – I dare anyone not to get onto Skellig Michael on a good day and not think that you are in one of the most magical places on this planet. I may be a bit biased, with my Kerry connections; I even chose green and gold for my company colours!

'It goes all the way back to that line, "Are you the person you want to be? And if not, what are you doing about it?"

'Travel broadens your horizons in a way that I think very few other things do. It's true when they say travel is the only thing that costs you but makes you richer.

'I haven't seen that priest since, but were I to ever meet him again I would simply say thank you – perhaps in a few of the languages I have picked up travelling around the world!'

WOMEN AT WORK

~

GETTING IT DONE
WITH GRACE.

The greatness of good intentions.

Caroline Downey

President, ISPCC and Music Manager

'The day I watched the news report of Ann Lovett's death.'

~

There are few indisputable facts in life. One of those undeniable truths is that the work of Caroline Downey has changed the landscape of fundraising in Ireland. She's the extraordinarily successful business-woman who is one half of the country's leading music promoter MCD Promotions, Director of the Gaiety Theatre, manager of Hozier and Hudson Taylor, President of the Irish Society of the Prevention of Cruelty to Children (ISPCC), and she's a mother of three.

~

Caroline's CV is a list of accomplishments as long your arm; she's a woman who built an empire through talent and grit, and who has segued into new careers twice in her adult life. She's also the woman who has raised €40 million for charities in Ireland, while always conveying a sense of immediate warmth, graciousness and joy. For the bulk of her life, Caroline has focused her energies on improving the welfare of others, in particular children, raising the sum mentioned from when her fundraising work began in the 1980s, spurred on by a tragedy she learned about on the news.

On 31 January 1984, fifteen-year-old schoolgirl Ann Lovett died in Granard, Co Longford. She died after giving birth to a stillborn child in a graveyard in the freezing cold of winter, alone in a grotto. Ann and her baby son were discovered by three local boys and she died later in hospital. Her sister Patricia took her own life at the age of fourteen just a few months later.

Hearing about Ann and her child changed Caroline's life for ever and, by default, that of generations of children afterwards who Caroline helped through the ISPCC.

'For me, everything that I have done on a philanthropic scale was after the day that Ann Lovett died,' she explains. '*The Late Late Show* reviewed the papers, as they did back then, and I remember Gay Byrne [who hosted the show from 1962 to 1999] reading it out, saying this girl had died in a graveyard. He then said, "Nothing terribly exciting there" before putting the newspaper on the floor and carrying on with the show.

'I remember thinking, "How did this happen to a fifteen-year-old girl? How did no one know she was pregnant?" The whole community then closed ranks and wouldn't discuss it. Now, you read stories about people who managed to conceal pregnancies, but I remember thinking how lonely it must have been to die in a grotto. And how terrified she must have been. When I tried to have a conversation with people at dinner parties about it, no one would discuss it. They didn't discuss child abuse in Ireland at the time, either, and it really bothered me.'

~

At the time, child abuse in particular was swept very definitely under the carpet in Ireland; the Catholic Church's grip was firm. Contraception was only legalised in some forms in 1980, Mother and Baby Homes were in operation around the country and Magdalene Laundries were deemed a viable solution for so-called 'fallen women'. There really was no place to go for a teenage girl in distress.

In that context, the idea that Gay Byrne – or anyone in his position – would toss aside a newspaper and dismiss it as 'non-news' is not a surprise. Ann Lovett's death wasn't the catalyst for change in Ireland, but another tragic example of a society letting its women and children down.

> When I tried to have a conversation about it, no one would discuss it ... and it really bothered me.

In recent years, as we look back through the lens of lived experience and new compassion, Ann's death is remembered and used as a benchmark for how far Ireland has come.

Caroline couldn't forget the story of Ann's death, and when she became pregnant with her eldest child, Zach, two years later, she still couldn't quite shake that feeling in her gut telling her to do something, to *act*.

'When I was pregnant with Zach, who was born in December 1986, Ann's death struck an even deeper chord with me. She kept coming back into my head, how she must have felt. I had a lot of anxiety. Here I was in a private hospital ... I was twenty-five years old, giving birth, and I kept thinking of how cold it must have been for Ann, giving birth outside in January?

'It really bothered me that she had nowhere and no one to turn to and neither did her sister Patricia, who took her own life four months after Ann's death.

'Jane Hogan, a friend of mine, said, "If you feel this strongly about it, you should join the ISPCC, which has been at the forefront of children's protection for over one hundred years. It's a voluntary organisation and it's not dependent on the State, so we can ask questions that charities receiving a lot of money from the State can't challenge." I walked into the ISPCC head office on Molesworth Street and said, "My name is Caroline Downey and I want to start fundraising for you." And here I am, thirty-two years later, president of the ISPCC.'

The ISPCC has functioned in an independent capacity since the 1980s, replacing its UK counterpart NSPCC (National Society for the Prevention of Cruelty to Children), which operated in Ireland until the 1950s. Every year, ISPCC Childline, a 24-hour counselling service which is one of the flagships of the organisation's myriad services, answers more than 300,000 phone calls from children in distress; the most recent statistics show a child called every minute on Christmas Day in 2018.

When Caroline first joined the charity, it was moving towards a new wave of actionable plans, and they were trying to secure funding to set up Childline. Caroline explains:

'We started fundraising specifically for that, because I always felt if Childline had existed when Patricia and Ann Lovett were struggling, would they have phoned? Maybe if they had phoned, somebody could have helped them'.

As Caroline began fundraising, she was also becoming increasingly successful professionally. MCD was taking off and Caroline was building relationships with some of the biggest names in international music. Over the course of the next three decades, Caroline would remain at the forefront of the industry, utilising every celebrity connection she had to raise money for worthy causes; and the ISPCC was always at the top of the list.

Throughout the 1990s, she produced pretty much every major show you can think of. Have a favourite pop culture music moment? Chances are, Caroline was involved in it. From the annual International Fashion Show at the Point Theatre (now the 3Arena) where supermodels Naomi Campbell and Christy Turlington took to the runway, to rugby and football tournaments with Irish legends like Brian O'Driscoll and Robbie Keane – you name it, Caroline's done it.

'At the height of the Celtic Tiger, we were making €1 million at every ISPCC Ball. The bulk of the money was raised through the auction and I stole the idea from Elton John's White Diamond and Tiara Ball that I would attend with Louis [Walsh, the music manager] each year. He of course has a wide-reaching celebrity network. David Beckham would teach you how to play football or Martina Navratilova would teach you how to play tennis. Sting did an Ashtanga session.

'They were simple ways of fundraising and the celebrity involved could raise a huge amount of money by just giving up their time. Sometimes people who were incredibly wealthy would want to purchase something normally unattainable. So, I would ask members of the Irish rugby team to coach someone at their school or Padraig Harrington would teach a golf lesson in his home.

'It all went to a really good cause and nobody ever said no, because why would you say no to the ISPCC and Childline? Fundraising seemed easy for me because the people I talked to . . . none of them can comprehend why children are abused.'

In the late 1990s, Caroline launched the Childline Concert at Dublin's 3Arena. It's a venture that's still going strong and where pop stars of the day perform to an audience made up nearly exclusively of children (and their parents). Every performer involved gives up their time free of charge. Westlife have always been staunch supporters of the cause, as have Little Mix, Boyzone, Girls Aloud, The Saturdays, Sophie Ellis Bextor, Alexandra Burke and many other Irish and British pop artists.

'The concert was effective. Boyzone and Westlife, and every other pop band that came along, would call out the Childline number and the audience would repeat it back. It was a way for children to know the number and it was a way to take any stigma away from phoning Childline.

'This was important because there used to be a huge stigma around calling Childline because it was so strongly associated with abuse. However, the reasons why kids use Childline vary – true, it could be for more serious cases of abuse, or for bullying, or anxiety over exams, suicidal thoughts or confusion around sex and relationships. All of these issues are massive to a child.'

The Childline service was the brainchild of the ISPCC's former chief executive Cian O Tighearnaigh. He first identified the need for an outlet where children could speak honestly and openly.

But it wasn't as simple as introducing a new phone service and getting children to call. Phone bills, for a start, were a real problem initially. Any call made in a household would appear on the phone bill – number and all. Children couldn't make calls anonymously.

'Mobile phones were yet to be invented, so if a child wanted to ring without their parents or guardians finding out, they'd have to find a phone box. In response to this problem, Telecom stepped up and made sure the Childline number wouldn't appear on the bill and they have paid for all the landline calls since Childline was formed. They didn't want any recognition for it, they just did it.

'Now technology is vastly different, so children can text, call for free from a mobile, log in for 1-2-1 online chat and email, but we do still have the same arrangement with mobile companies now – you don't need any credit to call Childline and calls don't show up on the bill.

'I proud that Childline is very much at the forefront of my work, and Ann Lovett is the reason for it. She's always with me.'

During this time, Caroline gained quite a knack for production, which proceeded to lead her down another parallel career path: 'Running events for the ISPCC gave me confidence in turn to produce plays at the Gaiety and Olympia Theatre.'

By this point, Caroline's children – Zach, Jett and Storm – had grown up and were getting ready to fly the nest. She had also separated from her husband, Denis Desmond, after thirty-two years of marriage. She threw herself into her work and was open to each and every opportunity that arose; and with decades of experience in the industry, she could recognise potential early on. This path led her to managing Hozier.

Caroline's children had all attended St Gerard's secondary school in Bray, Co Wicklow. When her daughter, Storm, came home from a transition year retreat one day full of stories about a boy in her class with a powerful voice, Caroline was intrigued.

The teenage boy was Andrew Hozier-Byrne, who is now simply known as Hozier, the Grammy-nominated singer who debuted at number one on Billboard's Top 200 charts in the US in 2019. And to refer to him as a superstar-in-the-making is not hyperbole.

To cut a long story short, Hozier sent Caroline some demo tapes and she loved what she heard.

Caroline sent everything to Rubyworks (the Dublin-based record label to which Hozier is now signed, and with which she is also involved), and they brought in Rob Kirwan, a producer and sound engineer, to start recording tracks.

One of these tracks was *Take Me To Church*; which, in 2015, would become an anthem for a generation, in particular the LGBT community it was aimed at and those millennials and Gen Z'ers who felt disenfranchised from the sins of the Catholic Church's past haunting their present.

And the music video – which cost only €1,500 to produce – was a hit. It has been viewed more than 800 million times to date and the song itself has been streamed over one billion times on Spotify, a feat achieved by only a few dozen artists.

~

How Caroline came to manage Hozier was as natural a partnership as it gets.

'I had mentored Andrew, we signed him to Rubyworks, but when it came to who would manage him, I was really struggling with who I would recommend. People assumed I would be his manager, which is something I hadn't considered, but where I was in my life at that moment, I felt that I would try and be the best manager I could.

'I'm really practical in what I can achieve and what I can't achieve and so I felt that if I couldn't do right by Andrew [Hozier], if I wasn't a good manager, I would know my limitations and bring someone else in.

'I'd seen enough in thirty-five years to understand what made a good – and a bad – manager. I just couldn't find anybody who I felt was right for him as he's quite a unique person. He's super talented, but he also has huge empathy for people.

'I feel a lot of management is about common sense and going with your gut . . . and a good bit of luck, being in the right place at the right time with the right song.'

And so, Caroline threw herself into her work.

'As Andrew came along, I took over the Gaiety and renovated the Olympia Theatre at the same time. I went into overdrive. I mustn't have had a life, I just didn't know it. Now it's so much calmer.'

Success is never a guarantee and, in spite of her well-documented accomplishments, Caroline credits her achievements as being the result of never being afraid of failure – or of hard work.

'If you think anybody succeeding in their own business is working Monday to Friday nine-to-five, it's not going to happen. I don't know anyone who is successful who you can't speak to at the weekend at any time. That applies to all aspects of life'

Growing up, Caroline says she never understood her purpose: at school, you're raised to believe that academia is the only path to success; but her undiagnosed learning disability meant school was never a positive experience and, after finishing secondary school, she certainly wouldn't be seeking further education now that she was no longer obliged.

'I was born in Ireland, but raised between Australia and South Africa; I went to seven different schools and I'm dyslexic. I didn't know I was dyslexic until they diagnosed Jett; I just thought – and was told – I was stupid,' she says.

'I moved back to Ireland when I was sixteen and I was definitely not going into another school again. I couldn't bear it. I waitressed, modelled and did a whole load of jobs, then I met Denis when I was nineteen and began working alongside him with MCD.

'Circumstances throughout my life have led me down the path I'm on now and watching that news report about the tragedy of Ann – and later Patricia – both of whom were let down by the system, compelled me to want to make Ireland a safer place for children.

'But through her and her sister's death, I trust and hope that lots of other young people's lives have been saved.'

She reached for the stars.

Norah Patten

Aeronautical Engineer

*'The day I visited the Kennedy Space Center at fifteen
and realised my dream of visiting space.'*

~

There are few better introductions than 'Dr Norah Patten is on course
to become Ireland's first astronaut', and every time she hears it, Norah
is delighted.

~

Space travel is, for most of us, entirely out of reach; it feels like the
exemplification of a childhood dream that so few in human history
can ever be lucky enough to see through. All children are curious and
will relay fact after fact of new learnings to just about anyone who
will listen, but Norah is bringing that twinkling childhood ambition
into an adult reality.

Norah is an aeronautical engineer from Ballina, Co Mayo, and
she knew from an early age that space would be the great love of
her life.

As a child, she spent most summers visiting family in the United
States. Her first introduction to space was at aged eleven when she

visited the Glenn Research Center in Cleveland, Ohio, a NASA centre which tells the story of space to people of all ages. It was love at first sight, but it wasn't until Norah was fifteen years old and she visited the John F. Kennedy Space Center in Florida that she realised her heart was full with galactic ambitions.

She understood then that she had the potential to make what would oft be dismissed as a frivolous pursuit into a very realistic career path.

'For me, life has been a build-up of experiences, but the day that changed my life is probably when I visited the Kennedy Space Center, NASA's primary launch centre for space flight, when I was fifteen.

'I had been really interested in space before that, but when I went to NASA in Florida the sheer scale of what they have there astounded me. I knew it was the only thing career-wise I wanted to do.

'Being exposed to something like that was so cool – the rockets and photos of astronauts. It was such a different world from what I had known. There were amazing pictures and displays of spacecraft and astronauts. I was fascinated and that fascination has never left me.'

She was already a dreamer, but Norah never grew out of her childhood obsession: she was drawing pictures of spaceships and hanging them up in her room, her collection ever growing. It was all standard fare for a child's imagination – that typical trait of dreaming of life beyond what is known – made all the more interesting when you remember this already ambitious dream was somewhat out of the ordinary in rural County Mayo in the 1990s.

As time went on, Norah's curiosity only grew and she wasn't going to let a little thing like geography stand in her way. At age fourteen, she saved her babysitting money and bought her first telescope. By fifteen, after that NASA visit, she was strategising about realistic ways to get into the space game as an adult.

She wrote to NASA in Cleveland, Ohio, asking for advice about how to enter a career in space, even naively – and endearingly – enquiring about the possibility of taking up an internship there during her transition year in secondary school. NASA internships are extraordinarily competitive, but living thousands of miles away in Ireland would prove to be Norah's biggest barrier when it came to enacting her space dream.

'It was much harder back then to get your hands on information because it was before the internet. Now we have so much access to so much information, which is great, but it wasn't like that when I was a young child. I had to make more effort to find out what was going on,' she explains.

'I hand wrote a letter to NASA and put it in the post. I asked how I could work at NASA and they sent me a booklet on careers you need to pursue to work in the space sector or become an astronaut. I still have that letter.'

Their correspondence was exactly what she needed to hear. Instead of being told no, she was given a clearly laid-out map of options by the gatekeepers themselves. And she would stick to that map with admirable tenacity – a tenacity that would carry her through the twenty-plus years she has spent working towards her goal.

'Space exploration is so vast, there are so many things you can do to get into the field whether it's medicine, science, engineering, technology,' she says. 'I loved space but I wasn't overly sure what aspect of it was going to be my thing. I saw the rockets and I wanted to know more about flying and physically getting to space, so I started researching astronauts and what they studied.

'So, NASA instilled in me a couple of elements that fed into my decision to study aeronautical engineering at the University of Limerick (UL).'

While most Irish teenagers might attend an open day at a third level institution, fill out their choices through the Central Applications Office (CAO) form and hope for the best, Norah did her research well in advance. 'I wrote to the department head asking them to send me information on the course so I really spent my time doing the homework on it. My focus was on getting the points needed and getting into the course.'

Aeronautical engineering, a branch of engineering that considers the design, development, testing and manufacture of aircraft, space-craft and missiles, was Norah's first choice, but the ever-prepared astronaut-in-training also had two back-up options in case it didn't work out as she planned. (It did.)

Focus and determination are two of Norah's most enduring personality traits, characteristics she picked up as a child and held on to in a world which likes to maintain the status quo and doesn't always encourage dreamers. She possesses the kind of pleasant stub-bornness that only the successful seem to hold.

Her sister, Emma, often reminds her that since they were children, 'If someone told you that you couldn't do something, you were the type to not let it stop you – you'd do it anyway.'

Norah says, 'I didn't want to listen to anyone telling me I couldn't do something.'

This focus is admirable in any environment, but all the more impressive when you remember she grew up in the rural Ireland of the early to mid-1990s. Long before the internet, the idea of a young woman speaking so determinedly about visiting space would have been as common as . . . landing on the moon.

After all, it was only in 1990 that NASA's *Voyager One* took its first picture of the entire solar system. It may have been more than thirty years since the moon landing, but that type of lunar activity was seemingly reserved for the Neil Armstrongs and Sally Rides of the world.

'You have to put this in context. Nowadays, the whole idea of space is a lot more open and people can get involved who would never have been involved before, which is fantastic, but twenty-five years ago, growing up in Mayo, people thought I was mad,' she says.

'But I was just obsessed. I didn't care what people thought and I was going to fight for my dream, I was going to make it happen.'

> I didn't want to listen to anyone telling me I couldn't do something.

Norah's parents, Pat and Bridie remained unfazed by her regular announcements that she was one step closer to becoming the first Irish person in space.

However, not living stateside was something of a disadvantage for her progress, but where there's a will, there's a way. After completing her undergraduate degree in 2006, Norah went straight into further study and began her PhD in Wind Tunnel Testing at her alma mater UL, that same year.

'I did different courses and programmes and I learned very quickly after my undergrad that I'd have to study internationally to pursue what I wanted,' she says. 'At the time, there was very little going on in Ireland that was related to space.'

In 2010, she studied for three months as part of the Space Studies Program (SSP) at the International Space University (ISU), which provides interdisciplinary educational programmes for students and aspiring space professionals at varying levels of application in both the private and public sector. As an aeronautical engineer with a speciality in wind tunnel testing, Norah was a particularly attractive candidate; a victory made all the sweeter on a personal level as she was one of the few Irish people to attend the course.

'That was my real foot-in-the-door in terms of an international setting and it was one of the best things I've done. Our core lectures covered everything you could want to know about space – the body and business of space, space law, astronomy, stars, rockets. I was crying when I had to leave because I felt a real sense of purpose there.

'I often think back to how much pressure we put on ourselves after an undergraduate degree: there's a huge weight on you about what you're going to do, you need to get a job, and so on. I was questioning where I was going but when I got to ISU, I knew I was doing what I loved.'

After that, it wasn't quite back to the drawing board as Norah now had rather illustrious credentials to her name and became more aggressive in her search for further space-related education.

'I was always on the lookout. You can't just sit back and expect opportunities to fall in your lap because it doesn't work that way. After leaving ISU, I made sure I was going to do my best to stay involved with them.

'I finished my PhD and I applied to go back as a teaching associate in 2011. That summer, I went to Austria for eleven weeks.' And by 2012, Norah was made associate chair at SSP which was hosted at the Kennedy Space Center, where it had all began for her more than twenty years before.

'It was like coming home,' she says.

She came armed with the knowledge and determination to coordinate an Irish programme with NanoRacks, a private company which has access to the International Space Station (ISS) for research purposes.

'In 2013, while working at the Irish Composites Centre, I raised some funding to run a national competition in Ireland allowing transition year students to compete to design an experiment that would be sent to the ISS and tested by the astronauts on board. The ISS is an orbiting laboratory – and what an awesome opportunity for young Irish students. This was the first time that Irish teenagers had an opportunity to do something like that.'

Norah was beginning to realise that the biggest doesn't always mean the best and that her little tiny country of Ireland could have a seat at the table in space, but it wouldn't come easily and she would have to be the driving force behind it.

'You have to get involved in as much as you can until that right opportunity comes up. Doing the NanoRacks programme was such a positive thing for me – I represented Ireland at the International Astronautical Congress (IAC) in 2015, the biggest space conference in the world and I got an emerging space leaders grant as part of that.

'It was special to share what we've achieved in Ireland with no space agency and limited space activity. If you're willing and determined to make something happen, you can.'

By 2017, she had acquired all the theoretical knowledge required for space exploration, but still needed more physical experience in the field. Enter Project PoSSUM (Polar Suborbital Science in the Upper Mesosphere).

PoSSUM is the first and only crewed suborbital research programme, and is designed to teach candidates the skills required to effectively conduct research on the next generation of space vehicles.

It involved wearing a spacesuit inside a flight simulator to best understand the physical difficulties of moving and working in such a uniquely confined space. Norah believes it's the most realistic career option for getting to space – it was another carefully chosen opportunity that she grabbed with both hands.

Norah applied for PoSSUM, was selected and joined ten other international team-mates in 2017 and is the first ever Irish person to taken part in the training.

'It was exactly what I needed to do if I had any chance of getting to space. You have to possess a very wide mix of experience and skills.'

She says, 'The programme that I'm doing – our plan is to get commercial suborbital flights like Virgin Galactic or Blue Origin, rather than a space agency like NASA or the European Space Agency (ESA). I just don't see Ireland having an astronaut through ESA for another couple of years, partly because of the funding we put in compared to other countries.

'For me, this is the most realistic route.'

It's now a question of 'when' rather than 'if' Norah's space dream will become a reality. She has clearly mapped out her own destiny her entire life and she was lucky enough to start to realise it at the age of fifteen. Now, with the eyes of Ireland on her, she holds an even greater responsibility as a national treasure in the making.

'After all these years, to finally see my dream through to completion will be amazing,' she says. 'It's the biggest ambition I can have and I feel the whole of Ireland is behind me. That's a huge responsibility to try and make happen for both myself and everybody else who has supported me.

'It's a work in progress and you have to constantly chip away at it with your eye on the prize. There are a lot of opportunities now that there weren't ten to fifteen years ago, particularly in space, when even just twenty years ago, it was nearly exclusively government-focused.

'Little kids send me letters with their drawings of rockets – with us in a rocket together. Parents message me a lot and say lovely things about the way they speak about me in their house. I didn't plan for any of that at all; it's been a wonderful surprise.

'Imagine the impact it will have in Ireland when I finally travel into space. When I was eleven this whole dream seemed impossible, so the idea that it's finally become plausible is incredible to me.'

She won her badges of honour.

Orla Barry

Paralympic Medallist and European Champion

'The day I won my first competition when I was nine.'

~

It goes without saying that women's sporting accomplishments are still largely under-reported, and when that sport also involves a woman with a disability, hard-earned victories might not always get the recognition they deserve.

~

Orla Barry, a 29-year-old from Ladysbridge in east Cork, is a bonafide Paralympian superstar: she has a bronze medal for the discus throw from London 2012, a silver medal from Rio 2016 and an additional seven medals from European and World Championships over the years.

Orla first got a taste for competition – and victory – at the age of nine when she competed in her first athletics competition in Co Kilkenny, before she eventually found her calling in the discus throw, for which she broke the world record in the F57 classification in 2013.

Orla, born in 1989, is a double above-the-knee amputee and her determination to succeed can perhaps be summed up in her own succinct description of her disability, which gave her the chops to beat the first record of her life. 'I was born with both legs but I didn't have kneecaps or shin bones so I wouldn't have been able to support my weight. When I was eleven months old, we amputated and I was walking before my second birthday with artificial legs.'

> " I can't overstate how important it is to build your own self-confidence. It took a long time for me to do that.

Orla's parents, Tom and Nuala, instilled in her from an early age the importance of adaptability, a crucial tool in her arsenal for sporting success, but a skill she has also applied to every aspect of her life. But none of her achievements – or the wisdom she has to impart – would be possible without her realising her athletic gift twenty years ago, when she took part in her first competition.

'That's where it started for me,' she explains. 'I gave everything a go – I tried track and field, all the throwing instruments like shot put, discus and javelin and I came away from the discus knowing that I would definitely go back again. I started at the bottom and climbed my way to the top.'

She had always indulged in some type of activity, whether it was swimming in the hydrotherapy pool at Enable Ireland or her work with a physiotherapist as a child in order to help her to walk. When she was a young girl, swimming gave her a special kind of confidence. From an early age, Orla and her parents attended events organised by the Irish Wheelchair Association, which organises sporting competitions for both children and adults with disabilities.

As it turns out, she was something of a prodigy.

'There were a good few kids my age there, all with different disabilities. It's a good way for kids to meet each other and understand disabilities and see what someone else does in their life and how they're learning to adapt. It's also great for the parents. You might think there isn't much available for people with disabilities, but there is when you go looking. You have to be prepared to travel and work a little bit harder to find something out there for you, but it's there if you want it.

'After my first competition, I came away wanting to immediately try the next one. I had spent the days with older athletes and hearing them speak about their own training routines – like competitions abroad and warm weather training – I somehow started to instantly mentally prepare for the Paralympics. It was a whole new world and I wanted it to be my life. I came away from that day knowing I wanted to win a Paralympic medal.'

Orla's road to greatness was, of course, paved with a few bumps, but her laser-sharp focus would help see her through the more difficult days. In her sport, the three major titles that can make or break a career are the European Championships, the World Championships and the Paralympic Games.

Before she reached double digits, she was mapping out a plan – equal parts ambitious and realistic – to get herself to those three events. Her promising talent, coupled with her unbridled motivation to win, were the ingredients behind her formula for long-lasting success.

'It took a long time. I started when I was nine and then, from the age of thirteen upwards, I was going to senior championships abroad. I knew I was good enough, even at that age,' she explains.

'At fourteen, I went to my first Europeans and, at fifteen, I was at my first world championship. I don't know if I was bit naive or young, but it takes time to develop to being a top level athlete. You have to learn the tricks of the trade and how to mentally cope with competition, as well as physically.

'I can't overstate how important it is to build your own self-confidence. It took a long time for me to do that. It wasn't until 2012 that I won my first championship medal, at the Europeans, just before the London Paralympics in September.'

Athletes peak at different ages depending on their sport, position, age and other factors. Orla credits constructive feedback and performance analysis as the tools that got her onto the podium.

'It took a lot of disappointment, of accepting it wasn't meant to be that time and going back to the drawing board. I would ask myself, "Where can I make my changes, what are my gains?" You have to learn after each experience. You do your own debrief and focus on the negatives and positives of your performance. You're trying new things to get better and better, and eventually that was what led to making it onto the podium.'

In 2012, at the age of twenty-two, Orla won her first major championship when she took home gold at the Europeans.

'I had built it up so much in my head – it looked so big and I just needed to break that mental seal and believe I could do it. Once I broke it, that was it. I've never missed a podium finish since – but it took that first mental unlocking for me to get there.'

That gold medal, the culmination of more than a decade of hard work, was proof she wasn't just a rising star or unworthy of the hype, but rather it signified the deserved victory of an impressive young woman here to stay.

'In one sense, you can say that everything happened organically in that I took every step of the ladder. I wasn't a flash in the pan. I was a slow burner. But, as a result of that, I've enjoyed some really successful years. Since 2012, I've always had podium finishes and I've never been disappointed in my performance. That comes from working from the bottom up.

'At the end of the day, I'm there on my own. I'm in the circle, I have to throw the discus as far as I can and nobody else can help me. If I do my best, well, then, that's all I can do. It's all about me, although I do have an amazing team behind me – my coaches for technical throwing and strength and conditioning (S&C), my physiotherapist, my nutritionists, my psychologist, my parents and my family. They are all part of my team and, without them, I'd be lost.'

Orla's advice to anyone reading and aspiring is beautiful in its simplicity: love what you do and do it well.

'I didn't start this journey saying, "I want to achieve this many medals or records in this many years;" my goal was always to win a Paralympics medal and now that I've done that . . .

'As well as the medals and everything people see when you're on the news for a few seconds after a big win, there are all the other bits, other parts of the training, that people don't see. I like to talk about those, too.

'I love the aspects people don't see. I love the training. It's my life. I don't know any different. I never really had a job as this has always been my job.'

And it's a job that one would need to have an innate passion for with the hours and the travel required. Training full-time means three throwing sessions per week, two to three gym sessions and two to three cardio sessions per week, plus a Pilates session once a week. Orla supplements that with niche training such as her S&C, which requires a two-hour drive each way to nearby county Limerick and visits to the Institute of Sport in Dublin – a four-hour trip each way again. Sundays are her one day off per week and they remain sacred.

Orla's 'just get on with it' attitude comes from her parents, who never allowed her to see her disability as an obstacle, but rather a challenge; specifically, a challenge she can overcome. And growing up with an older sister and two younger brothers, Orla was never treated any differently to her siblings.

'As a child, it can be challenging when you have a disability to go to school and make friends, play in the yard with everyone else, take part in PE classes, or go on school trips – you're always trying to keep up with everybody else.

'But if you see something as an obstacle, it becomes an issue.

'It doesn't need to be an issue. Get on with it. There's an awful lot to be said for just *getting on with it*. Everyone has challenges in life. If we all rolled around saying "poor me", we'd never achieve what we want. If you just get on with it, you can get over these challenges – and you will achieve whatever you want.

'This is the way I was brought up. I wasn't brought up to be any different from my brothers and sisters – they had chores, so I had chores. When my parents had a child with a disability, I'm sure it was confusing for them for the first few weeks – especially because I was the first child to ever be born like that in Ireland, and they didn't have anyone to talk to who'd been through it too.

'They had this big decision to make: will we or won't we amputate? If we do, will it work? If we don't, will we be sorry? They only had doctors to talk to and would have loved to have spoken to other parents about what they did, what worked for them and regrets they may have had. I think when they made that decision, they adopted that attitude of, "This is the decision we've made, and we're going to make the most of it."

'They made sure I would walk and make the best of what I have. I adopted that attitude, too.'

Orla wears her success in the Paralympics as a badge of honour, not only because of the two medals that hang proudly in her home as a result, but because she personifies hope for anyone with a dream, with aspirations that extend beyond the ordinary.

'A lot of people say, "You're the Olympic girl," but I'm not. I'm a Paralympian, not an Olympian. I'm a Paralympic medallist. I'm proud of that.

'I'm proud of the fact that I have a disability and didn't let it get in my way, I came through the challenges. The only way you can cope with a disability is to adapt. I'm proud that I was able to adapt, and I feel it can get lost sometimes because some people think I'm the "Olympics girl".

'I wasn't going to stop competing until I won a Paralympics medal, whether it happened in 2012 or 2016, or if I had to wait until 2020. Now I have two of them! Now I just take each year as it comes, my body is breaking down a bit because I'm getting older. You have to look after your body . . . I don't know how much more I'll get out of this. I'll just have to see.'

While Orla's not at the end of her career, she has been focusing on readjusting her outlook on life both in sport and the next chapter that awaits her when the time comes. In further proof of her jaw-dropping motivation for personal achievement, she has been studying full-time for a Master's in Education, which she completed in early 2019.

She also has the levels of self-awareness usually reserved for those on the outside looking in and not a professional who has spent her entire adolescent and adult life polishing her craft – a craft she will one day have to leave.

'To be able to bow out and to still have been the best would be nice,' she says. 'I have never been world champion or Paralympic champion. It would be great to say my ultimate professional goal is to be number one in the world, but the girl who is number one is ten per cent ahead of me. If I have three more years left, I still don't know if I'll be able to catch her. She's incredible and explosive at what she does, and she's more explosive than I am. I have great technique, she has great explosive power and that's what makes her better than me. I don't know if I'll ever catch her.

'Maybe there will be a day I could catch her, but, because she's so far ahead, I wouldn't set that as my goal. It's not. I don't want my goals to be controlled by other people. If I create a goal, I want it to measurable and realistic. For me, goals are my own and to beat myself. I can't control anybody else.

'I want to always be on the podium and to leave sport when I am ready to leave it. I think it will get to a point where I won't enjoy it as much any more; I might feel it's the end of this chapter and it's time to start a new one.'

Orla's words of wisdom come with a sense of grandeur so rarely seen in women her age, as we now know of the blood, sweat and tears she went through to achieve them.

And her parting words?

'Try everything and do what you love because you love it. It can always be done.'

If in doubt,
always do the right thing.

Breege O'Donoghue

Former Chairwoman of Primark

'There are too many days to choose from ...'

~

Breege O'Donoghue is, to put it lightly, a force to be reckoned with. For thirty-seven years, she worked at Primark (which trades in Ireland as Penneys); spending much of it as director and board member, overseeing with others more than 350 stores worldwide and in excess of 80,000 employees from the company's Dublin headquarters.

~

When we speak of her unwavering influence on the retail behemoth that Penneys is in Ireland, Breege is typically modest and speaks of the team effort involved in turning the brand into one of such repute as a Mecca of affordable fashion, homewares, and accessories. She didn't invent the #ThanksHunPenneys hashtag, but she is responsible for the culture that inspired it.

When Breege left her post in 2016 at the age of seventy-two (although she continues as a Primark ambassador and undertakes some project work), she left a legacy of genuine inspiration behind her; so it's of little surprise that when asked to pick the day that changed her life, she cannot whittle it down to just one, but rather she chooses three days.

~

'The day I went on my first trip abroad to Switzerland.'

Fresh from finishing her secondary school education, Breege began working in hospitality at the Great Southern Hotel Group, a former chain of eleven hotels around Ireland, including the Russell Court in Northern Ireland. She had happily worked in hospitality, but her eyes were opened to the potential that lay in wait during her first trip abroad. She was tasked with travelling to Switzerland for training. Once there, she was exposed to different languages, cultures and experiences which would leave an imprint on her life for ever.

'I clearly remember, back in 1963, when I went to Switzerland for the first time,' she remembers. 'To me, that was really significant as I was learning an entirely new culture, in a country where they spoke four languages and you kissed people on both cheeks when you came to work in the morning.

'I arrived in the wintertime and, as you can imagine, it was really cold, and I was travelling an hour and a half away from work every day to start work at 6.30 a.m. These were all culture shocks. It's something that, to this day, is still very much in my mind. It turned out to be a very rewarding experience.'

In fact, Breege fell in love with the country and life in continental European in general, and this motivated her to become multilingual.

'I have a great love of culture and languages, not just French and

German, but others, too. I think Switzerland embedded that in my mind,' she says. 'Ireland is really a small country, a little island, and here was Switzerland, also a small country, in the heart of Europe with different cultures and languages; it made a mark on me.'

Made a mark it did: Breege brushed up on her school French to become fluent, before picking up conversational German and other languages throughout her life.

'I made many friendships with people in the hospitality sector. I went on to be on the board of the Shannon College of Hotel Management and I chaired that board for eight years and that was all perhaps influenced by my experience and life in Switzerland. I sent many young people for skills and experience training to the best hotels in Switzerland and Germany for periods of between six and eighteen months, which bridged the gap between seasons.'

~

'The day I graduated from commerce at UCD after four years at night school.'

To quote W.B. Yeats: 'Education is not the filling of a pail, but the lighting of a fire.' Breege, a devoted believer in the freedom and empowerment that education can give, referenced this when accepting one of her many awards recently. Her belief in that sentiment is so strong that it inspired her decision to pursue third level education later in life.

In 1972, she graduated with a Bachelor of Commerce from University College Dublin (UCD) after studying for four years as a night student – a time that also changed her life. (Breege says she was privileged to be the recipient of a UCD Lochlann Quinn School of Business Alumna of the Year award in 2015.)

At the age of thirteen, Breege was sent to be educated at the Sisters of Mercy in Gort, Co Galway.

'I was born in a very different time,' she explains. 'We had the hedge schools of the 19th century, I went to school before Donogh O'Malley's [Fianna Fáil's Minister for Education in the 1960s] re-education plans in 1967 and the bus and school transport system, which is why many pupils from my generation didn't complete primary education. In 1950, fourteen was the school leaving age.

'I was brought up in the countryside and I'm lucky I had a stable foundation at home,' she says of her childhood on a farm in Boston, near Tubber, Co Clare. 'The farm was idyllic. It was also hard work and I milked the goats before I went to school.'

Breege had the ambition and determination to further educate herself, beyond the level at which her circumstances would allow during that era, and her degree from Dublin's distinguished university increased her confidence in business.

'I didn't have the opportunity, for economic reasons, to go to university when I finished my Leaving Cert, but I had the aspiration,' she tells me. 'That was an important event in my life. It was significant because education acts as a bridge between the worlds of work and the worlds of academia, and I'm really a great fan of the lifelong educational model.

'I'm still very grateful to UCD as they were really the first university to have a night degree to suit students with other commitments.' It would seem that UCD were grateful, too, as they awarded Breege the Smurfit Patrons of Excellence in 2017, and she is a board member of the UCD Michael Smurfit Graduate Business School.

For four nights a week and on a Saturday morning, Breege would cycle from her eight-to-five workplace and travel to the UCD campus in Belfield, south county Dublin.

'I was in business and interested in business, so it was a suitable fit,' she says. 'It was a wonderful experience. I made good friends, many of those are still good today. It gave me a love of education.'

And thus Breege's love of lifelong education was born. Her BComm was her first foray into formal third level education and she would continue to learn and study a whole range of subjects throughout her life to ensure her skills were always at the level they needed to be.

'I acquired a firm foundation across academia and it's stood me in good stead,' she says. 'I've taken a number of short courses at Harvard and other business schools. I did my chartered director qualification just eighteen months ago; I had practical experience but I wanted to make sure I learned the theoretical part – and that I was fully briefed. I learned a number of languages sufficient to do business in each of the European countries in which I was involved – I think that's important in terms of dignity and showing respect for a culture.'

~

'The day I joined Primark in 1979.'

Eight years before she became the only female member of the board of Primark in Dublin, Breege was recruited to head up Penneys' new human resources department.

'After seventeen years of working with the Great Southern Hotel Group, I joined Primark in October 1979. Primark at that stage was expanding in the UK and this was a new horizon for the company. I was influenced by the fact that Primark had a plan to expand. Reflecting on gender equality in the 1970s, she adds, 'I was very lucky because I worked with wonderful men.'

When she joined Primark, Breege knew she had ambitions outside Ireland. Until then, she had worked in Ireland and Northern Ireland, but she had bigger dreams. During her time at Primark, Breege led the company to a number of international conquests across Europe and the United States, with an emphasis on new markets. (At the time of her retirement in 2016, she was Group Director of New Markets and Business Development.)

Her career highlights include: the opening of the first store in Spain in 2006, followed by the first store in the Netherlands, Portugal, Germany, Austria, France and Italy. Another key launch was in September 2015, opening the first store in Boston, Massachusetts.

'Going to another country or continent to work requires due diligence, preparation, understanding the market, customer behaviour, culture – they're all challenges. Promoting the Primark story, the promise, the value proposition and customer experience ... we worked hard to nurture trust with the countries' governments, business influencers, businesses, educational establishments, universities, colleges, schools of fashion and local media,' she explains.

'The opening of Oxford Street in April 2005 was a particular high moment. We had a dream to be on London's premier street and it was a rather big moment opening a major store there. But initially it was a nightmare. There were 3,000 customers waiting, the police were on horseback and Oxford Street was closed for much of the day.

'That was quite extraordinary insofar as we hadn't anticipated that so many people would turn up. It's still very much talked about in major publications. It was an event in the calendar. The media talked about the "battle at Primark", "panic at Primark" and many other entertaining captions in the press,' she laughs.

During her time at Primark, Breege was able to create a support system for women in business at all levels. In 2008, she had an important role in launching a special project in Gujarat, India in order to empower women there with financial independence, and with others she curated roles for women in Primark's Sustainable Cotton programme.

'In conjunction with NGOs and the local Self-Employed Women's Association, we developed a project for 1,150 women and, at the end of three years there, their profit had increased substantially,' Breege says.

'The cost of input had gone down, as had the use of chemical ferti-liser and water usage. I sat with these women in Gujarat, working in 45°C heat, and I asked what they were doing with the profits. They had bought tractors, acreage, irrigation equipment, but, overwhelming, 95 per cent of them said they were using it for their children's education.

'The women were empowered. The project was extended to another 10,000 women for another six years. That was really very significant. And the merchandise subsequently – in 2016 – the merchandise was in various stores using the cotton produced from that pilot project.'

In the ever-growing world of 'fast fashion', of which Penneys is a market leader, Breege emphasises the importance of ethical practices and leaving behind a tradition of principled methods of production in addition to the cost-saving ones.

'It's about value for money; giving the customers what they want and ensuring all the products are made ethically,' she says.

'I wear a lot of Primark products and I'm proud to do so because I know they're not made at the expense of the workers of the supply chain. We work with tremendous partners in other countries; we share factories with 98 per cent of other high street brands. It's a great business; we provide a lot of employment both directly and indirectly, and in some cases trade revenue is greater than aid revenue, in those countries. We've also played our part in various partnerships and training schemes for the suppliers who make Primark garments.'

When it comes to the nitty gritty of what makes Penneys so special, and seemingly leaps and bounds ahead of all its retail competitors, both online and in its brick and mortar stores, Breege says the formula for success is one that's been perfected over the course of several decades.

'There's a lot going on when I say Primark is a business that thrives on being relevant, adaptable, using lean operations, due diligence, ethically produced products and trending fashion at great prices,' she says.

> We'd like more women in business ... Women are resourceful, adaptable, solution focused.

'The organisation is very much based on trust; it's passionate and energetic, it innovates and improves every day. The focus is on value, on support and empowerment; we hire smart people and they tell us what to do. These values were and continue to be our influences along the way.'

With a lifetime littered with accomplishments and awards, the highlights reel of Breege's career serves as a reminder that sometimes talent and intellect supersedes gender expectations. She is living proof of the accomplishments possible from a generation in which women were expected to remain in the home, or at least away from the boardroom.

Breege is deservedly proud of her many achievements, but gives particular distinction to the first board to which she was appointed

(Aer Rianta in the 1980s), her honorary doctorate from the Technical University Dublin in 2016 and the Chevalier de la Légion d'Honneur in 2016, the highest civilian merit in France, which she was awarded by former French President François Hollande. Oh, and she was also named Iconic Businesswoman of the Decade by the Women's Economic Forum, an accolade with which she was presented in Delhi, India.

'You like to feel you can give something back, I think that's really important. In regards to women, I think women have a lot to give – we've also got to recognise that women have the right to make a choice if they want to stay in business, rear their families, have a work/life balance and that has to be afforded to each woman,' she says. 'That, to a degree, is why we'd like more women in business.

'I'm aware of many women who have made many sacrifices running their home, raising their children, working hard in their businesses and going up the ladder, keeping all the balls in the air. Women are resourceful, adaptable, solution focused. Bringing up a family is also a special part of life.'

Her focus remains steadfastly on the support of women; she works to establish and back a network which empowers women in the workforce.

'I do some work for Primark, I work as an ambassador and on project work, I'm on the Primark trustee foundation as well as the board of pensions,' Breege tells me. 'I chair three companies; I'm a non-executive on a couple of others; I mentor women in particular and I work with Going for Growth, sponsored by Enterprise Ireland and KPMG. The programme this year was seven women over seven days and seven months. We set objectives and review each month, each of those organisations do a deep dive and we, as a group, act as consultants. Women are wonderful at sharing their most trusted secrets in relation to business and I believe I get more out of it than they do.'

Her leadership principles were ones so far ahead of their time that they set the tone for a number of supportive policies in practice today. Going forward, Breege believes that the major challenges will be culture and technology.

'I think I was often in the right place at the right time. I think I'm a reasonably good coach and good at dealing with the realities of the here-and-now. I can make a decision, if it's a bad decision, then that's better than no decision. In Primark, we had outstanding employees, young employees managing major businesses. It was all about support and development, empowering employees to use their experience and cultivate their strengths.

'Being able to take a risk is really important. Hire smart people, they'll teach you what to do. My motto is that, "If in doubt, always do the right thing."'

SLIDING DOORS

~

WHEN DESTINY AND YOUR DREAMS ALIGN.

She's committed to helping
women feel good.

Sonya Lennon

Fashion designer and broadcaster

'The day I agreed to co-host Off The Rails.'

~

The term 'modern Renaissance Woman' may very well have been coined for Sonya Lennon. She is freshly fifty years old and has spent the last thirty years of her life making women feel good, whether it be through her eponymous fashion line, her advocacy, her position on the cross-party parliamentary committee on gender pay in Leinster House or her charity – it's all in a day's work for Sonya.

~

But none of these accomplishments would have come to fruition if she hadn't taken a leap of faith and agreed to co-host *Off The Rails*, a television makeover show which aired on RTÉ and was extremely successful in its many forms throughout its eleven-year run.

'I didn't know it at the time at all, but it changed my sense of my place in the world. It changed my relationship with fear and it set in motion a domino effect, a course of events that have pretty much transformed my life.'

She had reservations about taking on the role to begin with, not because of any jitters about presenting, but because, at forty, she was a leader in her field – she hadn't just reached the upper echelons of fashion styling in Ireland, she established what those metrics of success were. For most people, the opportunity to be on television – if even for a flicker – is too much to resist, but not for Sonya.

'I was really apprehensive about accepting the role from a business point of view; it was 2008, I had built up a portfolio of clients over twenty years, I was a very successful freelance stylist and creative director, working in advertising, movies, music videos. I had a lovely life. I was making a really good income. I had a high degree of control and a great amount of respect. I had

> It changed my relationship with fear, it set in motion a domino effect, a course of events that has pretty much transformed my life.

basically furnished myself with the lifestyle that I wanted,' she says.

'When RTÉ asked me would I present the show with Brendan [Courtney, her close friend and long-standing business partner], there was a risk for me that I would lose that foothold in the industry. Everything I'd worked so hard to create could fall away and somebody else would take it from me. Then, after grappling with it for about a month, during which time I did screen tests and had various conversations, I came to this epiphany that it was an opportunity that would never come back if I said no. A prime time, national broadcast show does not come knocking twice.

'At that stage, I thought, I'm going to do it. I'm not sure if it's the right thing to do, but it's an opportunity and I feel duty bound to pursue it. If I don't like it, I'll walk away and I'll pick up the pieces again.'

After taking a leap of faith, there was another worry – would television producers, as they've been known to do – try to mould her into something she wasn't?

'I was really desperately afraid that I would be perceived as something other than I was. I was afraid that a move to TV presenting would actually damage my substance and intelligence in business. But that was something I put on myself.

'Nobody else had any grand plan for me about making me fluffier or blonder or less smart. That was a bias I brought to the table that was thankfully smashed by somebody who was very bright.'

The show, which aired weekly for three years while Sonya and Brendan hosted it, was a runaway hit and, by the time the first season aired, she was a household name and a new voice in broadcasting – and she had every intention of using this profile for greater means. Part of her appeal was not only her unwavering self-assuredness and the twenty years' experience which informed her expertise, but that she was also a 39-year-old mother of twins (Evie and Finn) on a second wave of her career.

'When I started doing the show and the profile of it rose, and my confidence grew in a way that I wouldn't have previously thought possible! That in turn then gave me a sense of place – of belonging – within my work. I was forty when I started the show. I wasn't a young buck coming to the table. I had a career behind me, I was already a mum, and so a lot of charitable organisations approached me to host fashion shows, lend my name or be an ambassador. That was the moment I felt that I couldn't take this new responsibility lightly.'

She realised she could be a force of good in the world, or, at least, in Ireland. I've known Sonya long enough to say, without question, that her passion for women's rights goes far deeper than the ladies-who-lunch crowd. Her mother and father, Deirdre and Donal, raised her to recognise her strength from an early age and Deirdre in particular always encouraged her daughter to have financial independence.

'My mother was a firebrand and she would say, "Always have your running-away money and have the ability to make choices, make your own living and don't depend on a man." At the time, this opinion was considered very avant-garde and was an unpopular, and uncommon, view. My mother worked all through mine and my sister's childhoods, so she walked the walk as well.

'My dad was similarly inclined – he was at my birth in 1968 at a time where having the father present was practically unheard of. He actually went to a nun who delivered me for prints afterwards because she was so impressed! He was intensely proud of that and always very forward thinking. There was a strong set of values instilled in us children from an early age.

'I thought, if I have the power to be a voice, I need to be very clear what that voice needs to say, and that's when I read about Dress for Success. Their mission tapped into every value I was brought up with.'

Dress for Success is an international non-profit founded by Nancy Lublin in New York in 1997. It aims to empower women to enter or return to the workforce by providing them with appropriate clothing and also training them in interview preparation and offering a support network. It has branches in thirty countries, and Sonya brought it to Ireland in 2011.

'It took about a year and a half of heartache, writing action plans, business plans, identifying board members, sourcing premises, fundraisers, and so on; it was the most gruelling thing and, looking back on it now, I'm pretty sure they designed it to be that way to test your metal and see you have what it takes to keep going,' Sonya says.

'I wouldn't have done that without *Off The Rails*, I know that for sure. What Dress for Success did for me was take my self-belief and validation to a different level.'

Not only had she created an organisation doing much-needed work, but the gruelling process led to her light bulb moment when she realised the skills she'd developed were transferable.

'I suddenly realised I'd created an organisation that hadn't existed before. It was a not-for-profit business, so surely, I thought, I could take the same principles and apply them to a profit-making business. Dress for Success gave me the confidence to own my trajectory, to control that and be strategic in terms of what I was doing and not be dependent on other people.

'You are an active participant in your life as opposed to a passive one. That's the big choice you make, I think, in this life. You can't control everything, but you can control a lot and you can manage the rest.

'From there, everything grew. By now, I was attracted to doing things that made me fearful and it became a bit of an adrenaline rush to try things that were risky or not as easy as other options. None of that would have happened without the unexpected swerve of agreeing to host the show to begin with.'

Early in her career, Sonya learned an important lesson and it's one which I ask you to withhold judgement on before reading the next few paragraphs. It is this: *nobody cares*. Sonya first learned of the power she could harness from appreciating this when she underwent media training for the first time. She was full of anxiety, unsure of the decision she had made. The person conducting the training noticed she was uneasy and asked what was wrong.

'I said, "I'm really worried. I don't know if I'm making the right decision. I'm committed to giving it a shot but it might not be the right thing for me. My career is very important to me and I don't want to mess it up." He said, "I just asked your series producer what her vision was for you and she didn't know, so it's really back on you." At that moment, I realised that nobody cares. Nobody has enough room in their brain to have a grand plan for you. It's entirely up to you.

'I made a commitment to myself: that if I was to do anything in a public arena, I would do it as myself. That "nobody cares" idea sounds like awful advice, but it's true. You experience everything through your own prism; it's not the same for everybody else. If you mess up really badly and it feels like your world is crashing down around you, nobody else sees it the way you do, they don't care. They have their own problems.'

By this time in the story, Brendan is the Des to her Lucy and the Fred to her Ginger. Before *Off The Rails*, they knew one another through mutual friends, but to say they clicked when working together would be an understatement. They have set up a number of businesses together, many of which have proven successful, but like all entrepreneurs, they've had their hearts broken more than once along the way.

And the idea that 'nobody cares' would carry Sonya through a difficult time; namely when they made the decision to close their app Frock Advisor, a shopping tool which paired customers with independent boutiques, in 2016.

'When we closed one of our businesses, we decided to do nothing in terms of telling the rest of the world. We had to let seventeen people go, it was horrific,' she recalls. 'We had to close the doors. It was awful. At the time, a number of other tech businesses had closed and people were sending out press releases and speaking publicly about it, but Brendan and I made a decision to keep the platform on life support and do nothing. We spent the whole summer licking our wounds, trying to find lessons to take with us and accept the positives. By the end of the summer, the emotion had dissipated, the pain had receded and we realised that nobody cared!

'It was the same lesson ten years later. As long as you're not mean or cruel, and you acknowledge we're all doing our best, we can accept that we mess up, then we move on and we keep on going. The picking-yourself-up business is the hardest, but it's the most important part.'

Her and Brendan's friendship is ten years old, meaning that there's a sense of intrinsic trust between them, built over that decade with its highs and lows.

'We really get on. We really trust each other. We've had each other's backs on a number of occasions. We've tested the boundaries of our relationship as individuals and as professionals. We know we would never do anything to ever harm each other.'

When *Off The Rails* didn't return for a seventh season (in its fourth year), Sonya and Brendan weren't going to rest on their laurels, recession or not. It was 2011, Ireland was still some time away from more stable economic recovery and they took a risk and started their Lennon Courtney clothing line, a contemporary women's fashion range which first launched in Arnotts in 2013 and has been stocked in Dunnes Stores since 2015.

'We set up Frock Adviser and Lennon Courtney at the same time, which was absolute lunacy at the height of a recession,' Sonya says. 'Lennon Courtney was created in response to a niche that we saw. We were dressing women every week on *Off The Rails* but we couldn't find what we were looking for. We knew we wanted a range of clothing that would do a certain thing: it would be smart, form-flattering regardless of your size, and aimed at the type of woman who has obligations to perform and doesn't want to be foofing around with fashion decisions in the morning. Her brain is too full for that.

'We had been playing around with the idea of launching a range of magic knickers at that time as we knew we needed to commodify the trust, expertise and profile we had built. We wanted to do something we could control and preferably create an income that would earn while we were asleep and didn't rely on us being in the room. Because, at that point, everything we did relied on us being in the room.'

The Lennon Courtney collection was an instant hit: *British Vogue* covered its launch during London Fashion Week in 2014 and *Elle* magazine gave it the seal of approval. It was stocked in Harvey Nichols, with a further thirty boutiques as stockists and, from the outside, they became a prestige brand riding high on their well-earned success.

In reality, they were haemorrhaging cash.

'It just wasn't working. The model wasn't working, it was eating itself. We never took a penny out of it. Nothing! It was like a really expensive hobby. If we started Lennon Courtney again, if I'd known then what I know now, would I have done it? Probably not. It was so hard. If I did do it again, I'd do it with a bit of knowledge about how to navigate certain things first. We learned everything on the hoof.'

They decided that they needed to adapt.

'It was quite a rigorous discipline to create clothes with very little resources. It was really hard – just before we were stocked in Dunnes Stores, things were really tough. We couldn't afford to cash flow the business, nobody would invest in fashion and so, we had to remodel it. We knew the value was there and that's how the conversation started with Dunnes. It's been transformative. It's growing every season and more women get to know about what we do in different countries, talking about us all over the world.

'It's real. It's a proper, accessible "solution collection". That's what it is and always needed to be. I think it would have been very different if all this happened to either of us on our own. We're basically accountable to each other for everything that we do, which makes it very potent. Neither of us would have any interest doing it on our own.

'I do things on my own – Dress for Success is mine – where the opportunities present themselves to work with Brendan as a partner, I would always err in favour of working with him than without him. Partly because of the accountability, partly because we fit hand in glove and complement each other's skill set.'

Sonya describes the day that changed her life as a literal sliding doors moment. If, in 2008, she had chosen option B, which was continuing on with her successful styling career, when the financial crisis plunged Ireland into a brutal downtown, she would have lost everything she was so scared of losing.

'It was 2008, so the advertising industry fell apart. Nobody was making, doing or promoting anything, so my income would have been decimated. It would have been a different path. You can't guess. You can't legislate for the future in that way.'

Sharing the courage to
live in the moment.

Andrea Nolan

Principal and Vice Chancellor of Edinburgh Napier University

'The day my daughter Maeve was born.'

~

Andrea Nolan is many things: a veterinarian, a professor, the principal and vice chancellor of Edinburgh Napier University, one of Scotland's most prestigious universities, one of the few Irish women to hold an OBE (Order of the British Empire) and a trailblazer; but she is, most importantly, a mother.

~

Andrea, originally from Raheny, a suburb in Dublin's Northside, has been living in the UK since 1980; she moved there shortly after she graduated from Trinity College Dublin with an MVB in Veterinary Medicine.

Her first love was academia, a courtship which would see her work in a number of prestigious third level institutions around England and Scotland, before meeting her husband Brian Morris and starting their own family in what would become her life's truest love story.

The day that changed Andrea's life wasn't becoming a mother for the first time, although each of her children brought her insurmountable joy, but, more specifically, it was giving birth to her third child Maeve in 1994, who has Down's syndrome.

At the time of Maeve's birth, Andrea was working as a full-time lecturer in veterinary pharmacology at the University of Glasgow and was on the cusp of a professional change.

'Maeve was born in Glasgow and, when she was born, neither I nor my husband noticed anything different about her – I didn't know she was going to be born with Down's syndrome. The doctors took her away about twenty minutes after she was born because her hands were quite blue, which was quite stressful at the time. We didn't see her for about three or four hours after that, and then a consultant came in and told us that our daughter had Down's syndrome, and, in addition, cardiovascular problems. It transpired she had a hole in her heart.

'That was the day that changed my life in a hugely enriching way.'

Until her second daughter's birth, Andrea had very little experience with and exposure to people with disabilities – at the time, those with physical and mental challenges were usually educated at separate schools and no one in her family had Down's syndrome.

But she was, as mothers tend to be, head over heels in love with her new arrival. Maeve's birth opened her eyes to a world of possibility and, over time, Andrea began to see everything differently.

'It's hard to describe the early times with Maeve. Because we didn't expect it – it was challenging,' Andrea says. 'Falling totally in love with her and watching her grow has opened my mind to what it is to be human, what it is to be vulnerable and what it means to have amazing courage and strength. I feel that I derive so much courage from her.

'Maeve's presence in my life has made me more aware of how we, as a society, truly view people who are vulnerable. I don't want to focus completely on Maeve's vulnerabilities, because she has enormous talents and strengths, but the question is: how do we utilise those talents and strengths as a society?

> Falling totally in love with her and watching her grow has opened my mind to what it is to be human, what it is to be vulnerable and what it means to have amazing courage and strength.

'Throughout her life, I have fought and battled to get Maeve the support and recognition she deserves. I have felt such huge joy simply sitting at parties with our friends or going on trips, at watching her in special needs judo, at appreciating the richness and joy of those people who others might think are disabled and don't realise how much they have to contribute.'

Maeve's birth proved serendipitous not only in the ways she changed the family dynamic, but also in leading Andrea down the extraordinary career path she now finds herself on.

'Maeve changed my personal life, but also my professional life,' Andrea says. 'It has changed our family life and I wouldn't be in my current job, which I love, had she not been born. My career had been on a different path and Maeve's birth changed its route completely.

'There have been lots of days in my life – when my parents died, when I had breast cancer eight years ago, when I had a mid-term miscarriage – that have been really hard. But nothing or no one has transformed the way I live and view the world around me in the way Maeve has.'

When Maeve was born, Andrea was already a mother to her two

eldest children, Sinéad and Owen, both under four. At the time, working in academia was becoming increasingly stressful, owing to sustained budget cuts across third level institutions by the UK government in the 1990s. Her workload had steadily increased, though the staff count had dropped and the number of students at the university continued to rise. Her husband Brian was finally rid of 'one of those precarious academic contracts' and she made the decision to transition into part-time employment to a role with more consistent hours and less stress.

Andrea planned on leaving academia and applied for a job at the Home Office, a ministerial department in the British government, to work as a veterinary surgeon overseeing the care and welfare of animals undergoing experiments. She was interviewed for the position when she was eight months pregnant and was offered the job just a few days after Maeve was born, a job she already knew she could no longer accept because of the significant changes in her personal and family life.

Not only was her daughter born with significant disabilities, but Andrea was also suffering from what she believes now, in hindsight, to have likely been a form of postnatal depression – something she'd experienced after the birth of her first two children, too. She knew she wasn't in the right frame of mind to make a life-altering decision such as accepting a new job.

'If Maeve hadn't been born with Down's syndrome and her heart issues, I would have accepted the job at the Home Office. It was part-time and life would have taken me in a completely different direction. But I felt so strongly that it wasn't the right time to make that kind of decision when I felt I was all over the place.

'So, I stayed in the job I was in and became a very successful academic. I achieved my professorship and I ended up leading the veterinary school at the University of Glasgow, and then I became vice-principal and then the deputy. I then went on to be the leader of the Edinburgh Napier University. Professionally, it was extraordinary.

'I had another child, Sean, after Maeve. I've had a great career, one which has opened up a whole world to me that is new, interesting and challenging.'

In talking about her daughter, Andrea describes Maeve's condition as quite severe. For example, she has difficulty with her speech and people who aren't familiar with her methods of communication can struggle to understand her; she cannot travel independently, tell the time, cross a road safely and so is dependent on effective support to live a healthy and rich life, and access a wide range of opportunities and experiences.

Although her prognosis at birth was good – in that her family were told she would be able to both walk and talk – the implementation of effective communication techniques has been essential to Maeve's quality of life. It has allowed her to feel appropriately supported and able to connect with her parents, siblings and loved ones.

When Maeve was a child, the family used Makaton, a form of sign language which uses signs and symbols to help people communicate, but once she went to the local mainstream school, the teachers did not take this on board. But they grew to respect and value her and she thrived. Her experience in a mainstream denominational secondary school was not good, which prompted a move to a special needs school, where she grew in confidence.

Andrea recognises that today Maeve's educational experience most likely would have been different, and that the schools would now probably be more accommodating to her unique needs.

'She would develop a habit then that if she wouldn't speak or if you asked her a question, she would close her eyes and turn her face away,' Andrea says, 'almost as a way of saying *you can't see me* ... She knew she couldn't make herself understood.

'I have seen people laugh at her. People stare at her. And, every day, Maeve picks herself up and carries on. She's adapted to her life and is just brimming with enthusiasm for life and emotional intelligence.

'I've watched her at judo competitions and drama performances, or even ordering in restaurants – when people stare at her. It takes so much courage for her to step up there and go out and stand in front of people ... I draw my own strength from that. I think Maeve recognises that many people view her differently,' Andrea says. 'Especially now that she's twenty-five years old.'

Andrea credits her daughter's willingness to live a fulfilling life as the impetus behind her own courage. Maeve practises judo, attends drama clubs, learns the piano and vibraphone, and faces her fears head on. She empowers her mother to do the same.

'I don't have role models or heroes. I think heroes are the everyday people who do amazing things and fight their fears. I've frequently seen Maeve climb her own personal mountains and, if I'm facing difficulty at work or speaking to a large crowd, I think of her. She would just go for it.'

In this way, it seems entirely apt that Maeve was named after Queen Medb of Connacht (The Warrior Queen), one of the most revered characters in Irish mythology, a strong-willed and ambitious woman who inspired troops to fight in her honour and ruled for many years.

'Maeve has a severe learning disability,' Andrea says. 'But what is interesting is the complexity behind what we call a learning disability. Maeve can't add one and one together, for example. She might get the answer "two", or she might not. But she's been here on this earth for twenty-five years and she has the dreams and ambition of many 25-year-olds. She wants to live independently. She doesn't want her mum and dad to be with her all the time.

'She wants her own flat. She has her own desires and needs. She's got incredible emotional intelligence. She connects with people's moods and will understand if I'm distressed or anxious. As a person, she's hugely complex, her character is rich and underpinned with immense strength and bravery. It blows me away.'

Andrea's children are all on their own life journeys now, but she says, during their childhoods, Maeve's additional needs enriched all of their lives.

'I cuddled her just like I cuddled my other children,' Andrea recalls. 'Of course I did. She was a baby and that was it. We loved her.

'How has Maeve's disability impacted on my children's lives? Someone once said to me that a disabled child is a burden for your other children and I thought, "How can you think of a human being like that?" I hope I've brought my children up to realise that everyone can be vulnerable and you all have to look out for each other.

'My son, who was born after Maeve, perhaps found it the hardest when he was very young. But he's fantastic with her and he looks out for her. They're a close group. I have no shadow of a doubt that when myself and my husband are gone, they will be there for her — and she for them — and they will support her. I hope they, in time, reap and reciprocate the rewards from Maeve that I have had and that she gives to others.'

Andrea, as principal and vice-chancellor of Edinburgh Napier University, understands the specific pressures of leadership (she is head of more than 15,000 students), but still she learns techniques about how best to handle responsibility from her daughter, who epitomises mindfulness practice.

'Leading an organisation is challenging and can be stressful at times, but one thing I have certainly learned from Maeve is that she lives in the moment,' Andrea says. 'She anticipates what she's doing next – yes – but she feels genuine joy every day. I can see her savouring every minute of life.'

'I'm always worried about my next meeting, my next everything, but Maeve lives in the moment, is *present* in it and savours it, which I think is a lovely quality.'

Andrea is a female leader in a famously male-dominated field, and is also a vocal supporter of young women in STEM (Science, Technology, Engineering and Mathematics) subjects towards which men are most traditionally encouraged.

Throughout her career, which boasts a somewhat intimidating list of accomplishments – none of which would have been possible if she'd segued from academia and research as planned – Andrea has been at the forefront of her field. In the 1980s, when she was practising as a veterinarian, animals weren't given pain medication, but she was part of a revolutionary team which changed that.

'In the 1990s, I developed research on the physiology of pain, pain measurement and how you assess pain,' she says. 'My work encouraged vets to change their practice around pain, and thousands of animals are now treated better. I sometimes think about what I've contributed working with others – and what an amazing impact we can have on the world through science. Sometimes those positive results can gets lost, or forgotten about. I think we don't promote the varied achievements of our engineers and scientists enough.'

Her stellar contribution to veterinary science led to her colleagues nominating her for an OBE, the Most Excellent Order of the British

Empire, an accolade rewarding civilians for their contributions across many different fields.

Andrea was awarded her OBE for services to veterinary science and higher education in a ceremony in 2013 at Bute House in Edinburgh by former First Minister Alex Salmond. There was one complication given her Irish heritage: although she's lived in the UK for nearly forty years, Andrea still holds her Irish passport and, as such, she was given an honorary OBE as all recipients must be British passport holders. Even so, she is one of just a few Irish women to hold this honour!

'It felt lovely to me that my peers had recognised my work,' she remembers. 'It was so unexpected – a real surprise. It's quite an extraordinary process because you have no idea someone is putting you forward, so the first you know of it is when you get a letter in the post. I was absolutely bowled over.

'I received my award alongside about twenty women in leadership and science roles in Scotland. We had a fabulous celebration of women in science.'

It's remarkable, but none of that would have happened without Maeve. You may not believe in a divine plan, but it's hard not to believe in fate and its unexpected gifts when you hear Andrea speak about her youngest daughter.

Find your tribe.

Eimear Varian Barry

Blogger and Photographer

'The day I left what I thought was
my dream life in New York.'

~

How would I describe Eimear Varian Barry?

She's a mother to three beautiful children – Saoirse, five, Harper, three, and Lennon, one; and she's a photographer, stylist and creative. She is most identifiably, though, an 'influencer'.

~

Eimear makes her income online, targeting ads at her 90,000-plus followers on Instagram, working on lucrative brand partnerships and hosting in-person events and social media management. She is the epitome of a confident, cool modern woman.

But Eimear never knew what life had in store for her – adventure, love, travel and financial stability – especially when she was growing up and trying to fit in any of the boxes society was putting her in. She didn't have the attention span for academia and a chance interview led her to drop her life in her native Cork and move to New York for what she thought would be the culmination of a lifelong dream of 'making it' in the Big Apple; when in fact leaving the city would be the day that really changed her life.

Eimear started working from an early age: her mother Sareen recognised that studying wasn't her strength and wanted her to build on her self-confidence outside of school, so she began sweeping hair and shampooing clients at a hairdresser in Cork city.

'I was a really intense teenager – I've always been a little intense – I just *feel* a lot. Some people feel on the surface and are much more expressive and others don't, but I'm very expressive about my feelings,' she says. 'Growing up, as a middle child and a teenager, I was a bit difficult to live with, so my mum asked if I could get a job at a hair salon through a friend. At that stage, I felt like I was thirteen going on thirty.

'Working at the hair salon really influenced me because it was the 1990s and hairdressing was completely changing; funky mullets were coming into fashion, there was colour experimentation and traditional hairdressing had changed into this new, creative art form.

'I was spending time with these amazing, cool hairdressers who were travelling to Ibiza a lot during the Ibiza heyday and I felt really comfortable. You feel really liberated when you find your tribe. There was no limit to what I thought I could do, but I never ever thought that anything I wanted could ever become a reality, I was ... I am ... a huge dreamer. I'm Eimear the Dreamer.'

Eimear always sensed she was creative; she had the imagination of an artist and the work ethic of a CEO, but never quite knew her place in the world. She never wanted for anything growing up, but felt she couldn't cross an invisible socio-economic line.

'My parents didn't have money,' she says. 'I thought the media and fashion industry were for a certain class. I'm not saying we were hungry because we certainly weren't – I had a brilliant childhood

– but my parents didn't have the money for me to do what everyone else was doing in order to "make it".'

Making it, in this case, meant doing either an unpaid or low-paying internship – opportunities Eimear couldn't take without financial help. She needed to work full-time to support herself and had immediately scratched off RTÉ's Cork base off the list. ('There was no way you were going to get a job there unless you knew someone!')

Financially, moving to Dublin wasn't a realistic idea. At the time, she was nineteen years old and enrolled in St John's Central College in Cork City, studying filmmaking.

'I lived around the corner from UCC [University College Cork], so it was expected of me to go there. I put Drama and Theatre Studies down on my form, but did I get the 500-plus points required for it? Of course not!

'I knew I wanted to work in media, so I bought some phone credit in the shop and called Red FM, which is the second biggest radio station in Cork, and asked if they were looking for any work experience candidates. I got three days confirmed for *The RedFM Breakfast Show* and three days after that, I was offered a producer job.

'I said, "Show me everything and I can do it!" And they knew I could.

'You had to get that work done because it was a live environment, which is really good training for life. It was also good training for respecting the hard work that goes into making your dreams come true. I still think I've held that live environment training with me in my work now.'

In her work, Eimear met and interviewed a stylist called Mallory Schilling, originally from Mississippi, who was living in New York City. Eimear asked if she could do work experience with her for a week; when Eimear arrived in New York, Mallory encouraged her to stay there full-time and really give her all to chasing the American dream.

'Mallory hooked me up with a lawyer so I could pay my visa costs in instalments, which was amazing. I remember meeting her on 28th Street and 7th Avenue in the Flower District. I needed a sponsor in order to stay in the country for my work visa, so she put me in touch with her friend Diana Warner, a jewellery designer.

'I realised that staying in America was a plan that was going to work out. I couldn't believe it! I had a long-term boyfriend and a life back in Cork, but this was something that was happening with relative ease.

'Once it hit me, I started shaking profusely and felt like vomiting. I was panicking because things were working out so well – things that had always been easy for some people in life had been so far from my reach until then. Everything was pointing in the direction of a new start.'

When she got home to Cork, she told her boss at the radio station she was moving to New York in three weeks, with €500 in her pocket. She secured her visa with Diana's sponsorship and began sleeping on Mallory's couch because she couldn't afford to rent an apartment on her own. She was working at the jewellery studio every day, yet found herself feeling lost.

'I was really unhappy in the job – I went from media into jewellery design. The umbrella over all this of course was that I didn't know what the hell I wanted to do and I was lost. I knew I had skills. I had confidence in producing, but I didn't know anyone in radio there.'

Life stayed this way the entire time she was in New York. On the surface, she had it all: she was young, beautiful and energetic, working with a designer in one of the greatest cities in the world; but her work wasn't satisfying her either professionally or financially.

She fell down the rabbit hole that often besets lonely girls in big cities and started partying too hard. She lost her way.

'I was so lost – and what often comes with that? When you're in New York on your own and you're lost career-wise, you're surrounded by people who are there working and earning a lot of money and seem so focused? You become depressed, right?

'I was drinking a lot. I wasn't doing drugs, but I was too easily led. I was mad for attention and longing. I hadn't been home for a year and a half and I think that affected me as well.

'I befriended some southern girls; we were living in a studio in the West Village, which sounds fabulous – let me tell you, it was not. I was getting home at 2 a.m. every night after working briefly at an Irish bar in midtown. It was like something from the movies. It was the textbook New York story.

'I was full of enthusiasm, love, passion and open-mindedness while scrubbing grime and mouse poop. I would tell myself, "I've made it, I'm in New York," over and over.'

A weekend trip to Florida with her American girlfriends would prove to have a life-changing impact. Eimear hadn't left the city in nearly two years and was suffocating under the pressure to perform and trying to force something to fit that just wasn't working.

'I can't help but feel a bit disheartened by the experience when I look back,' Eimear says. 'If that was me now, I'd so be ready for the city. If I was to go back there, I'd be so focused and would take on anything that came at me. I'm so comfortable in my own skin; I know who I am. Then, I was starving myself. I would cancel plans with people because I knew I had to go out and eat. I would stay in that apartment and just smoke and starve myself. I was so obsessed with self-criticism.'

She would tell herself she was a failure if she didn't stay until the very last minute when her visa expired.

'I put a constant pressure on myself, because I always dreamed of building a wonderful life for myself and making it work. I accepted I was thoroughly depressed, so booked a one-way ticket to Melbourne, Australia. It was such a horrible time for me, but it was also the best. I'd never be able to do what I do today without that experience.'

There was 'no way' she was returning to Ireland, so she and her sister Doireann booked tickets to Australia (Doireann still lives in Perth) together, then went their separate ways. Eimear began working as a hostess at a colourful cocktail bar called Madame Brussels and she began to feel at home again among her artistic tribe.

'I went through a really interesting fashion phase where I was convinced I was from the 1940s. It was weird,' she laughs. 'Everything was from the 1940s – my bedroom, my hair and my clothes, my whole appearance; I wore white makeup with red lipstick. I never had a Goth phase as a teenager, so Melbourne was very intense in that way.'

Personally, she was still struggling with her mental health, but the new setting did wonders for her mindset. ('Compared to the way I am now, I was still all over the place in Melbourne. It's been a long journey.')

In Australia, the government dictates that visa holders can extend their stay in the country by doing three calendar months in an eligible industry such as fishing, farming, mining or construction.

'I got word there was a job on an oyster ship in Darwin, which is the other side of the continent, and flew six hours to my interview. I was booked into a hostel and thought I'd have my *Eat, Pray, Love* time. When I was there, I was planning on reading a good book and confirmed to myself that I wanted to give up drinking because I realised it wasn't good for me. I still don't drink that much these days.

'I was sitting in the corner of the hostel drinking a chai latte and I noticed some really hot English builders. I just walked over to them and asked if I could join them. Three kids later . . . that's how I met Daniel.'

Daniel (who asks that his surname remain private) is her partner of six years and the father of her three children. It was love at first sight for both of them.

> It was such a horrible time for me, but it was also the best. I'd never be able to do what I do today without that experience.

'I went for the interview, but remember I was still in my 1940s phase, so I went to the office wearing a vintage dress with red lipstick. There was no way I was going to get that job on an oyster ship out at sea!

'I only had three weeks to find farm work and, through a friend, I heard about a job at a Seedlings Farm, which is twenty kilometres from the nearest tumbleweed village of Bowen. I bought a bike for a fiver in a charity shop and started cycling between the two. I lost a load of weight because I wasn't drinking and was cycling those twenty kilometres all the time. I started work on the farm at 5 a.m. every day. Daniel moved to Melbourne for me, but he got really homesick because he's a real home bird.'

Daniel is originally from Surrey, England, and they decided to move back to the UK together in 2013; a perfect fit for Eimear to put down roots in somewhat familiar territory without having to return home with, in what she felt would be, her tail between her legs.

Their romance was a whirlwind: they had only been dating for a few months when they decided to move to England and, a week later, she found out she was pregnant.

'We were living in his tiny old childhood bedroom,' she recalls. 'I had no job. I had £500 in my bank account – again, I wouldn't advise moving country without money. It was really hard because I was really sick. I was going to interviews, pretending I wasn't pregnant because I knew I wouldn't get hired if they knew I was pregnant. It was really difficult because I didn't realise England is so structured; when I was in New York, I'd meet someone on a night out and I'd be on a movie set the next day. When I came here, I thought, "What's a second interview?"

'I'd talked my way into my radio job and all my other jobs just happened organically, so that was daunting for me,' she says. 'They do everything right here, which I love, but it came as a shock. I was going through agencies asking them to give me anything.

'It wasn't working for me. My worst interview was for a social media editor role with Net-a-Porter [the luxury online retailer]. A girl I knew from Cork recommended me for it, but I had no idea what I was talking about – I didn't even have an Instagram account at the time!

'I'd love to see a tape of it. That interview must have been horrendous because I never heard from the girl from Cork ever again – and we used to talk before that,' she laughs.

But bills needed paying and she wanted to plan for her family's future as much as possible.

'I was temping with charities and doing customer service jobs,' she remembers. 'When I was heavily pregnant, I worked in a call centre for £5 an hour where I had to get two trains to get there, selling e-cigarettes over the phone to retailers. I knew I had good experience and skills, but it wasn't enough to get a job. Daniel was on £80 a day doing labouring. We were so broke and we were on housing benefits for about a year. We were people who had qualifications and really wanted to work, but we were in that situation at that particular time.'

However, the lost feeling that had haunted most of her twenties disappeared as time went on, in particular, the joy she felt at becoming a mother grounded her in a way she's never experienced before.

Eimear began taking pictures of her outfits and sharing them on Facebook and Instagram, which was originally intended as a means to stay in touch with friends and family, but grew into a fully-fledged business. She started selling clothes on Depop, a shopping app for pre-loved clothes preferred by bloggers and influencers, and generated an income stream of her own. It was a page straight out of Nasty Gal founder Sophia Amoruso's origin story. And Eimear was good at it.

'I'd pay for the food shopping by selling vintage clothes on Depop. For my birthday one year, Daniel gave me £100, so I took a suitcase to Brixton and used the money to buy good vintage stuff. I knew by that time what would sell well. I used a mirror we bought for 99p on eBay to take selfies to show off the clothes.

'People started following my Instagram. When I had around 10,000 followers, a woman called Emma Hart from Push PR invited me to an event for London Fashion Week, where I was surrounded by the big-name bloggers. That really inspired me; I realised I could actually make a living with what I was doing. I could work from home and be with my babies and make this happen.'

As it turns out, she had a knack for photography and styling – that, coupled with her no-nonsense approach to her life and her charming family, was the perfect formula for digital success. Now, she makes a healthy living from brand partnerships and advertising through her website and social media channels. It's no wonder Eimear felt so lost growing up; her job didn't even exist until the 2010s.

'I didn't know what I wanted to do and didn't realise what I was really good at until I was about thirty-one. We just bought a house for half a million quid. I'm really proud of us and how we turned it around so quickly.'

She came back stronger.

Derval O'Rourke

Athlete

'The day I became a World Champion.'

~

'Go bravely, go deeply or do not go.'

While putting together this book, I came across this quote and thought that its meaning rang true for sprinter Derval O'Rourke. At 23 years old, she rose to international prominence overnight when she was crowned a world champion in the 60 metres hurdles at the 2006 IAAF Indoor World Championships in Moscow.

~

For those on the outside, Derval's rise to the global stage was seemingly out of the blue, but for Derval, it was a culmination of a particular twelve months of sheer grit and a lifetime of training, rooted in unwavering self-belief. It was the day that changed her life.

'For me to talk about another day would be trying to make another day more important,' she says. 'That day in Moscow had the most significant impact on the direction my life would go.'

Her victory at the championships in 2006 put Derval on the world map, but she was already familiar with the ins and outs of track and field at an international level. She'd made it to the 2004 Summer Olympics in Athens and regularly qualified to represent Ireland at international competitions, but, after years of training, she still hadn't reached the upper echelons of the sport. And so, she took out an insurance plan on her future – she studied arts at University College Dublin, graduated with an MA in Business Development from the renowned Smurfit Business School, and balanced her academic studies with running.

After graduating and watching her classmates move into the roles they had spent years training for, Derval began a campaign all of her own: she would become a world champion.

'I was good enough to be at the Olympics and a regular in the Ireland team, but I wasn't good enough to be globally successful or in the top eight in the world,' she says. 'I was conscious that I wasn't at the level where I could make a career out of it. About six months before the world championships, I made a decision to take a job that had nothing to do with my background in business, and, instead, was one that would facilitate my athletics career. I was working a minimum wage job in a gym, selling memberships, and I completely changed my coaching set-up. I started to believe at that point: I made a decision to believe I was world class even though I had no reason to.'

If necessity is the mother of invention, then sheer willpower was the source of Derval's determination. At the same time she was going to put all of her eggs in her running basket, Athletics Ireland informed her they were about to cut her funding because she wasn't advancing enough to merit the financial support of the organisation. 'I was making a decision to go all in and they were making a decision to pull out of it.

'They told me I had to be top twelve to be funded. I said, "What if I win?"'

She was facing the World Indoor Championships, a notoriously difficult track and field competition with the crème de la crème of athletes from around the world, and the only championship that legendary Irish runner, and Olympic gold medallist, Sonia O'Sullivan hadn't won a gold medal at in her illustrious career as a long-distance runner.

'Ireland traditionally makes distance runners,' Derval explains. 'So the fact that I was doing a completely different event to what Sonia would have done meant that there was no belief outside of me – and among the few people who were helping me – that I could do it.'

'I went into the competition following a brilliant few weeks of training. It justified the fact that I had backed myself and put my non-athletics life completely on hold. On the day itself, I remember waking up and thinking, *I'm going to win this. I'm going to win this world championship.* I went down to the track and met with the other athletes and I said, half-joking, "I'm just going down to win the thing."'

Derval's straight-down-the-line thinking was crucial to her eventual victory: she didn't overcomplicate it. In the build-up to the competition, she had put literal blood, sweat and tears into transforming herself into the best possible athlete she could be and that was enough to give her the confidence to compete with a winner's attitude.

After her morning heat, she landed a place in the semi-finals, which she won, and broke the Irish record in the process, before doing the same in the final.

'One of the girls in the warm-up said to me, "You're never going to break your record in the final now because you broke it in the semi," and I was like, "I'm going to go faster, that's my plan." I had never been in a final of any major championship. It was the first time I was ever in the top eight, so even if I had come last it would have been a massive step forward but it wasn't what I wanted. I wanted to win it.

'When I got to the final, I had absolutely no doubt I was going to win. All I had to do was just get out of the blocks and go to the line. I never thought about what would happen after I won, I just knew what I had to do to win. I finished in 7.84 seconds and I set another Irish record. I only won by two hundredths of a second.'

Derval's secret to long-standing success remains her unwavering self-belief. Athletes of all disciplines require gargantuan levels of psychological strength, just as much as their physical prowess; even tennis superstar Serena Williams acknowledges that a huge factor in her success is the formidable mental toughness which enables her to come back stronger than ever when she's been down, whether in sport or in life.

'It was an outrageous level of backing myself when it probably didn't make a huge amount of sense,' Derval says. 'There's been no other day in anything else that I've done – whether it be athletics or anything else – that I've found the same level of self-belief as I did that day.'

Throughout her career, she also looked to other successful sportspeople, like Irish rugby star Ronan O'Gara and footballer Roy Keane. 'It didn't make sense that he [Roy Keane] should be that good but he made a decision and went after it. I liked that.'

Derval's victory was a surprise to nearly everybody outside her inner circle, including the world's press, who scrambled to find out just who this plucky record-beating Irish woman was; but for Derval it was a self-fulfilling prophecy.

'I think it had been building for a lot of years,' she says. 'It's not like I'd gone from someone running in Cork County – I had been to an Olympic games, I'd been to the Worlds, I'd been to the Europeans. I was always a student of my event. I always looked at all the other women. I had an incredible amount of respect for anyone I raced against because I knew how hard it was. I was like a sponge, I absorbed everything from everyone who was better than me and implemented it.

> There's been no other day – whether it be athletics or anything else – that I've found the same level of self-belief as I did that day.

'I got to a point where I felt ready to stand above the crowd. Something just clicked.'

But still, a significant part of her triumph was down to her decision to pause her life and focus exclusively on running. When she wasn't selling gym memberships, she was training hard and often to fuel her 'side hustle', which was world domination. 'I took some ownership and responsibility for those six months before . . . maybe I was putting my eggs in too many baskets – business school and the Olympics – instead of thinking that I want to be the best runner in the world. That was hard to do: pin your colours to the mast and say, "This is what I'm going to do. And by this date, I'll know if I was right to back myself."' And she was.

'It changed everything because, from the moment I passed the finishing line, everyone suddenly knew who I was,' she says. 'I went from struggling to get by as an athlete, to companies suddenly trying to get me sponsorship deals. Agents wanted to sign me and the bank even talked to me about buying a house! It completely changed the direction of my career. If I'd made the final that would have been a great step, but to be world champion took it to a different level. Even now, if I'm introduced, the first thing they say is: "Derval O'Rourke, former world champion."'

'On the day that changed my life, I was really calm because my plan was to win. It just took everyone else longer to realise it.'

That night was one of unbridled celebration, but Derval had been so laser focused on becoming a world champion that her parents and coaching team chose not to attend the race in Moscow, so as not to heap any more pressure on her. Her running agent, the late Andy Norman, who was on the sidelines, was moved to tears by her win.

'He had a soft spot for an underdog,' she says. 'He was such a mentor, helping me with my career since I was a kid and he liked me because I was the underdog. He had all these other brilliant athletes who would have made him loads of money and I was making no money because I wasn't that good. But I was spirited and he liked that.'

That spirited will to win was unquestionably the secret to Derval's remarkable success. It's the reason she is a household name in Ireland today. However, it was tough to maintain this spirit in the face of relentless naysayers – some coming from a place of concern hoping to manage her expectations and others who just didn't see what she saw in herself. In the weeks beforehand, Derval was undefeated, 'which was unusual,' she says, but other competitors had taken notice and some questioned the quality of her wins.

'People who'd been in the sport a long time were making comments about things going well, and that the bubble would burst. That made me even more determined for it not to happen.'

'I've rarely been in a position where any of the things I've succeeded at have been guaranteed,' she states. 'I've always had to work hard and I wasn't handed anything. There are so many Irish athletes who are more talented, but my talent is that I'm very resilient. I definitely grew as a person from that external doubt and negativity. I have my own business now, it's not an easy thing, but it's something I really enjoy. I'm really ambitious with it and that probably doesn't make sense to people on the outside. Athletics was the first step in giving myself permission to really believe in and back myself, and when I won that world championship, it was the first time that my ambition got me to where I wanted to go.

'I think it's harder for women to back themselves. We grow up in a society that doesn't really encourage us to do that. I'd been on the circuit for five, six years before I started making those decisions to really give myself a go. To completely believe in myself.'

Unlike with team sport, which relies on the support of the many to bolster one another during hardships, running is a singular, isolating sport. You have only yourself to blame for failures and thank for successes; these are the reasons why Derval surrounded herself with Andy, her coaches and a tight-knit circle of friends, none of whom were involved in sport.

'The night before I flew to Moscow in 2006, I went to dinner with one of my best friends, I said to her, "I think I can win this and that's my plan." My friend had some wise words: "You're the only one who can determine it. You've put everything in place. These races come down to hundredths of seconds. When it comes to the final, whoever backs themselves the most will succeed because, at that point, it's about who can keep their head. You have seven seconds not to make a mistake and you can only do your best."

'The only reason I shouldn't have won it was history. No Irish woman had won it, the male athletes had won few medals and a European athlete hadn't won it in a while; it was going to the

American and Jamaican athletes. History was the only thing telling me I couldn't win. Well, I figured that was the past so it was time to change the future.'

This mindset is the secret ingredient in the Derval O'Rourke formula for success, which she applies to her business as the #FitFoodie, and raising her three-year-old daughter Dafne.

'My priority is Dafne's level of joy and quality of life. When I won at the Worlds, it was because I loved doing it; I loved running that fast, I loved the process, it was sheer joy. Even if no one had known that I'd won, I'd have gotten the same level of joy out of it. I probably transfer that to Dafne. I also think she needs to be tough and resilient, I think most girls and women do. I want her to be really joyful but also stand up in the world and get what she wants because it's a big bad world out there.'

Derval takes the responsibility that comes with fame seriously; her laser-focused sense of self is contagious. Throughout our conversation, I feel as if I too can be a world champion if I believe in myself hard enough. But what of the others who look up to her?

'I hope they look up to me and realise my success came off a lot of hard work and a different type of attitude; it's not that I'm really talented and they're not talented,' she encourages. 'Everybody is capable of doing certain things. My world championship is somebody else's going to college. It depends on what works for you.

'Finding your *why* is really important,' she asserts. 'Why do you want to do something? For me, I knew all the reasons I wanted to win at the Worlds, so every time it got hard – and it got ridiculously hard at times – I came back to why I was doing it. If you do that, you'll always have a good foundation and a good answer. Whatever situation you're in now doesn't have to be that situation in the future. You have to be really solidly based in what you want to do and be honest with yourself and only then put a roadmap of your life together.

'If you put a roadmap together without knowing why you're doing it . . . you'll just give up when it gets hard. Athletics got hard for me and I knew why. But when I retired, it felt really easy. I'd had such a good career, why would I be devastated about something that was such a gift? *There's no unfinished business here*, I thought. I was ready to move on.'

A natural on air.

Doireann Garrihy

Broadcaster

'The day I filmed my first TV pilot.'

~

Doireann Garrihy is a very modern example of very modern success. She's an experienced broadcaster, reformed actor and social media sensation – but influencer she is not. At twenty-seven, she's achieved more in her work in media than most do in a lifetime; she's a talented host with unparalleled comic intuition.

~

There's no two ways about it, Doireann is an 'It Girl'. She currently hosts one of the most coveted gigs in all of Irish broadcasting: a breakfast radio show with co-host Eoghan McDermott on RTÉ 2FM – her first full-time national job. On the side, she stars in her own digital comedy series available on the RTÉ Player, which she also writes, and works alongside her sister, Aoibhín, on her wellness brand BEO.

Every successful woman has a trail of incredibly hard work in her wake. The day that changed Doireann's life was the moment she realised she could take stock of one of her proudest working moments, acknowledging the difficulties she overcame to get there, and still be blissfully unaware of the abundance of professional success that lay ahead.

'The day that changed my life was the moment I was standing in front of the camera, about to shoot the pilot for *The Doireann Project* for RTÉ Player,' she says. 'It might seem trivial, but it was just so surreal for me.'

A number of challenges had to be overcome for Doireann to reach this moment. Rewinding back to the beginning of Doireann's adult life, while studying at university, pursuing her dream of training to be an actor, her family was experiencing difficulties at home. When Doireann's parents', Clare and Eugene's, business fell on hard times, she was the only bird who hadn't flown the nest and therefore put pressure on herself to be the comic and emotional relief at home.

For nearly three decades, the Garrihys ran a successful construction business, but during the economic crash in 2008 and subsequent recession, their business faced the same fate as so many others. They endured for two years, but in 2010, Clare and Eugene put their business into voluntary liquidation.

'My parents had been in business in construction for twenty-six years,' Doireann says, 'and my dad had his own company Castleknock Construction and my mom worked alongside him. The Celtic Tiger was very good to us. We wanted for nothing. We always went on two holidays a year; my parents are from Co Clare so we spent our summers there. That was all we knew.'

But then Doireann found herself lost, as many young women in their twenties can find themselves, searching for a personal and professional purpose.

'It's only recently that I've thought back on my college and post-college time,' she says, 'and realised I went through a lot. First of all, I didn't know what I was going to do and what path I would go down, but also because my parents were going through their own troubles, I felt I had to be behind them. My eldest sister Aoibhín was living in Clare with her now-husband, my sister Ailbhe was living between Amsterdam and Sydney, and because I was the one at home, I felt the need to be there for them.'

Doireann adds that 'everyone lost the run of themselves then', referencing the excess spending of the Celtic Tiger heyday, which comprised much of her adolescence. But lessons were learned and the Garrihys were down, but they weren't out. Studying at university at the time, Doireann put a pause on any extracurricular activities to help her father get his new business – Dublin Bay Cruises, which hosts boat trips from Dún Laoghaire City Centre and Howth – off the ground, and spend quality time with her mother.

She cut short her time in the J-1 programme, a time-honoured tradition among Irish third level students who spend three months working and living in the United States as part of the Summer Work and Travel Programme. Exploring Europe through interrailing wasn't possible either. Rites of passage reserved for students with the desire and means to travel simply weren't an option for her because of the pressure she put on herself to repay the generosity her parents had shown her for her entire life.

'It took them about two to three years to figure out their Plan B, but the time in between that was just awful. The business was their independence; it was how they funded our school, college ... everything. It's only recently now that I'm well past that stage that I realise how tough it was. My parents never made me feel this way, but I lived at home when I was in college. Most people leave when they turn eighteen and they don't really properly come back. I lived at home and I would feel guilty if I wanted to stay out on weeknights because my mom may have made dinner – she would often say I was the person who made her laugh and kept her going during that time.'

It's clear Clare and Eugene are the defining force in Doireann's life, the unwavering influences who have guided her through the stratospheric highs of her career now, aware of the less well-known stories of what it took to get there. They supported her desire to pursue a non-traditional career path and always advised her to follow her heart. It's of little surprise she wanted to return the favour when they needed support.

'They've given me so much. From day one, when I said I wanted to act, they could have just said no. I know people who wanted to do music or art and they were told to do law or medicine. My parents let me do what I wanted to do,' she explains.

Doireann went to great lengths, pondering the answer to the existential question asked of everyone in this book – 'I'm twenty-seven and I haven't had much tragedy in my life at all. I've been so wildly lucky so far,' she tells me – and found herself always coming back to the moment in December 2017, filming the pilot for her own show. It was a lifelong ambition come to fruition.

Doireann grew up wanting to act: she was a student at the prestigious Billie Barry Stage School, which counts actress Angeline Ball and singer Samantha Mumba as alumni, and eventually took Drama and Theatre Studies at Trinity College Dublin to fine tune her craft. Her sister, Aoibhín, is a well-known actor, with an impressive theatre background who rose to national prominence in the evening soap opera *Fair City*. As the eldest of the famous Garrihy Sisters, Aoibhín was a strong influence on Doireann, the youngest, as they were growing up. Aoibhín was able to warn Doireann about the less-than-glamorous reality of being a working actor, especially in Ireland, which has limited opportunities in the industry.

'I wanted to act my entire life; it was all I ever wanted to do. Aoibhín geared me up for how tough it was going to be, but I still wanted to do it. So, I graduated from college and gave it a go for six months. I got a good agent, the same one that represents Gabriel Byrne and the Gleeson brothers, so I thought it would all happen – "Oscar in six months", the whole thing.' She laughs.

It would be cruel to rule out any Oscar nominations, but her acting career was derailed when she became fully entrenched in the industry, facing rejection day in and day out and expected to brush herself off and move on, waiting for her big break. Charlie Chaplin, the legendary silent film actor and arguably the world's first movie star, captured the acting experience best when he said, 'Actors search for rejection. If they don't get it they reject themselves.'

It wasn't meant to be for Doireann. While some aspiring actors can dust themselves off and walk away, Doireann, a self-proclaimed sensitive soul, began questioning herself and her abilities; the constant rejection caused her to self-doubt and lose confidence. After six months, she couldn't handle it any more and she knew that auditioning for parts, which made her question everything about herself, wasn't conducive to a healthy life.

'Most people are at it for at least three years before they might cave and give up, but I just couldn't hack it. The rejection was too much. I started to doubt myself: "Was I ever good? Could I ever act? Am I too fat? Am I too ... whatever?" No matter how much someone tries to prepare you for it, you're never ready for that much rejection. I really doubted myself.'

Doireann was twenty-two years old and at the first real crossroads in her life. She'd prepared to be an actor her entire life, so she needed a Plan B. Aoibhín told her about the Today FM School of Radio and Podcasting, a first-of-its-kind course run by experts at Ireland's largest commercial broadcaster.

'I was instantly bitten by the radio bug,' she explains. 'I never thought to do radio, which is funny because Ian Dempsey [legendary radio broadcaster] from Today FM is my godfather and I've listened to him my entire life, but it never occurred to me that it would be something I'd be good at and something I could enjoy. The beauty was that it didn't matter what you looked like, you just sat in the front of the mic, have the craic and be yourself. That came at such an important time for me.'

> I was instantly bitten by the radio bug.

After completing the ten-week course, Doireann began doing shifts for AA Roadwatch, reading traffic reports across radio for a year; doing split shifts, 5 a.m. starts, late-night finishes and anything else that was required. In May 2016, she began working as an entertainment reporter in Spin 1038, the Dublin-based youth-oriented radio station.

Radio jobs are hard to come by and even harder to keep long-term, but she was a natural and just about every programme director at every radio station seemed to agree, which, I must clarify, are not Doireann's words as she won't allow herself to comfortably accept such praise.

But Doireann did recognise the value in bolstering her social media presence at a time when Snapchat, Instagram, Facebook and Twitter were at war to become the most influential medium of communication in the world. She figured out a way to incorporate her acting skills into her new work: impersonations. More specifically, impersonations of some of the biggest names in blogging, then at its peak.

'If I wanted to be noticed in radio and get my own show, it's good to have another string to your bow. I thought, "Why don't I use my acting skills to my advantage here?" I started doing impressions of Irish bloggers and uploaded them and it took off from there. I was tempted to say that was the day that changed my life, but that wasn't really the start.'

Doireann chose five big 'names' online: Pippa O'Connor, a former model and mother who now runs a lifestyle and fashion empire off the back of her following; Suzanne Jackson, a fashion and beauty blogger who has a lucrative cosmetics line; James Patrice, famous for his own impressions of his mother; and Marissa Carter, the Cocoa Brown CEO who built a loyal following independent of her business with her no-nonsense beauty advice.

Together, their combined following went well past the one million mark, and just about everyone on social media knew their names and their trademarks. But only Doireann could mimic them to perfection. Her impressions were uncannily good and she became famous in Ireland within a few weeks. People began wondering who this plucky young woman, who could portray someone so accurately, was, and why hadn't they heard of her sooner?

Her family were all too familiar with the Doireann Show growing up, though. As a child, she would make them sit together on the couch so she could act out sets – they had to pretend they were students and she would relay bang-on impressions of her teachers. ('My mom always said she could never get over my powers of observation, as she calls it, even when I was three years old.')

It was the perfect storm for success: the timing was right, but Doireann also had the credentials to inform any career perspectives.

'It came at a time where people were starting to question some of blogger culture,' she says, before adding, 'I'm part of the culture now! I uploaded my first video the night Donald Trump was elected [as US president]. I think it was important it was that day – first of all, everyone was online because they were following the Trump situation and then, they needed a laugh because it was depressing for a lot of people.'

Within the space of four years, her career catapulted. She was given a higher position with her employers at Spin 1038, promoted to co-hosting *The Zoo Crew* with Martin Guilfoyle. In 2018, she was chosen as the new host for the resurged *The Podge & Rodge Show* on RTÉ One. (That same year, she left Spin because she was over-worked, overtired and too worn-out for a then-26-year-old.)

Fast forward a few months later to 2019 and, in May, she landed her current breakfast hosting gig with an audience of more than 150,000 listeners. But her heart remains with *The Doireann Project*; the day her life changed, or at the very least, when she realised it had.

After weeks of negotiations, Doireann was commissioned for a ten-minute pilot that would be released exclusively on the RTÉ Player, as part of the broadcaster's digital expansion. On the day she filmed the pilot, she stared at her name above her dressing room, knowing her name would be in the title of the show and suddenly, it all made sense.

'There was something so surreal about it calling it *The Doireann Project*,' she says. 'In my mind, I thought it would be a random thing that would sit on the Player – some people would watch it and some people wouldn't. But then it was the most watched original pilot on the Player ever. I couldn't believe it! It just goes to show that people liked what I was doing, which was a massive boost for me. It wasn't until I was back standing in front of a camera to film my own show, my name was in the title and my name was over the door – I was doing what I always wanted to do, but I had gone about it in such a roundabout way,' she explains. 'It changed everything and opened so many other doors after that.'

She is an ardent believer in back-up plans, perhaps a belief that she inherited from her parents' fortune and subsequent misfortune, and their enduring work ethic. Doireann finishes with a few parting words, sounding wise beyond her twenty-seven years:

'What's meant to be will be and you will find your path. It may be something you never expected to happen or dreamed you would enjoy, but go with the flow. It made our family stronger and our work ethic stronger. I think I am where I am now because of it. Plan Bs are good, Plan Cs are good. Even if it's Plan F! It will come.'

Parting Words

The hardest part about putting *The Day That Changed My Life* together was making the choice as to which thirty-one women to feature. Ireland is a country rich with talent across all its professional, political, cultural and sporting activities, replete with global leaders and titans of industry; and all the while there is a vibrant tapestry of brave women making choices of courage and integrity in their daily lives. Selecting a relatively small number was no easy task, but it was a pleasure to explore the endlessly inspiring women in this small country and beyond.

I believe we are all storytellers; some of us just express our voice in different ways. And it's true that we can often underestimate the comfort in sharing our stories and knowing the complexities of femalehood extend beyond the individual.

When I first pitched this book all those stories ago, I said, 'I want women to feel they can take on the world after reading this.' And I sincerely hope you do.

Finally, this book is for the women who do not feature and whose stories have not been told; you have not been – nor will you ever be – forgotten.

Thank You

Thank you, first and foremost, to the women in this book who helped make it a reality:

Áine Kerr, Amy Huberman, Andrea Nolan, Breege O'Donoghue, Caroline Downey, Cassie Stokes, Christina Noble, Ciara Griffin, Derval O'Rourke, Doireann Garrihy, Evanne Ní Chuilinn, Georgie Crawford, Minister Helen McEntee, Joanne Byrne, Judith Gillespie, Kirsten Mate Maher, Minister Katherine Zappone, Kathy Ryan, Louise O'Reilly, Mary Ann O'Brien, Norah Casey, Norah Patten, Orla Barry, Sabina Brennan, Sarah Tobin, Sonya Lennon, Tara Flynn and Terry Prone.

You are all extraordinary. Thank you for helping make this dream a reality; I sincerely hope it does the good we all so very much want it to. A special thank you to the managers, PRs and advisers for getting my emails past the first hurdle and for your help in bringing this all together!

Thank you to the team at Black & White Publishing: Campbell Brown and Ali McBride for your belief in this book from the very beginning. You have been just as excited as me and it's been wonderful to share with you. Emma Hargrave, I am forever indebted to you for your thoughtfulness and expertise and for making me an infinitely better writer by being such a wonderful editor. Alice Latchford, thank you for your any-time-any-day willingness to help. You have all made this such a special experience for me, one that I will treasure for ever.

Thank you to my mother Regina who always encouraged this little girl to use her voice and after thirty-two years, I finally found it. And thank you to my father Jim, for all your understanding and support.

To my sister Maura, I probably won't ever be able to repay you for your life-long support and unconditional love, but I figured dedicating this book to you was a good place to start. To my niece Olivia, I can't wait to watch you grow up and see the young woman you become. Your cuddles made difficult days boundlessly better and I hope when your taste moves beyond pop-up books, you might find it cool that your aunt wrote this. And thank you, Thomas, for being a wonderful brother-to-be!

To my best friend, Laura Keenan: every day, you teach me strength and remind me to practise true kindness. Thank you for answering endless phone calls at times when I struggled to keep it together this year (and many times during many years before that). I know what true friendship is because of you.

Finally, thank you to my wonderful fiancé Guy Sinnott: meeting you changed my life in more ways than I ever knew possible. As one of the women in this book told me, 'To love and be loved makes everything else easy.'

Thank you for making everything else easy.

About the Author

© Emily Quinn

Caitlin McBride, proud resident of Dublin, is the executive style editor at Independent.ie, Ireland's biggest news website. She writes on everything from hard news to red carpet fashion, from body positivity to royal wedding hairstyles. Writing an anthology focusing on women's interests, through women's voices, has always been on her bucket list and, with this book, that dream becomes a reality.

If You Would Like to Talk

This women's stories in this book tackle some difficult topics. If you are affected by any of the issues and would like to talk, these organisations will listen in confidence and without judgement.

SAMARITANS
Helpline: 116 123
Website: www.samaritans.org/samaritans-ireland

AWARE
Helpline: 1800 80 48 48
Website: www.aware.ie

PIETA HOUSE
Helpline: 1800 247 247
Website: www.pieta.ie

WOMEN'S AID
Helpline: 1800 341 900
Website: www.womensaid.ie

DUBLIN RAPE CRISIS CENTRE
Helpline: 1800 77 8888
Website: www.drcc.ie